KIERKEGAARD'S
FEAR AND TREMBLING

Continuum *Reader's Guides*

Continuum's *Reader's Guides* are clear, concise and accessible introductions to classic works of philosophy. Each book explores the major themes, historical and philosophical context and key passages of a major philosophical text, guiding the reader toward a thorough understanding of often demanding material. Ideal for undergraduate students, the guides provide an essential resource for anyone who needs to get to grips with a philosophical text.

Reader's Guides available from Continuum

Aristotle's Nicomachean Ethics – Christopher Warne
Aristotle's Politics – Judith A. Swanson and C. David Corbin
Berkeley's Principles of Human Knowledge – Alasdair Richmond
Berkeley's Three Dialogues – Aaron Garrett
Deleuze and Guattari's Capitalism and Schizophrenia – Ian Buchanan
Deleuze's Difference and Repetition – Joe Hughes
Derrida's Writing and Difference – Sarah Wood
Descartes' Meditations – Richard Francks
Hegel's Philosophy of Right – David Rose
Heidegger's Being and Time – William Blattner
Heidegger's Later Writings – Lee Braver
Hobbes's Leviathan – Laurie M. Johnson Bagby
Hume's Dialogues Concerning Natural Religion – Andrew Pyle
Hume's Enquiry Concerning Human Understanding – Alan Bailey
 and Dan O'Brien
Kant's Critique of Aesthetic Judgement – Fiona Hughes
Kant's Critique of Pure Reason – James Luchte
Kant's Groundwork for the Metaphysics of Morals – Paul Guyer
Kuhn's The Structure of Scientific Revolutions – John Preston
Locke's Essay Concerning Human Understanding – William Uzgalis
Locke's Second Treatise of Government – Paul Kelly
Mill's On Liberty – Geoffrey Scarre
Mill's Utilitarianism – Henry West
Nietzsche's On the Genealogy of Morals – Daniel Conway
Nietzsche's The Birth of Tragedy – Douglas Burnham and
 Martin Jesinghausen
Plato's Republic – Luke Purshouse
Plato's Symposium – Thomas L. Cooksey
Rousseau's The Social Contract – Christopher Wraight
Sartre's Being and Nothingness – Sebastian Gardner
Spinoza's Ethics – Thomas J. Cook
Wittgenstein's Tractatus Logico Philosophicus – Roger M. White

KIERKEGAARD'S
FEAR AND TREMBLING

A Reader's Guide

CLARE CARLISLE

continuum

Continuum International Publishing Group
The Tower Building   80 Maiden Lane
11 York Road   Suite 704
London SE1 7NX   New York NY, 10038

www.continuumbooks.com

British Library Cataloguing-in-Publication Data
A catalogue record for this book is available from the British Library.

ISBN: HB: 978-1-8470-6460-8
PB: 978-1-8470-6461-5

Library of Congress Cataloging-in-Publication Data
Carlisle, Clare, 1977-
Kierkegaard's Fear and trembling : a reader's guide / Clare Carlisle.
    p. cm.
    ISBN-13:   978-1-84706-460-8 (HB)
    ISBN-10:   1-84706-460-4 (HB)
    ISBN-13:   978-1-84706-461-5 (pbk.)
    ISBN-10:   1-84706-461-2 (pbk.)
   1. Kierkegaard, Søren, 1813-1855. Frygt og bæven.
    2. Christianity–Philosophy. I. Title.

B4373.F793C37 2010
198'.9–dc22
2009052529

Typeset by Newgen Imaging Systems Pvt Ltd, Chennai, India
Printed and bound in Great Britain by CPI Antony Rowe Ltd,
Chippenham, Wiltshire

For Mark

CONTENTS

FOREWORD

At several moments during the course of writing this book, I have been visited by the question of why I am writing it. These visits have not always been especially welcome, and the question has been surprisingly difficult to answer. There are, I think, good reasons for producing a clear guide to Kierkegaard's *Fear and Trembling*: this is a challenging and enigmatic text, and even though some readers find it more captivating than many other works of philosophy, there is always a danger of becoming bored by a book one doesn't understand. Thus one reason for writing an accessible commentary on *Fear and Trembling* is to encourage readers to persist with it and to plumb its depths, in order not only to do its author justice, but also to be rewarded by a fascinating, profound and influential book that it would be a shame to miss out on.

However, when I was first asked to write this *Reader's Guide*, I was aware that excellent introductions to *Fear and Trembling* were already available. John Lippitt's *Routledge Philosophy Guidebook to Kierkegaard and Fear and Trembling* (2003) and Edward Mooney's *Knights of Faith and Resignation: Reading Kierkegaard's Fear and Trembling* (1991), for example, are both highly recommended, and the editorial introductions to various English translations of the text – such as those by C. Stephen Evans and Sylvia Walsh, Alastair Hannay, and Howard and Edna Hong – are all authoritative and illuminating.

So the question, it became clear, was about why *I* am writing a guide to *Fear and Trembling*. One plausible general answer to this question is: in order to discover that the text is more difficult than I thought it was, and that I understand it less well than I'd assumed. A more particular answer is: in order to think about courage. Before I was invited to write this *Reader's Guide* I had (I assure you) already read *Fear and Trembling*. In fact, I'd read it many times, and on each occasion it raised new questions and yielded fresh insights. I think I have always been intrigued and moved, without quite knowing why, by its author's suggestion that the person of faith is distinguished by 'a paradoxical and humble courage' – but re-reading it this summer, my attention was drawn far more than before to references to courage throughout the text. This compelled me to reflect on courage: on why Kierkegaard, in 1843, thought it was important; and on why we should think it is important now. In his 1784 essay 'What Is Enlightenment?', the German philosopher Immanuel Kant urges his readers to have the courage to understand things for themselves (*'Sapere aude!'*), but for Kierkegaard a further and perhaps more radical kind of courage is required when we reach the limits of our understanding; when knowledge, calculation and planning fail us; when we step out into the unknown. This domain of the unknown may include the existence and nature of God; the inner lives of other people, and even of ourselves; and also, of course, the future.

I offer these personal remarks not in order to tell you something about myself, but in order to say something about Kierkegaard and *Fear and Trembling* – and not just to point out the significance of courage for this thinker, and in this text. One of the starting-points of Kierkegaard's philosophical reflection on such themes as truth, freedom, selfhood, suffering, love, responsibility and spiritual growth – which are all, along with courage, integral to *Fear and Trembling* – is his recognition that to exist is to be in a continual process of becoming. *Fear and Trembling* ends with a reference to Heraclitus' remark that one can never step twice into the same river, and we learn most from this ancient piece of philosophy when we focus less on the river than on the person stepping into it.

On the first page of his book *Repetition*, Kierkegaard raises 'the question of repetition—whether or not it is possible, what importance it has, whether something gains or loses in being repeated', and this question is as pertinent to the act of reading a text as it is to other activities and experiences. I often advise my students to read a text at least twice before they even attempt to make a preliminary judgement about its meaning and value. But can a reader read the same book twice? Each time we read we are different, because we are continually formed, however slightly, by our actions and experiences. At the very least, the person who reads *Fear and Trembling* for a second time is, unlike the 'same' person who reads it the first time, someone who has read the book once before.

Perhaps if I attempted a second time to write a *Reader's Guide* to *Fear and Trembling*, this would differ as much from the present book as from those by John Lippitt, Edward Mooney, and future authors who will no doubt repeat the endeavour to introduce readers to this classic text. In any case, please remember that what follows is one possible interpretation of Kierkegaard's text, which is itself one possible interpretation of the biblical story of Abraham's sacrifice of his son Isaac. In other words, if you are a serious reader of *Fear and Trembling* then you will approach both this introduction and the text itself in a questioning spirit. Kierkegaard often envisaged a reader who, as a 'single individual', would take to heart his writing as an occasion to reflect on her own life. Of course, you may wish merely to understand *Fear and Trembling* better. But if so, I hope that this *Reader's Guide* will help you to recognise and to think through for yourself the many questions raised in Kierkegaard's text.

The majority of this book is expository and exegetical, rather than critical. This is not because I want to persuade readers to agree with Kierkegaard, but because *Fear and Trembling* contains much that requires explanation – and my primary aim is to contribute to a better understanding of the text. And in any case, however well we understand *Fear and Trembling*, it has an essential, and deliberate, open-endedness and ambiguity that makes its author's position elusive. For this reason, it is not entirely clear *what* we should assess and evaluate. In my final chapter, however, I will step back from the text and consider some critical responses to it. Readers who would like a shorter overall discussion of *Fear and Trembling* might miss out the lengthy section 'Reading the Text', and move straight to 'Reception and Influence' after reading the 'Overview of Themes and Context'.

I would like to thank Ben Morgan, Georgios Patios, Mark Sinclair, Dan Watts and Kate Wharton, who each read and commented on all or part of a draft of this book. I'm also grateful to my colleagues in the Department of Philosophy at the University of Liverpool, whose support enabled me to have a semester of research leave in autumn 2009.

A NOTE ON THE TEXT

All references to Kierkegaard's *Fear and Trembling* use the 2006 Cambridge University Press edition of the text, translated and edited by C. Stephen Evans and Sylvia Walsh. Like the 1985 Penguin Classics edition, translated by Alastair Hannay, the Cambridge edition is a slim volume that includes a good introduction and useful notes, and is ideal for use by undergraduate students.

The standard English-language scholarly edition of *Fear and Trembling* is the 1983 Princeton University Press volume, translated by Howard V. Hong and Edna H. Hong, which also contains *Repetition*. The Hongs' edition contains a short Historical Introduction, notes, and supplementary material relating to the two texts, much of which is taken from Kierkegaard's journals and papers.

CHAPTER 1

OVERVIEW OF THEMES AND CONTEXT

The majority of this book is devoted to reading *Fear and Trembling*, section by section, in order to understand, explore and reflect on the ideas and questions that it contains. This opening chapter offers just a brief overview of these themes, in order to give the reader a preliminary orientation, and also to convey a sense of the richness and complexity of *Fear and Trembling* – a text which manages, in little more than a hundred pages, to be 'about' many different things at once. I will also fill in some of the philosophical, theological and cultural background to the text.

An observant reader will notice, on opening *Fear and Trembling*, that the book appears to have two different authors. The front cover of any edition of the text will bear the name 'Søren Kierkegaard', but inside there will be a title page indicating that *Fear and Trembling* is 'A Dialectical Lyric' written by 'Johannes de silentio'. This name denotes not just a pseudonym, but a character created by Kierkegaard. Even though, as we shall see, *Fear and Trembling* is an extremely personal work, the fact that it is signed by Johannes de silentio puts some distance between the author and his text. We should not assume that the views expressed in the book are Kierkegaard's own. For this reason, when discussing *Fear and Trembling* I will attribute its content to the pseudonym, Johannes de silentio, leaving open the question as to whether it can also be attributed to Kierkegaard. It may be that the connections and similarities between this text and others that Kierkegaard wrote under different pseudonyms will persuade us that *Fear and Trembling* does belong to a body of philosophical work that is distinctively 'Kierkegaardian'.

Fear and Trembling was published, in Copenhagen, on 16 October 1843. Two other short books written by Kierkegaard were also published on this day: *Repetition*, written under the pseudonym Constantin Constantius, and *Three Upbuilding Discourses*, a collection of sermon-like talks based on biblical texts,

published under Kierkegaard's own name.[1] This book of religious discourses – which comprises two discourses on 'Love Will
Hide a Multitude of Sins' and one on 'Strengthening in the Inner
Being' – is one of six such 'edifying' collections published during
1843 and 1844, each of which is dedicated to Kierkegaard's
father, Michael Pedersen Kierkegaard. *Repetition* and *Three
Upbuilding Discourses* provide an immediate context for *Fear and
Trembling*, and it is possible to regard the three works as a kind
of literary triptych, for even though they appear to be very different kinds of text, written by three different authors, they share
in common at least some of the themes that are outlined in this
chapter, and discussed in more detail throughout this book.[2]

Sometimes scholars engage in debates about what *Fear and
Trembling* is 'really about'. This is itself an indication of the
text's enigmatic character, but it seems to me that *Fear and
Trembling* is clearly multi-layered, and indeed that this contributes to its enduring significance, and its appeal to many different
kinds of reader. For this reason, however, it is not always easy to
separate the themes of the text, but in this chapter I will attempt
to do precisely this, by organizing key themes under several
headings. The first three sections focus on aspects of Johannes
de silentio's analysis of faith: the idea of a relationship to God;
the fragility and impermanence that characterize the human
condition; the themes of fidelity, love and truth. The following
two sections deal with the question of the relationship between
religious faith and ethical life: I put this question in context by
showing how the category of the ethical is, in Kierkegaard's
thought, one of three 'spheres of existence', before turning to
consider how the question is addressed in *Fear and Trembling*.
Section 6 examines Johannes de silentio's critique of the modern
age, and of modern philosophy, and the final section glances at
the literary form of the text, and discusses its cryptic epigraph.

THE TASK OF FAITH: RELATING TO GOD

The theme of the individual's relationship to God, and questions about how this relationship affects her life and her way of
being in the world, are at the centre of *Fear and Trembling*. Like
many of Kierkegaard's works, the book takes biblical texts as a
starting-point for philosophical reflection. Most immediately
and obviously, the subject-matter of *Fear and Trembling* is the

story of Abraham's response to God's command to sacrifice his son, Isaac, which is narrated in Genesis 22. This story is sometimes referred to as 'the Akedah', which means 'the binding'. Abraham takes Isaac up to Mount Moriah, makes an altar, binds his son, and raises a knife over his body. This response has to be considered in the light of God's earlier promise that Abraham would be the father of a great nation: Isaac represents the fulfilment of this promise, and thus the demand that he be sacrificed conflicts with it. According to Johannes de silentio, Abraham's faith consists not merely in his obedience to the divine command, but in his continuing trust that God will nevertheless be true to his promise.

However, Johannes de silentio's analysis of faith moves between the Hebrew bible and the Christian scriptures. The title of *Fear and Trembling* is taken from one of the earliest Christian texts, Paul's letter to the Philippians. Paul urges the Christian community in Philippi to 'work out your salvation with fear and trembling; for it is God who is at work in you, enabling you both to will and to work for his good pleasure' (Philippians 2:12–13).[3] Paul's message combines a call to responsibility with a denial of human self-sufficiency: the spiritual life is 'enabled' by God's work, but each member of the community is urged to 'live your life in the manner worthy of the gospel of Christ', to 'stand firm in the Lord' (Philippians 1:27, 4:1). *Fear and Trembling* echoes this message, for it explores a tension between responsibility and humble receptivity that seems to lie at the heart of faith. It also resembles Paul's letter insofar as it directly addresses its author's Christian contemporaries in the context of a specific historical situation. As Kierkegaard once observed, 'Times are different and have different requirements.'[4]

Like most of his Danish and German contemporaries, Kierkegaard grew up within and practised the Lutheran form of Christianity. Martin Luther's reformation of Christianity in the sixteenth century was prompted by his view that the religious life had become too worldly, too focused on external observances, and dominated too much by the hierarchy of the church, which mediated between ordinary people and God. Luther emphasized that faith – that is to say, the individual's inward, personal relationship to God – was at the heart of the Christian life. By the nineteenth century, however, Lutheran Christianity had itself become an established church, and was the official state religion in Denmark. Kierkegaard, in an entirely Lutheran spirit, was concerned that this conventionalized public religiosity deceived people into believing themselves to be Christians as a matter of course, simply by virtue of being born into a Christian country and participating in its customs – going to church each Sunday morning, for example. In short, Kierkegaard thought that the culture of nineteenth-century Denmark fostered religious complacency.

Johannes de silentio uses the example of Abraham to explore the nature of the task of faith that confronts Christians living within this culture. One of the reasons why Abraham's faith provides a starting-point for Johannes de silentio is that it is, in a sense, a faith without religion: without doctrines, without institutions, without a religious community shaped by shared practices and customs. Abraham's faith consists wholly in his personal relationship to God, and the story of his life that is narrated in Genesis takes the form of an ongoing conversation with God. Just as Abraham's faith is tested to the utmost by God's command to sacrifice Isaac, so, in *Fear and Trembling*, Kierkegaard's pseudonym attempts to test the faith of his contemporaries by raising the questions of whether they would act as Abraham did, and whether they can even understand Abraham's faith. In this way, *Fear and Trembling* was written, like other Kierkegaardian texts, in order to provoke genuine reflection on the task of becoming a Christian. Part of Johannes de silentio's strategy is to show that Christianity *is* a task; that is to say, that people are not born into Christianity, but face the task of becoming Christians. Only at the end of *Fear and Trembling*, however, does this become explicit: the book's brief Epilogue makes many references to 'the task', announces the need to 'call attention to the tasks', and emphasizes that 'the task is always sufficient for a lifetime' [108].

The Epilogue to *Fear and Trembling* implies that the text as a whole is seeking to explore what exactly the task of faith entails. As we shall see, the interpretation of Abraham that is offered in the book suggests that faith is not just the highest task of a human life, but the most difficult. This, of course, is a view that readers may want to question – perhaps because they disagree with Johannes de silentio's reading of the story of Abraham;

perhaps because they do not share with his envisaged nineteenth-century reader the presumption or the aspiration to be a Christian, and therefore do not regard a relationship to God to be even relevant, let alone essential, to their lives. Even though Kierkegaard, writing in the guise of different pseudonyms, disputes the idea that people are born into Christianity, it is perhaps still right to say that nineteenth-century Europeans were born into the *task* of becoming Christians. By contrast, many of us who were born in the twentieth or twenty-first centuries have inherited different tasks – including the task of figuring out which tasks to undertake – but it may still be the case that Johannes de silentio's analysis of the task of faith is relevant to our own situations. In questioning the legitimacy of a Christian's claim to be a Christian, Johannes raises the more general question of whether, and how, we are true to the identities and roles we assume for ourselves.

Just for a moment, let us try to consider faith from the point of view of someone who believes in God, and who accepts faith as her task. Why might faith be difficult? Why might it be difficult to maintain a relationship with God, who is after all the creator and source of all things? In *Fear and Trembling*, Johannes de silentio shows that faith has to contend with two powerful forces: doubt and sin. Faith is the opposite of doubt, on the one hand, and it is the opposite of sin, on the other. Doubt undermines a person's belief and trust in the existence and the goodness of God. Faith is not knowledge, and thus it is always susceptible to being tested by doubt – perhaps because scientific theories about the beginning of the universe and the nature of the human being might seem to make the hypothesis of a creator God redundant; perhaps because the suffering, cruelty and injustice we find in the world seem to be incompatible with the presence of a loving God. In *Fear and Trembling*, Johannes de silentio envisages Abraham as plagued by doubts that cause him great anxiety.

Although the pseudonym does not apply the category of sin directly to Abraham, sin nevertheless plays an important role in the text – especially in Problem III – and more generally it is essential to any conception of Christian faith. The concept of sin is complex and has a long history, but it basically signifies a failure to relate properly to God. Sin means turning away from God in some way, and according to the Christian theological tradition this evasion of the God-relationship is a universal human tendency, even though it can express itself in many different ways. For Kierkegaard, becoming aware that one is in the state of sin – that one has a relationship to God which is not being honoured or fulfilled – is the essential first step in the task of becoming a Christian. In his 1846 text *Concluding Unscientific Postscript*, his pseudonym Johannes Climacus writes, in the course of a discussion of *Fear and Trembling*, that 'Sin is a crucial expression for the religious existence . . . Sin is the beginning of the religious order of things.'[5] Even a concept so steeped in the theological tradition can be understood as relevant beyond that tradition, so long as we bear in mind that it is primarily concerned not with doing something immoral, illegal, or disapproved of by the Church, but rather with a certain tendency to neglect what is, deep down, most important in one's life.

Readers who do not accept or understand the claim that they have, or might have, a relationship to God may find it easier to countenance the idea that they have a relationship to themselves. One of the interesting aspects of Johannes de silentio's interpretation of Abraham is the suggestion that it is difficult to distinguish between Abraham's relationship to God and his relationship to himself. Why does Abraham choose to sacrifice Isaac? 'For God's sake, and what is altogether identical with this, for his own sake' [52]. If it makes sense to say that one has a relationship to oneself – a relationship that might render meaningful the possibility of 'being true to oneself' – then the categories of doubt and sin need not be confined to a specifically religious task of faith. One might find oneself contending with self-doubt; one might have an obscure sense that one is ignoring or avoiding something within oneself that, if it succeeded in claiming one's attention, would turn out to be integral to one's being. And indeed, the doubts that Johannes de silentio imagines Abraham struggling with are not so much doubts about the existence and nature of God, but doubts about himself: whether he is mistaken about the divine command, whether he really does love Isaac more than he loves himself.

FAITH AND GIFT

Another important theme in *Fear and Trembling* is the connection between religious faith and ordinary life – between spirituality and what we might call 'the world'. In particular, Abraham's sacrifice of Isaac provides the occasion for Johannes de silentio to raise the question of family relationships. The pseudonym highlights 'a remarkable teaching on the absolute duty to God' [63] in the gospel of Luke, where Jesus says: 'Whoever comes to me and does not hate father and mother, wife and children, brothers and sisters, yes, and even life itself, cannot be my disciple . . . none of you can become my disciple if you do not give up all your possessions' (Luke 14: 26, 33). Johannes de silentio insists that this 'hard saying' should not be avoided. However, he also insists that Abraham exemplifies a faith that, far from withdrawing from the world, lives happily within it and gains great joy from human relationships.

Such faith involves receiving one's finite, earthly existence, in every little particular detail, as a gift from God. But this divine gift can only be given, and received, once the individual gives up her possessions – that is to say, gives up on the very idea that her life, and everything within it, belongs to her in the first place. On this view, the religious person's renunciation of worldly things does not itself constitute the task of faith, but is rather a preliminary movement that makes faith possible. Several of Kierkegaard's pseudonyms indicate that being absorbed in worldly concerns is a common and very effective way of ignoring one's relationship to God (or to oneself, considered as a spiritual being) – but they also emphasize that faith is itself a way of living in the world. Abraham's achievement, according to Johannes de silentio, consists in the fact that 'he believed precisely for this life' [17]; that 'he did not believe that he would be blessed one day in the hereafter but that he would become blissfully happy here in the world' [30].

Fear and Trembling offers a sustained exploration of the conditions under which the relationship to God is maintained; the conditions in which the religious life is lived. These conditions are simply those of human existence. In his interpretation of the story of Abraham, Johannes de silentio emphasizes suffering and loss, finitude and mortality. The theme of the gift is anchored just as much in this view of the human condition as in Christian theology. For example, one does not have to believe in a creator God to be struck by the thought that nothing in one's life is of one's own making. I did not create my body, my intelligence, my parents, the street or indeed the earth I live on. This is not to

7

deny that we make choices about our lives, that we build up friendships, families and careers through our own efforts and actions. But we do not create the people who become our friends or partners or colleagues, nor do we bring about our first encounters with them; we did not make the talents and capacities that enable us to pursue a certain career. We do not even create our own children: the fact that some people who want to have children are unable, for whatever reason, to do so suggests that this is also something that lies beyond our own power, whether or not we actually do become parents. And we are just as little able to hold onto what is ours once we have it.

Abraham's situation draws attention to this aspect of the human condition: he and Sarah are childless in their old age; when their son Isaac is born, he is a gift from God; Isaac is subsequently demanded as a sacrifice. The biblical story of Job, which is discussed in Kierkegaard's pseudonymous text *Repetition*, has a similar message. Job loses all his children, his animals, and his servants. Like Abraham, Job's possessions are eventually restored to him by God: Job is given 'twice as much as he had before' (Job 42: 10), just as Abraham 'receives a son a second time' [7]. Kierkegaard was clearly fascinated by the idea that one only is what one is, and has what one has, by virtue of a gift – and that what is thus given can also be taken away. In *Fear and Trembling*, this human vulnerability is vividly expressed by Johannes de silentio's reference to 'the sword hanging over the beloved's head' [43], an image which connects the climax of Abraham's story with the awareness of mortality and impermanence that haunts all human relationships. Kierkegaard returns to the theme of the gift in his 1843 religious discourses on biblical texts such as 'Every Good and Perfect Gift is From Above', and 'The Lord Gave, and the Lord Took Away; Blessed be the name of the Lord', which he published, under his own name, a couple of months after *Fear and Trembling* and *Repetition*.[6]

Although the word 'gift' does not actually occur in *Fear and Trembling*, it is, I think, an important theme within the text. However, Johannes de silentio frequently emphasizes that faith is not something that human beings can accomplish through their own efforts, and insists that Abraham's faith consists in his ability to receive Isaac, rather than in giving up his son in obedience to God's command. Perhaps the reason why Johannes doesn't speak in terms of gifts or grace is that, as we shall see, he is a character who struggles to make sense of the idea of a loving God, and who thus fails to understand *how* Abraham receives Isaac as a gift.

But what is at stake, philosophically, in the idea of the gift? This is a question that we will need to confront as we read *Fear and Trembling*, but here I will just point to the difference between the notions of gift and sacrifice, and the idea of human rights that provides the basis for much of our thinking about ethics and justice. The discourse of human rights implies a concept of entitlement that is foreign to the logic of the gift. A gift is most purely a gift when it is completely superfluous: when it has not been earned or worked for, and when it does not confer an obligation on the person who receives it. However, this superfluity seems to go hand in hand with, and perhaps even to depend on, a lack of security.

If, as Johannes de silentio suggests, human life is lived in the face of doubt and the expectation of losing what one loves, it is natural that people respond to this existential situation with fear and anxiety – with fear and trembling. For this reason, courage emerges over the course of the pseudonym's discussion as the most important of the traditional virtues that are regarded as elements of a good human life. There are references to courage throughout *Fear and Trembling*, and Johannes de silentio compares his own limited courage to the courage of faith that is, he suggests, beyond his reach.

SØREN AND REGINE: FIDELITY, LOVE AND TRUTH

Biblical texts are not the only point of departure for the discussion of faith presented *Fear and Trembling*, nor are Johannes de silentio's reflections confined to questions about the religious life. The biographical background to the writing of *Fear and Trembling* reveals another dimension to the text. As we have seen, Kierkegaard published both *Fear and Trembling* and *Repetition* on the same day in October 1843. These two books were written during an astonishingly productive three-week visit to Berlin in May 1843. Eighteen months previously, in the autumn of 1841, Kierkegaard had broken off his relationship with a young woman called Regine Olsen, to whom he had been engaged for a little over a year. This decision and its consequences had a profound effect on Kierkegaard's intellectual development as well as on his inner life, and *Repetition* uses the story of a broken engagement as a basis for philosophical reflection on questions of truth and ethics. Other pseudonymous works also indicate Kierkegaard's preoccupation with marriage and romantic love: *Either/Or*, published in spring 1843, depicts two contrasting attitudes towards marriage; *Stages on Life's Way* (1845) returns to the story of a broken engagement; much of Problem III, the lengthiest chapter in *Fear and Trembling*, focuses on the stories of various couples who face the decision of whether or not to marry.

Some commentators prefer to leave the story of Kierkegaard's relationship to Regine out of their analysis of *Fear and Trembling*, and it is certainly possible to read the book and reflect philosophically on its exploration of religious faith without knowing anything about its author's personal life. One of the reasons for overlooking this biographical background is a worry that regarding the book as 'about' the broken engagement undermines its philosophical significance. However, Kierkegaard's decision not to marry Regine was a stimulus for intense philosophical reflection about human freedom; about the existing individual's relationship to what he calls 'the ethical sphere'; about the possibility of making a commitment to another person in the face of an uncertain future. Indeed, it might not be entirely extravagant to claim that Kierkegaard's break with Regine determined the time and place of the birth of 'existentialism'. Be that as it may, when we read Johannes de silentio's discussion of Abraham with Kierkegaard's broken engagement in mind, it becomes clear that *Fear and Trembling* is concerned not simply with the individual's relationship to God, but with other relationships too. Reflecting on *Fear and Trembling* and *Repetition*, Kierkegaard's pseudonym Johannes Climacus asserts that 'a love affair . . . is always a usable theme in relation to what it means to exist.'[7]

Kierkegaard appears to have interpreted his break with Regine as follows.[8] He loved Regine. After asking her to marry him, he began to feel that he was not suited for marriage – because he had a highly-strung, depressive nature; because he felt unable to share his inner life completely with another person; because he wished to devote his time to thinking and writing – and that for these reasons, and possibly others too, he would not make

Regine happy as her husband. In 1843, he wrote, of the relationship, that 'I wanted it but was incapable of it.'[9] Both Kierkegaard and Regine were very distressed when he ended it; her father even begged Kierkegaard to reconsider. From an ethical point of view, breaking the engagement, like breaking any promise, was wrong. Moreover, Kierkegaard found it difficult to explain himself to Regine, and even thought it best to pretend not to love her in order to make the break-up easier for her to bear, so that he transgressed his moral duty to be honest as well as his duty to keep his promise.

From this situation emerged the philosophical question: are ethical requirements the highest claim on a human being? If so, then Kierkegaard's actions were simply wrong, insofar as they represented an assertion of his own interests at the cost of Regine's. But is it possible to regard his betrayal and deception as expressions of a kind of inner truthfulness: not just a decision to be true to his own developing feelings about what is right, but a decision to be true to his love for Regine? Might actions that fall short of ethical requirements be expressions of a love that transcends such requirements?

These are some of the questions that Johannes de silentio raises in response to the story of Abraham. The two situations clearly have some structural similarities. Johannes de silentio describes Abraham's decision to sacrifice Isaac as 'a teleological suspension of the ethical' [49], and in *Concluding Unscientific Postscript* Kierkegaard's pseudonym Johannes Climacus claims that both *Fear and Trembling* and *Repetition* concern a broken engagement and present 'the interpretation of the broken pledge along the lines of a teleological suspension . . . '[10] In 1849 Kierkegaard wrote in his journal that '*Fear and Trembling* actually reproduced my own life.'[11] Now, this does not mean that we should conclude that the story of Abraham is merely a substitute for the story of Kierkegaard's relationship to Regine. Indeed, one clear difference between the two situations is that it seems easier to regard Kierkegaard as motivated at least in part out of concern for Regine, while it is difficult to argue that Abraham has Isaac's interests at heart when he decides to sacrifice him. However, the fact that Kierkegaard evidently saw a connection between his experience with Regine and the discussion of Abraham in *Fear and Trembling* does suggest that

Johannes de silentio's analysis of faith has a relevance outside a specifically religious context – that it bears on questions about love and fidelity between human beings, as well on the individual's relationship to God.

For Kierkegaard, the break-up with Regine, like the story of Abraham, raised the question of what it means to 'remain true to [one's] love' [106]. His pseudonym Johannes Climacus suggests that *Either/Or* is 'a polemic against truth as knowledge'[12], and this description might be applied to Kierkegaard's work as a whole. Implicit in *Fear and Trembling* is an opposition between truths that are known (if, indeed, such truths exist) and truths that are lived – an opposition that is articulated more explicitly in its companion-text, *Repetition*.[13] Lived truth, or truthfulness, may take various forms, such as honesty, integrity, authenticity and fidelity. These are all subjective truths, in the sense that they are ways in which an individual exists, ways in which she relates to others or to herself. The possibility of fidelity is invoked by Johannes de silentio's claim that Abraham's achievement was to remain true to his love, but also, it seems, by Kierkegaard's reflection – recorded in his journal in Berlin in May 1843, while writing *Fear and Trembling* and *Repetition* – that 'if I had had faith, I would have stayed with Regine'.[14]

In Kierkegaard's philosophy, the theme of truth is tied to the theme of movement. Again, this connection is perhaps more apparent in *Repetition* than in *Fear and Trembling*, but nevertheless the latter text is full of movements. Indeed, Kierkegaard appears to have considered using 'Movements and Positions' as a title or subtitle for the book (another alternative was 'Between Each Other').[15] At one point in the text Johannes de silentio remarks that 'it would not be difficult for me to write a whole book if I were to go through all the various misunderstandings, the awkward postures, the slipshod movements I have encountered in my modest practice' [38], and he repeatedly describes faith as a 'double movement'. As well as such direct references to movement, the nature of faith is expressed through metaphors of movement such as Abraham's journey to Mount Moriah, and the leap of a ballet dancer. *Fear and Trembling* ends with a reference to ancient Greek philosophical debates about the possibility of motion, and *Repetition* begins by taking up this issue again.

One of the reasons why it might be difficult to 'remain true to one's love' is that, as Kierkegaard's pseudonyms often point out, existing individuals live in time, are always in motion, perpetually becoming. This thought is by no means particular to Kierkegaard; in Plato's *Symposium*, for example, we find the claim that

> during the period for which any living being is said to live and to retain his identity – as a man, for example, is called the same man from boyhood to old age – he does not in fact retain the same attributes, although he is called the same person; he is always becoming a new being and undergoing a process of loss and reparation, which affects his hair, his flesh, his bones, his blood, and his whole body. And not only his body, but his soul as well.[16]

If change and movement are integral to the human condition, this has important ethical consequences. When we relate to ourselves or to others, we do so *through time*: the self is not exhausted by its present being, but stretches back into the past and forward to the future. So, for example, when one makes a promise, one promises on behalf of the future self one is yet to become; one gives to one's future self the responsibility for being true to the present self who makes the promise. Indeed, through the very act of promising the 'present self' shows that its being is not, in fact, confined to the present moment, but includes a relationship to the future. But we do not know exactly who, or how, our future selves will be. In this way, as in others, the kind of truth that is at stake in fidelity is not accessible through knowledge – at least, not through knowledge alone.

SPHERES OF EXISTENCE: AESTHETIC, ETHICAL, AND RELIGIOUS

In many of Kierkegaard's pseudonymous texts a distinction is made – sometimes explicitly, sometimes less overtly – between three 'spheres of existence': the aesthetic, the ethical, and the religious. Johannes de silentio does not use the phrase 'spheres of existence', but nevertheless the distinction between aesthetic, ethical and religious standpoints, and the question of the relationship between them, is integral to his analysis of faith. The characterizations of these different spheres are quite fluid throughout

Kierkegaard's works, and the ethical sphere in particular varies from one text to another: it is sometimes depicted, as in *Fear and Trembling*, in a fairly narrow way as the domain of morality; in other texts 'the ethical' signifies, more broadly and perhaps more positively, a mode of life characterized by the exercise of freedom – by a willingness to make decisions and commitments, and to take responsibility for oneself. Viewed in this way, the ethical sphere contains elements that are also important for the religious life, although in the religious sphere these expressions of freedom are understood in relation to God, rather than in merely-human terms. But however it is delimited, the ethical sphere is for Kierkegaard always a domain of human autonomy, and it is always concerned with what he calls 'actuality': with real-life situations that often involve other people as well as oneself, in which decisions and commitments really matter.

The aesthetic sphere is distinct from the ethical sphere insofar as it lacks this actuality; it is often described as a form of 'ideality' or 'reflection', which includes imagination and fantasy as well as the kind of abstract thought that is purely intellectual or hypothetical. The aesthetic sphere is also associated with moods, feelings and inclinations, which are transient, in contrast with the ethical commitments that bring stability and constancy to a person's life.

One way of distinguishing between the three spheres of existence is with reference to the values that act as motivating principles within each sphere. The aesthetic form of life can only recognize as valuable whatever is pleasurable, amusing or interesting, and this means that it is subjective and relativistic, since such value depends entirely on an individual's personal tastes and preferences. Moreover, the fact that what is enjoyable or stimulating one day can become boring the next renders this kind of value mutable, unstable. An archetypal aesthetic charac-ter is a flirt or a seducer who chases a series of different partners, and either fails to get what she desires, or gets it but then becomes bored and so moves on to someone new. The first part of Kierkegaard's book *Either/Or* depicts a young man who lives in this way, and we find here, as in some of his later texts, the suggestion that there is no lasting satisfaction or fulfilment to be gained from a purely aesthetic life. In the ethical sphere, by con-trast, the highest value is moral duty, which is a longer-lasting and more objective, communal form of value. Within the religious sphere, the highest value is the individual's relationship to God – that is to say, her faith.

It is important to recognize that Kierkegaard's distinction between the aesthetic, ethical and religious spheres does not concern *what* people do, but *how* they do it. For example, one might distinguish between aesthetic, ethical and religious ways of being a Christian: in each case, a person engages in typically 'Christian' activities such as going to church, reading the bible, praying, professing belief in the resurrection, using a certain vocabulary, and so on. But for the aesthete this might be a passing phase – perhaps an experimentation or 'flirtation' with Christianity simply because it appears to offer interesting or enjoyable experiences; for the ethical person this would constitute a dutiful commitment to a certain conception of a good, moral life, and participation in a specific community; for the religious individual it would express a personal relationship to God. In other words, each of the three spheres of existence denotes a particular way of relating to oneself, to the world, and to others. In the context of the task of becoming a Christian which is the subject-matter of Kierkegaard's writings, this distinction between the three spheres provides a framework for analysing the illusions that, in his view, fed the complacency of his contemporaries. Authentically becoming a Christian means existing religiously, but identifying alternative existential spheres indicates how it is possible to deceive oneself by going through the motions of a Christian life while remaining within an aesthetic or ethical way of being.

An important question that faces the reader of *Fear and Trembling* concerns the nature of 'the ethical' – understood in the more specific sense of the sphere of moral conduct – that is invoked by Johannes de silentio. If we look back through the history of philosophy, we find many different accounts of morality. Philosophers do not just engage in debates about what is right and wrong, good and evil, but also attempt to explain how claims about moral values can be justified. Among the most influential accounts of morality are those which prescribe specific laws – for example, the Ten Commandments, or Jesus' commands to love one's enemies and abstain from judging others; those based on a more general, formal law such as 'treat others as you would wish to be treated'; those which focus on certain virtuous character traits, such as justice, generosity, courage and truthfulness; those which assess the moral worth of actions solely in terms of the overall happiness or harm that results from them; and those which emphasize the cultivation of wisdom that will lead to knowledge of 'the good', which is understood to exist objectively, independent of cultural norms and individual preferences. And one might regard the authority of a system of morality as grounded in human reason; in tradition; in nature; in divine revelation; or in an ongoing process of negotiation between different individuals and interest-groups.

As we will see, in *Fear and Trembling* Johannes de silentio considers the story of Abraham from an ethical perspective characterized by the claim that moral requirements apply to everyone, and are grounded in human reason. The pseudonym emphasizes that this 'ethical sphere' is self-contained: 'it rests immanently in itself, has nothing outside itself that is its *telos* [end, goal, good], but is itself the *telos* for everything outside itself' [46]. Having defined the ethical in this way, Johannes asks how it is possible to admire Abraham for being prepared to kill his son. He argues that if we judge Abraham's willingness to sacrifice Isaac according to ethical criteria then we can do nothing but condemn him as a murderer. For what could there possibly be to admire in a father who kills his innocent young son?

RELIGION AND ETHICS; FAITH AND REASON

By defining the ethical in such a way as to insist that it 'has nothing outside itself that is its *telos*', Johannes de silentio raises the issue of the relationship between ethics and religion. If the ethical sphere recognizes no values higher than rational, universal moral laws, then this means that it can accept religious beliefs and practices only to the extent that they accord with these laws. The German philosopher Immanuel Kant states that '*apart from good life-conduct, anything that a human being supposes that he can do to become well-pleasing to God is mere religious delusion and counterfeit service of God*', and he therefore argues that Abraham was wrong to obey God's command to kill his son.[17] Johannes de silentio agrees with Kant that Abraham's actions are morally reprehensible. According to the pseudonym, Abraham transgresses his ethical duty solely for the sake of his own relationship to God. This means that unless this relationship to God – this faith – can be recognized as higher than the ethical sphere, our only option is to regard Abraham as a murderer. Kant's view represents one horn of the dilemma that Johannes de silentio presents to his reader; but the pseudonym, unlike Kant, wants to keep open the possibility that Abraham's faith is admirable, even though it cannot be understood.

There are several reasons why Johannes de silentio wants to challenge Kant's view – a version of which was shared by Hegel – that true religious faith consists simply in fulfilling, to the best of one's ability, the ethical requirement of 'good life-conduct'. One of these reasons is that, for both Kant and Hegel, the ethical sphere is a self-contained domain, within which human beings give themselves a moral law to live by. Perhaps Kierkegaard – or Johannes de silentio – would agree that this seems reasonable enough. But should Christianity be confined within this autonomous, finite ethical sphere? Surely a person who really does believe in God will recognize that his power makes possible things that lie beyond the limited range of human action? As Johannes de silentio puts it, 'spiritually speaking, everything is possible, but in the finite world there is much that is not possible' [37].

It is interesting to compare Johannes de silentio's analysis of the story of Abraham with that offered by Martin Luther in his lectures on the Book of Genesis. Luther's interpretation of the sacrifice provides us with part of the historical background to *Fear and Trembling*, but it is important to point out how Johannes de silentio's discussion of Abraham differs from Luther's. Crude readings of *Fear and Trembling* can lead to the misguided view that its analysis of faith is essentially the same as the Lutheran account, which valorizes Abraham's unquestioning obedience to God and rejection of reason.

Luther emphasizes the contradiction between God's promise to make Abraham the father of nations and his subsequent demand that Abraham sacrifice Isaac, and indicates that 'human reason would simply conclude either that the promise is lying or that the command is not God's but the devil's. For there is a plain contradiction. If Isaac must be killed, the promise is void; but if the promise is sure, it is impossible that this is a command of God.'[18] For this reason, according to Luther, 'it is impossible for us to comprehend the greatness of this trial'; he confesses that 'I could not have been an onlooker, much less the performer and the slayer. It is an astounding situation that the dearly beloved father moves his knife close to the throat of the dearly beloved son, and I surely admit that I cannot attain to these thoughts and sentiments either by words or by reflecting on them.'[19]

Johannes de silentio echoes Luther in accentuating the contradiction faced by Abraham; in claiming that Abraham's faith cannot be understood; and in indicating his own inability to do what Abraham did. However, while the sixteenth-century theologian expresses unqualified admiration for Abraham, Kierkegaard's pseudonym is far more ambivalent: 'while Abraham . . . arouses my admiration, he appals me as well' [53]. The dilemma that Johannes presents to the reader of *Fear and Trembling* is never finally resolved: *either* we must conclude, with Kant, that Abraham is no better than a murderer; *or* we admit – as Luther does so readily – that religious faith transcends the requirements of ethics and reason.

Appreciating the ambivalence of Johannes de silentio's position should help us to recognize that *Fear and Trembling* is not simply promoting a 'divine command' theory of ethics, according to which 'the good' is identified with God's will. If this were the case, then Johannes de silentio would have no difficulty in admiring Abraham on ethical grounds, and he would not suggest that the sacrifice of Isaac involves a 'teleological suspension of the ethical'. Also, he would not distinguish the faith for which he admires Abraham from mere obedience to God's command, as he clearly does in 'Tuning Up', where he envisages alternative Abrahams who obey God without having faith. On the basis of a divine command ethic, all that would matter is that Abraham does what God tells him to, but this is certainly not Johannes de silentio's view. Luther's response to Abraham, on the other hand, seems to advocate a divine command ethic: in his Lectures on Genesis, he envisages Abraham explaining the situation to Isaac by saying, 'God has given a command; therefore we must obey Him.'[20] And elsewhere, Luther uses the story of the Akedah as an example to illustrate that reason should not challenge God's will, arguing that just as Abraham 'committed the entire matter to God's omnipotence and wisdom, knowing that God had many more ways and means of fulfilling the promises concerning the seed of Isaac than he could comprehend with his blind reason', so 'in the same way we are to believe with all humility and obedience the . . . commands of [God], without any doubts or arguments as to how it is to be reconciled with our reason or how it is possible.'[21] While many people – religious believers among them – would be suspicious of such unquestioning 'blind faith', for Luther it is reason that is 'blind' insofar it is incapable of attaining to the truth of divine reality.

Johannes de silentio's view about the relationship between faith and reason seems to be both more nuanced and more enigmatic than Luther's. The pseudonym describes Abraham's faith as paradoxical and absurd, something 'which no thought can lay hold of because faith begins precisely where thinking leaves off' [46]. But this does not mean that reason is 'blind', although it does indicate that the scope of reason may be limited and that faith might lie beyond these limits. Reason is required in order to recognize a paradox *as* a paradox – and once reason has done so, there is a choice to be made between rejecting the paradox as absurd, and recognizing the value or importance of something beyond reason. This represents another formulation of the dilemma that Johannes de silentio poses to his reader. Notice that according to this formulation, remaining within reason involves making a decision, just as much as transgressing its limits does.

We should be careful not to assume too quickly that we know what Johannes de silentio means when he insists that he cannot understand Abraham's faith. In the Preface, he argues that 'even if one were able to translate the whole content of faith into conceptual form, it does not follow that one has comprehended faith, comprehended how one entered into it or how it entered into one' [5]. Here, he seems to equate 'comprehending faith' with understanding *how* faith is acquired. It seems that Johannes de silentio understands what faith is – or rather, understands what it *would be*, if it exists at all – without comprehending how such faith can be accomplished. He states that, in contrast to Abraham, he is unable to make the movement of faith: 'For my part, I can very well describe the movements of faith, but I can-not make them. If one wants to learn how to swim, one can let oneself be suspended in a sling from the ceiling and very well go through the motions, but one is not swimming. Likewise, I can describe the movements of faith . . . ' [31]. The understanding that the pseudonym lacks is practical, rather than theoretical. This raises the question of whether there might be a difference between a theoretical or conceptual paradox, and a practical or existential paradox. As we will see when we consider the section of the text entitled 'A Preliminary Outpouring from the Heart', there are reasons for thinking that Abraham's faith is paradoxical and absurd in this latter sense. That is to say, when Johannes de silentio suggests that it is absurd, he means that he does not understand how to make the movements of faith, although he does grasp what these movements consist in.

Furthermore, we should perhaps be wary of supposing that Johannes de silentio has the final word on the question of the relationship between faith and reason. An entry in Kierkegaard's journal of 1850, concerning *Fear and Trembling*, suggests that the pseudonym, who admits that he lacks faith, has a particular perspective that would not be shared by someone who actually has faith:

> When I believe, then assuredly neither faith nor the content of faith is absurd. Oh, no, no – but I understand very well that for the person who does not believe, faith and the content of faith are absurd, and I also understand that as soon as I myself am not in the faith, am weak, when doubt perhaps begins to stir, then faith and the content of faith gradually begin to become absurd for me.[22]

Why would the absurdity of faith depend on a particular perspective? Why is faith not absurd for the believer? Is this simply because someone who believes in God has surrendered her rational faculties – precisely in order to enable her to believe – and thus cannot recognize that her faith is absurd? Or is it because a person who has decided to put her trust in God understands her life and her relationship to the world on the basis of this trust, so that faith has, in a sense, its own logic, its own form of understanding? Or perhaps personal relationships in general are not of a rational order, so that when one is inside a relationship the categories of reason simply do not apply – and faith is a personal relationship to God. Perhaps a relationship cannot be understood from the outside in the same way as it is understood from the inside. Or alternatively, if the question of absurdity pertains to the *how* of faith, then it might make sense to say that one person understands how to live in faith while another lacks this understanding, or that a single person might sometimes understand faith and sometimes fail to understand it. We may struggle to make sense of these possibilities, but in any case recalling Kierkegaard's suggestion that faith is absurd only from a perspective outside it can encourage us to keep in mind the question of Johannes de silentio's own particular position within *Fear and Trembling*. If he is trying to persuade the reader that Abraham's faith is absurd, why might this be? Notice that, according to the journal entry quoted above, a person who feels unable to understand Abraham's faith can conclude that she is not herself a believer. And so, if the reader comes to share Johannes de silentio's interpretation of faith as paradoxical and absurd, then she must also come to recognize that she shares the pseudonym's lack of faith. And this recognition may bring her closer to the decision about whether or not to take up the task of becoming a Christian.

CRITIQUE OF THE MODERN AGE – AND OF MODERN PHILOSOPHY

Kierkegaard was a perceptive commentator on the state of the society he lived in, and he inherited from the German philosopher G. W. F. Hegel – who died in 1831, while Kierkegaard was a student at the University of Copenhagen – an acute sense of history. But whereas Hegel thought that history was progressing, under the guidance of philosophy, towards a more enlightened world, Kierkegaard interpreted his times in terms of decline rather than progress – and he regarded modern philosophy as a symptom of this decline. His writings contain many comments about the problems of the modern age: in *A Literary Review* (1846), for example, he tells his readers that they are living in 'a reflective and passionless age' that 'leaves everything standing but cunningly empties it of significance'; such an age 'has no values, and everything is transformed into representational ideas . . . finally, money will be the one thing people will desire, and it is moreover only representative, an abstraction . . . The whole of life [becomes] ambiguous, neither moral nor immoral.'[23] These remarks indicate that Kierkegaard believed his times to be characterized by a crisis of values – and *Fear and Trembling* opens with precisely this issue. Johannes de silentio begins his Preface to the text by suggesting that 'not only in the commercial world but in the realm of ideas as well, our age is holding a veritable clearance sale' [3], and he returns in his Epilogue to this concern for declining values 'in the world of spirit' [107].

More specifically, Johannes de silentio is concerned that religious faith is held to be of little value. He regards the complacent assumption that faith is easy as one aspect of this attitude. Therefore, in order to raise the value of faith the pseudonym seeks to accentuate its difficulty. As we shall see, his interpretation of the story of Abraham aims to do just this. Having highlighted the horror, distress, loneliness and anxiety of Abraham's situation, and having emphasized that it is impossible to admire Abraham's willingness to kill his son from an ethical point of view, Johannes presents the reader with a dilemma that undermines any complacency about faith: either Abraham is simply a murderer, or his faith represents the highest task of a human life, but is absolutely paradoxical. This dilemma urges the reader to make a decision not just about the story of Abraham, but about herself: Does she really have faith? Does she really want to have faith, if *this* is what it entails?

Closely related to the concern that faith is declining in value is the idea that this process will end in the decline of religious belief itself. As Johannes de silentio puts it in his Preface, 'Everything is to be had so dirt cheap that it is doubtful whether in the end anyone will bid' [3]. In other words, although the devaluation of faith currently manifests itself as a complacent assumption that everyone has faith, eventually people will give up on faith altogether. When we now look back on the nineteenth century, we do indeed see it as a period in which religious beliefs were put into question and rejected by many people. In Europe today, Christianity is no longer the dominant force it once was, even though it continues to condition our culture in many ways. Scientific developments such as Charles Darwin's theory of evolution, and intellectual developments such as Karl Marx's analysis of capitalism, can of course be regarded as causes, or as symptoms, of this process of secularization. Towards the end of the nineteenth century, the German philosopher Friedrich Nietzsche famously proclaimed 'the death of God', by which he meant the giving up of religious beliefs – upon which, Nietzsche emphasized, rested faith in moral values, in the possibility of knowledge, even in the value of truth itself.[24] But we find in *Fear and Trembling* an anticipation of this event, for Johannes de silentio describes a situation in which 'the whole existence of the human race rounds itself off in itself as a perfect sphere and the ethical is at once its limit and its completion. God becomes an invisible vanishing point, an impotent thought . . . ' [59].

According to Nietzsche, there is something inevitable about the death of God: it is not that people just decide to give up their faith, but that Christian belief becomes impossible to accept. Notice that there may well be a tension between Johannes de silentio's concerns about this death of God, on the one hand, and the declining value of faith, on the other. If his attempt to raise the value of faith by accentuating its difficulty has any impact, then its effect might be to hasten the process of secularization. Johannes de silentio may be right to suggest that if prices fall too low then no one wants to bid – but very high prices might also be discouraging. Readers of *Fear and Trembling* who accept the pseudonym's suggestion that belief in God lacks a rational basis – that it is, in fact, absurd – are just as likely to respond by giving up on the task of faith as by applying themselves to this task. Perhaps Johannes de silentio's analysis of the story of Abraham succeeds only in giving faith a final push over the edge of reason.

Kierkegaard was not the only person in nineteenth-century Copenhagen to suggest that his society was suffering a crisis of values. In fact, his diagnosis of the modern age in part echoes that of the Danish Hegelian writer Johann Ludvig Heiberg, whose 1833 essay *On the Significance of Philosophy for the Present Age* identifies a crisis of religion and culture and a decline into nihilistic relativism.[25] However, Heiberg believed that Hegel's philosophy represented the solution to this situation, whereas Kierkegaard regarded the popularity of Hegelian thought as one of the symptoms of decline. In many of Kierkegaard's texts, including *Fear and Trembling*, the question of the value of faith in the modern age is connected to a critique of modern philosophy, and especially of Hegel's ideas.

Although Kierkegaard was influenced by these ideas, he disagreed with some of the fundamental principles of Hegelian thought. These include a progressive interpretation of history, and an aspiration to incorporate everything – nature, religion, art, ethics, politics – into a rational system. According to Kierkegaard, Hegel's attempt to translate the content of Christian belief into conceptual form contributed to the devaluation of faith: he represents Hegel and his followers as believing philosophy's task of understanding the world to be more difficult, more important and more worthwhile than faith's task of existing in relation to God. Kierkegaard was particularly hostile to certain Danish Hegelians, such as Heiberg and Hans Lassen Martensen, and his pseudonyms' polemics against 'the System' often seem to be targeted more directly at these figures than at Hegel himself. When Johannes de silentio complains in the Preface to *Fear and Trembling* that his contemporaries presume to have reached faith and to have moved beyond it, instead of regarding faith as a life-long task, Martensen is probably his target. Martensen, for his part, wrote in his autobiography that 'in many ways [Kierkegaard] sought to disparage me, my abilities, and my work . . . His writings of course contained all sorts of polemical and satirical attacks on speculation [i.e. Hegelian philosophy], a portion of which were directed at me.'[26]

TELLING STORIES – AND WHO IS JOHANNES DE SILENTIO?

Fear and Trembling contains many stories. Although Johannes de silentio exploits Abraham's special status within the Judeo-Christian tradition as the 'father of faith', he approaches Genesis 22 as a literary text, and he develops imaginative variations of the story of Abraham and Isaac just as he suggests alternative versions of non-biblical texts. He also considers other biblical figures alongside characters from plays and folk tales, without distinguishing between sacred and secular genres, nor between fiction and historical fact.

The story of Abraham is first introduced as part of another story about a man who longs to witness Abraham's journey to Mount Moriah and his preparations for the sacrifice of Isaac. In the course of his interpretation of Abraham's story, Johannes de silentio discusses Euripides' play *Iphigenia in Aulis*; Shakespeare's play *Richard III*; biblical stories from the Book of Judges and the Book of Tobit; the Danish legend of Agnes and the Merman; the German tale of Faust, who sells his soul to the devil; a story, from Aristotle's *Poetics*, about a bridegroom who decides at the last minute not to get married – and the pseudonym makes brief references to numerous other dramas, myths and legends. And then there is the untold story of Kierkegaard's engagement to Regine. Moreover, Johannes de silentio might himself be regarded as a character in a story.

At the beginning of this chapter I drew attention to the fact that Kierkegaard published *Fear and Trembling* under a pseudonym. In fact, using a pseudonym was a common literary and journalistic convention in Kierkegaard's Copenhagen – but, as I have suggested, 'Johannes de silentio' is not merely a pen-name, but the name of a fictional character. This allows us to make a distinction between two versions of *Fear and Trembling*: the one written by Johannes de silentio, and the one written by Kierkegaard, which includes the pseudonym among its characters. The words, sentences and chapters that compose these two texts are identical. But Johannes de silentio's role differs depending on which version we read.

At the beginning of the chapter entitled 'A Tribute to Abraham', Johannes reflects on the roles of hero and poet, or storyteller. Insofar as he is regarded as the author of *Fear and Trembling*, the pseudonym is a poet who tells the story of Abraham, his hero. As we shall see, Johannes de silentio's style of storytelling often involves reinterpreting an original story for his own purposes: he does not just recount the story of Abraham, but uses a 'poetic licence' to develop his own version of the Genesis narrative. And moreover, to describe Abraham as the pseudonym's 'hero' is not unproblematic, since even though Johannes often expresses admiration for the Hebrew patriarch, his discussion of the story accentuates the difficulty of understanding Abraham and raises the question of how it is possible to admire a father who is willing to kill his son. Perhaps his concern is less to praise Abraham's actions than to challenge the conventional Christian view, still prevalent in the nineteenth century, that Abraham ought to be revered as the 'father of faith'.

However, insofar as Kierkegaard is the author of the text, *he* is the poet – and this gives rise to the possibility that Johannes de silentio is, in fact, his hero. It is, of course, natural to regard Abraham as the hero of *Fear and Trembling*, even though we are continually brought back to the question of how it is possible to admire him. Abraham, we are told, is a hero for all those who aspire to have faith. But what kind of hero might Johannes de silentio be? Because he is a character who confesses that he does not have faith, and that he can understand neither Abraham nor his belief in God, he might be regarded both as an exemplary Christian, and as an exemplary philosopher. His acknowledgement of his own limitations is, from Kierkegaard's point of view, an essential part of the task of becoming a Christian. And his recognition that he cannot grasp Abraham's faith indicates that he at least understands the difference between what he does and doesn't understand, which is an essential part of the task of becoming a philosopher.

These reflections on the role of the pseudonym suggest one way of interpreting the enigmatic epigraph at the beginning of *Fear and Trembling*: 'What Tarquin the Proud communicated in his garden with the beheaded poppies was understood by the son but not by the messenger' [2]. This quotation comes from the writings of the eighteenth-century German thinker Johann Georg Hamann, who was much admired by Kierkegaard. (In one journal entry, Kierkegaard traces to Hamann the germ of his own 'thesis', namely, 'to comprehend that faith cannot be comprehended or (the more ethical and God-fearing side) to comprehend that faith must not be comprehended.'[27]) Tarquin the Proud was King of Rome in the fifth century BC, and the quotation from Hamann refers to Tarquin's response to a message from his son asking how to deal with the city of Gabii, which was at war with Rome. Distrusting the messenger, Tarquin simply cuts off the heads of the tallest poppies in his garden with his cane; when the puzzled messenger returns and relates this incident to Tarquin's son, the latter understands that he is being told to execute the leaders of Gabii. This story thus conveys the idea of a messenger who delivers a silent message that he does not himself comprehend. Might Johannes de silentio be a messenger who does not understand Kierkegaard's unspoken message to the reader of *Fear and Trembling* – a messenger who thinks he is a poet, but who is in fact a hero, created in order to communicate a message about the limits of philosophy and the impossibility of faith?

An alternative reading of the epigraph, which also regards Johannes de silentio as the uncomprehending messenger, is to consider *Fear and Trembling* as delivering a secret message to Regine Olsen. This interpretation works insofar as Johannes de silentio never mentions Kierkegaard or Regine, so that his name itself might be a reference to his silence about their story, which nevertheless, as we have already glimpsed, resonates through the text. On this view, Johannes de silentio thinks he is just discussing Abraham's situation, but is actually discussing Kierkegaard's situation in relation to Regine as well.

Another possibility, however, is that the messenger to whom the epigraph alludes is not Johannes de silentio, but Abraham himself – and according to this reading, both Kierkegaard and his pseudonym can be regarded as the sender of the message. This makes sense insofar as the story of Abraham is used to convey to the reader a message about Christian faith. As we will see when, in the chapters to follow, we consider in more detail Johannes de silentio's interpretation of Abraham's faith, the story of the sacrifice of Isaac can be understood, in retrospect, as having a Christian significance of which Abraham is unaware. This can actually work on two levels. Some Christian readers of the Hebrew bible regard the story of Abraham's sacrifice of Isaac as having a prophetic dimension that anticipates God's sacrifice of his son, Jesus.[28] Alternatively, Abraham's faith pre-figures Christian faith in terms of its form rather than its content: it is not that the author of Genesis somehow anticipates the Christian gospel, but rather that Abraham's personal, trusting relationship to God in the face of conflicting demands provides a model for the Christian's spiritual life. This latter option is, it seems to me, more applicable to *Fear and Trembling*. In the same 1850 journal entry that we considered above, Kierkegaard writes that 'Abraham is called the father of faith because he has the formal qualifications of faith, believing against the understanding, although it has never occurred to the Christian Church that Abraham's faith had the content of Christian faith which relates essentially to a later historical event.'[29] This seems to rule out a prophetic anticipation of Jesus' death and resurrection, although in fact Kierkegaard's denial that thinkers within the Christian Church have attempted such an interpretation is surprising, given that Luther himself reads Genesis 22 in a specifically Christian way.[30] Be this as it may, within *Fear and Trembling* Abraham is used to convey a message to nineteenth-century

Christians about the difficulty of faith, and a warning against the tendency – formalized in the philosophies of Kant and Hegel – to assimilate the religious life into a merely-human ethical sphere. In Problem II, Johannes de silentio compares Abraham's situation with that of Jesus' disciples: not because they shared the same beliefs, but because deciding to follow Jesus, like deciding to sacrifice Isaac, involved the choice to recognize a religious claim as higher than ethical requirements.cv

CHAPTER 2

READING THE TEXT

PREFACE

It can be tempting to ignore or rush through a book's preface, under the impression that it is merely an incidental formality, or a rhetorical flourish. Sometimes this impression is justified, but the Preface to *Fear and Trembling* is indispensable. The Preface and the Epilogue to the text mirror one another, not only because they discuss the same themes and employ the same metaphors, but also because neither of these sections contains a reference to the story of Abraham that is the focus of the book as a whole. Instead of introducing or concluding the story of Abraham, the Preface and Epilogue provide a contextualizing framework for the interpretation of this story that is developed in the pages between them. Once the Preface is properly understood, it provides the key to reading the text.

Having said this, the contemporary reader certainly faces challenges in understanding the Preface itself. In addition to contending with the pseudonymous voice of Johannes de silentio – wondering why Kierkegaard chose not to write the book in his own name, and puzzling over the possible differences between Kierkegaard and his pseudonym – the reader has to decipher veiled allusions to certain thinkers who appear to be criticized in this opening section of the text. Instead of referring by name to Danish Hegelians such as Hans Lassen Martensen, Johan Ludvig Heiberg, and Rasmus Nielsen, the pseudonym uses certain phrases that would have been associated with these figures by readers in the 1840s, but which may easily pass unnoticed and uncomprehended today. So, as well as putting into question his own identity as author, Kierkegaard also obscures the identities of his opponents! Another challenging aspect of the Preface is the way it gestures indirectly towards important themes and ideas, instead of discussing them explicitly and straightforwardly.

Doubt and faith

Fear and Trembling begins with a comparison between the world of commerce and the world of ideas: in both these worlds, suggests Johannes de silentio, 'our age is holding a veritable clearance sale' [3]. A mirror-image of this metaphor is used in the Epilogue, where the pseudonym, having recalled an incident in which Dutch spice-merchants sunk some of their cargo into the sea in order to inflate the price of the remaining stock, suggests that 'we need something similar in the world of spirit' [107]. Taken together, these commercial metaphors indicate that the modern age – that is to say, the culture of nineteenth-century Europe – is characterized by a decline in value, and that something should be done in order to reverse this trend. In the 'world of commerce' value is monetary, but in the 'world of spirit' the value in question is of a different and less easily identifiable order: it is, presumably, a question of spiritual value. But what might this mean?

The interpretation of the story of Abraham that is put forward in *Fear and Trembling* represents precisely an attempt to arrest and reverse a perceived spiritual decline, comparable to the merchants sinking their spices in the sea. But what, according to Johannes de silentio, is falling in value, and needs to be bolstered? A preliminary answer to this question comes a little further on in the Preface, when the issues of doubt and faith are introduced.

Doubt and faith may appear to be opposites. However, we should note that – at least according to Kierkegaard's understanding of Christianity as it is presented over the course of his authorship – doubt and faith belong together, insofar as both are equally opposed to knowledge and certainty. If I know something with absolute certainty, then I do not doubt it; likewise, I would only claim to believe or have faith in something if there were some degree of uncertainty. So, for example, if I were a Christian then I might either have faith in, or doubts about, the continuity of my existence after death, which is something I cannot know about before I die; by contrast, it would seem strange to say either that I have faith, or doubt, that I am currently alive, or that I am female, since I know these things for sure.

Johannes de silentio suggests that modern philosophers have not only doubted everything, but 'go further' than this. He has in mind here a very specific intellectual context, which is twofold: first, the work of the seventeenth-century French thinker René Descartes, who is often regarded as the founder of modern philosophy; second, the way Descartes' philosophical method was discussed, in the nineteenth century, by Hegel and his followers. Descartes, recognizing that one's assumptions, opinions, beliefs and prejudices do not provide a sound basis for the pursuit of knowledge, decided that in order to attain certainty he must first doubt all that he had previously held to be reliable and true. Having called into question his sense-perceptions and even his grasp of mathematical truths (such as '2 + 2 = 4'), Descartes arrived at his belief in his own existence, and attempted to doubt this too. However, he saw clearly that if he was doubting then he must be thinking, and if he was thinking then he must exist. Thus he established, through his method of universal doubt, a bedrock of certainty from which he could proceed to secure knowledge of other truths.

Johannes de silentio's references to Descartes' methodological doubt are by no means incidental. The pseudonym quotes two passages which, each in its own way, appear to limit the practice of doubt. The first passage, from Descartes' *Principles of Philosophy*, suggests that doubt is not in fact universal, since 'whatever God has revealed to us must be accepted as more certain than anything else ... we must ... put our faith in divine authority rather than in our own judgement'. This claim runs counter to other tendencies in Descartes' thought: here, the French philosopher undermines the autonomy of human reason – its self-sufficiency; its independence from God, scripture and Church. But this autonomy does, however, seem to be asserted elsewhere in his work, such as in his attempt to arrive at a basis for knowledge entirely through his own efforts, by means of rational thought alone.

The question of human autonomy is central to *Fear and Trembling*, and from a historical point of view it is a question that becomes particularly important in Descartes' philosophy. Descartes is a transitional figure between the medieval and modern worldviews, and the shift between these two historical periods turns on the issue of autonomy. The medieval intellectual tradition was characterized by respect for traditional authority – in particular, that of scripture, Church, and canonical Christian thinkers such as Augustine – and by the subjugation of philosophy to theology, for in this period philosophy was viewed as a method for clarifying and articulating religious truths. Of course, there were many different medieval schools which disputed between themselves on the question of the extent of human beings' dependence on God, but it is still possible to offer this general characterization in order to explain how the modern period was distinguished by a new assertion of human autonomy. For example, in his *Meditations* Descartes attempts a demonstration of God's existence that in its formal structure resembles the 'ontological argument' put forward in the eleventh century by Anselm. However, although Descartes and Anselm reach similar conclusions, they have different starting-points. Anselm's argument is offered within a text, the *Proslogion*, which takes the form of a prayer directly addressed to God, and which repeatedly expresses the author's inability to seek God – let alone to find Him – without divine guidance. By contrast, Descartes' version of the argument follows after the process of methodological doubt that enables him to put his trust in his rational powers, and thus to base his demonstration of God's existence on a prior affirmation of his own intellect. On the one hand, then, Descartes breaks with the medieval submission to religious authority; on the other hand, he still appears to want to maintain an appeal to divine revelation, as evidenced in the first quotation cited by Johannes de silentio.

As a transitional and thus ambiguous thinker on the issue of autonomy, Descartes' presence in the Preface signals Kierkegaard's concern to put this issue into question. If we look again more closely at the particular passage cited, we can see that the transition, ambiguity or tension between the medieval and modern worldviews is actually articulated in it: 'although the light of reason may, with the utmost clarity and evidence, appear to suggest something different, we must still put our faith in divine authority rather than in our own judgment.' In *Fear and Trembling*, however, the question is not just about the extent and limits of human autonomy, but also about the implications of the assertion of autonomy that, if only partial in Descartes, became increasingly radical in the philosophies of his eighteenth- and nineteenth-century successors. Is there a connection between this historical development, and the decline in the value of faith hinted at in the opening lines of the Preface?

While the first quotation from Descartes challenges the view that doubt should be universal in the sense of being applied to everything, the second undermines its universality in a different sense. This quotation, from Descartes' *Discourse on Method*, suggests that the French philosopher's method of doubt was not intended as a universal prescription, to be followed by everyone, but rather met a personal need – that it 'had importance only for himself', as Johannes de silentio puts it. On this issue, as well as on the question of autonomy, an implicit critical comparison is being drawn between Descartes and the Danish Hegelians. It is very likely that Johannes is alluding to Martensen in particular, and that such allusions would not have been missed by contemporary readers. Martensen repeatedly used the Latin phrase *'de omnibus dubitandum est'* ('everything should be doubted') in his writings – including his 1837 dissertation *On the Autonomy of Human Self-Consciousness*, in which he identifies the notion of autonomy as characteristic of modern philosophy – and also in his popular lectures at the University of Copenhagen.[1] A few months before writing *Fear and Trembling*, in the winter of 1842–3, Kierkegaard began to write a work entitled *Johannes Climacus; or, De omnibus dubitandum est*: this unfinished text is a philosophical satire narrated by a student who is captivated by his teachers' exhortation to doubt everything, but, in attempting to put this principle into practice, ends up pushing it to the point of absurdity. Again, Martensen is probably the target of this satire.

For Kierkegaard, Martensen is associated not only with Cartesian doubt, but with the aspiration to 'go further' than doubt that is several times alluded to in the Preface to *Fear and Trembling*. This aspiration is a particular instance of a general tendency among Hegelian thinkers of the time to take as their starting-point the conclusions of their predecessors, and to seek to move beyond them – a tendency that was rooted in Hegel's own idea that history progresses towards an increasingly clear and complete grasp of the truth. (Even though Martensen was by no means a wholehearted advocate of Hegel's philosophy, and indeed on many occasions distanced himself from it, he was undoubtedly influenced by Hegel and was often regarded as a Hegelian by his contemporaries.) In his Preface, Johannes de silentio commends Descartes' 'modesty' and 'humility', while implying that Martensen's claims to improve on his philosophical achievements are grandiose and conceited. In this way, the pseudonym articulates Kierkegaard's vehement opposition both to the arrogance of his Danish contemporaries' aspiration to surpass the tradition's greatest thinkers, and, more importantly, to the underlying belief that successive generations advance closer and closer to the truth. We will return to this last point shortly. In response to the charge of arrogance, it is important to note that, whatever Martensen's character and attitudes may have been, the historical progressivism he seems to have taken from Hegel has an entirely philosophical basis in the idea that truth is always articulated from a historical perspective embedded in a particular society, culture and form of life, and therefore does not remain static, but develops through time. Attributing the claim to move beyond an earlier philosopher to a psychological factor such as arrogance risks missing the philosophical point – but Kierkegaard probably was well aware of this, and deliberately conflated the two issues in the service of his satirical polemic against Martensen's Hegelianism.

Although there are continuities between the critique of Martensen attempted in the unfinished *Johannes Climacus; Or, De omnibus dubitantdum est*, and Johannes de silentio's remarks about doubt in the opening pages of *Fear and Trembling*, there seems to be a shift in the latter work from a focus on epistemology (the area of philosophy that deals with the validity, scope and methods of knowledge) to a concern with more existential issues. These existential issues are not identified and explored in the Preface – they are the subject-matter of the discussion of Abraham that follows it – but it is significant that here doubt is coupled with faith. The pseudonym remarks that, just as his contemporaries think they have moved beyond doubt, so 'in our age nobody stops at faith but goes further' [4]. If we assume, provisionally, that the faith in question here is religious faith, then we can recognize that the kind of doubt that is coupled with faith, and with which faith contends – for example, the committed Christian's doubts that God is truly loving, that He heeds her prayers, or even that He exists at all – are quite different from the methodical doubt employed by a philosopher. The religious person's doubts are not strategic; they are not just intellectually challenging, but emotionally and existentially testing, for they are accompanied by anxiety and despair, by 'fear and trembling'. However, having made this distinction between epistemological and existential doubt, we should note that it is not clear-cut: in the case of a person who, having been tricked by a con-man, or betrayed by a close friend, calls into question both the reliability of others and her own judgement as to what is true and false, her experience of doubt may have something in common with that of the philosopher *and* with that of the religious person – her trust in humanity might be shaken profoundly and painfully, and she might also adopt a strategic principle of disbelieving everything that others tell her.

The time of history and the time of life

Both doubt and faith are described in the Preface as 'tasks'. Three key claims that are made about faith are that it is not an intellectual task; that it is a difficult task; and that it is 'a lifelong task' [5]. As I suggested in the previous paragraph, faith is existential rather than intellectual, and what this might mean is indicated by Johannes de silentio's claim that 'even if one were able to convert the whole content of faith into conceptual form, it does not follow that one has comprehended faith, comprehended how one entered it or how it entered into one' [5]. The attempt to 'convert the whole content of faith into conceptual form' is associated with Hegelian philosophy in particular, and Kierkegaard opposes this intellectualization of faith. An important aspect of the latter's philosophy is the distinction between 'what' and 'how'; in the 1846 text *Concluding Unscientific Postscript*, this distinction is formulated in terms of the contrast between 'objective' and 'subjective' truth. In the case of faith, what a person believes is distinguished from the manner in which she believes it. The 'how' of faith – its subjectivity – is a matter of a person's relationship to faith: entering into and existing within it, or appropriating it, taking it to heart. It is this subjective relationship that Johannes de silentio wants to depict as a difficult and 'lifelong' task. At this point in the text we have not been told what is meant by faith, and what its task consists in, but there is already a hint that it is difficult because the existential stakes are high. And faith is a task for a whole lifetime not just because it is difficult to accomplish, but, more essentially, because faith is itself a way of living one's life, from day to day and even from moment to moment. For this reason, the task begins afresh each day and can never be completed until life itself is over.

An important issue in the Preface, then, is the contrast between two orders of time: the time of history, and the time of an individual's life that begins with her birth and ends in her death. Of course, these orders of time cannot be separated since each individual's lifetime unfolds within and as history, and since the time of history is apprehended and understood by existing individuals in the midst of their own lifetimes. However, without denying this relationship between lifetime and history, Kierkegaard is concerned to shift the process of attaining truth from history to life. Or at least, he wants to raise the question: In which time do we learn? In which time do we attain truth? His pseudonym disputes the Hegelian view – which may be a simplification of Hegel's own philosophy of history – that the pursuit of truth is like a relay race, with each generation passing the baton of knowledge to the next, all the time drawing nearer to the finish-line of 'absolute knowing'. The distinction between the two orders of time suggested in the Preface prepares the way for the more explicit challenge to this Hegelian progressivism that is articulated in the Epilogue, where Johannes de silentio argues that 'no generation learns the genuinely human from a previous one. In this respect, every generation begins primitively, has no other task than each previous generation, and advances no further . . . Thus no generation has learned to love from another' [107]. As this passage suggests, the interpretation of truth – of what it is our task to learn – that is presented in *Fear and Trembling* not only attempts to shift this task from the stage of history to that of the individual's existence, but also proposes an alternative conception of truth itself: instead of the truth as knowledge, the *telos* of a human life should be the truth of love. The significance of Abraham's story, for the pseudonym, is that 'he remained true to his love' [106].

As well as questioning the historical understanding of truth that he attributes to the Danish Hegelians, Johannes de silentio offers in the Preface his own interpretation of history, which, in opposition to his contemporaries' progressivism, emphasizes decline. The decline in value that we discussed above is situated in an historical context: the pseudonym suggests that earlier thinkers – the ancient Greek sceptics, and even Descartes – were nobler philosophers than those of the present time. He describes both Descartes and the Greeks as 'venerable' [3, 5], while his attitude to his contemporaries is sarcastic and contemptuous.

In the name of Johannes de silentio, Kierkegaard presents a diagnosis of 'our age', a phrase that is repeated several times in the Preface and which indicates that he is influenced by Hegelian historicism at the same time as he wishes to criticize it. Indeed, the oblique references in this section of the text to the Danish Hegelians suggest that these thinkers are a symptom, if not the cause, of spiritual decline – a view that is expressed more directly by Johannes Climacus, the pseudonymous author of Kierkegaard's *Concluding Unscientific Postscript*:

> Before an outbreak of cholera a kind of fly comes along that is not otherwise seen. May not the appearance of these incredible pure thinkers be a sign of a disaster in store for humankind, such as, for example, the loss of the ethical and the religious?[2]

But why exactly does Kierkegaard think that his present age is one of spiritual decline? What is the problem he perceives? His point is not just that his contemporaries are mistaken to think they have fully understood doubt and faith, and moved beyond them, since faith is really a task for a whole lifetime. He also believes that this mistaken assumption is a sign of a dangerous complacency – dangerous because it misses the most essential concerns of human life, and thus undermines its value. According to Kierkegaard, this complacency is not confined to modern philosophers, but is shared by the urban middle-class Danes with whom he mixed in Copenhagen – people like himself, in fact – and so, for instance, Johannes de silentio envisages a sleepy, comfortable congregation listening to a sermon about Abraham, assuming they understand it, and secure in the assumption that they are faithful Christians. The problem, then, is that because people do not raise the question of whether they have faith, let alone the question of what it would mean to have it, they do not recognize that faith is a task, and by no means easy. Again, we can look ahead to *Concluding Unscientific Postscript* to see how this view is articulated explicitly in relation to Christianity:

> Now, we have almost reached the parody that to become a Christian is nothing, while to understand Christianity is a

very difficult and laborious task. Everything is thereby reversed: Christianity is made into a kind of philosophical theory, the difficulty then being quite properly that of understanding it. But Christianity relates essentially to existence, and what is difficult is to become a Christian.[3]

Just as in the *Postscript* the pseudonym Johannes Climacus aims to accentuate the difficulty of Christianity in order to encourage his readers to confront the task of becoming a Christian, so the strategy of *Fear and Trembling* is to emphasize the difficulty of faith. The interpretation of the story of Abraham put forward by Johannes de silentio is part of this strategy, since he suggests that Abraham's faith is extremely difficult – perhaps even impossible – to attain.

In response to these ideas, we should raise the question of whether there is a tension between Johannes de silentio's attempt to detach individuals' spiritual development from their historical situation – as when he argues that 'every generation begins primitively' – and his own version of historicism, which interprets history in terms of a decline in the value of faith. Is this two-fold attack on Hegelian philosophy an inconsistent attempt to 'have it both ways'? Are individuals' inner lives conditioned by history, or aren't they? One possible way of defending Johannes de silentio from this charge of inconsistency would be to understand him as claiming that the task of becoming a Christian is always a task for individuals to begin anew for themselves, but that the historical situation in which this task is faced can make it more or less difficult, and may even obscure the nature of the task. Nevertheless, the account of the significance of history in *Fear and Trembling* remains ambiguous, and this may be a weakness in the text.

'This is not the system'

In the final paragraph of the Preface, the pseudonym offers some remarks about himself. His main concern here is to insist that he is 'not at all a philosopher' [5], and to distance himself from 'the System', which refers to Hegelian philosophy. Adopting an excessively deferential tone that, in its sarcasm, clearly conveys his contempt, Johannes de silentio concludes his Preface by declaring: 'This is not the System, it does not have the least thing to do with the System. I invoke all the best upon the System and upon the Danish investors in this omnibus . . . ' [6]. In 1843 the 'omnibus' was a topical issue, since this form of public transport had been introduced in Copenhagen about three years earlier. By repeating the commercial metaphor with which he began the Preface, the pseudonym indicates that, in addition to signalling a decline in value, the metaphor implies that contemporary thinkers are motivated by a self-interested worldliness. So, in emphasizing his distance from 'the System', he expresses not only his disagreement with the details of Hegelian thought, but also his disdain for 'Philosophy', understood as a worldly, professionalized intellectual discipline. It might be argued that this kind of disdain for the worldly ambitions of his contemporaries – and of Martensen in particular – betrays Kierkegaard's own ambition, and his resentment of Martensen's success. Perhaps it is true that Kierkegaard's motivations were less noble than those he attributes to his pseudonym, but what is important is that he raises these issues in his diagnosis of the spiritual decline of his age – a diagnosis that might only be strengthened by proof that Kierkegaard himself was willing to enhance his reputation at the expense of his rivals.

The concluding paragraph also includes some remarks about the possible reception of *Fear and Trembling*. This is quite usual in Kierkegaard's writings: he is remarkably self-conscious about his literary output, his status as an author, and his relationship to and impact on his readers. Here, Johannes de silentio envisages at least three possible responses to his book: that he will be ignored; that he will be repeatedly subject to 'zealous criticism' [6]; and that 'one or another enterprising summarizer . . . will cut him up into paragraphs' [6]. (It is striking that the pseudonym here absolutely identifies himself with the text.) The first and second alternatives contradict one another, and yet Johannes claims to 'foresee' both of them; the third possibility, on the other hand – which he 'dreads' as 'even more frightful' than the others – seems especially pertinent, and places me in an uncomfortable situation as the author of an introduction to *Fear and Trembling*. As we work through each section of the text in turn, am I as writer, and you as reader, caught in the act of fulfilling the pseudonym's dreadful premonition that his book will not be read as he wishes it to be, but rather subject to detached scrutiny and analysis? How *does* Johannes de silentio wish to be read?

TUNING UP[4]

If the Preface to *Fear and Trembling* stands, in a sense, outside the text as the key to its orientation and purpose, then the section entitled 'Tuning Up' marks a second beginning insofar as it introduces the story of Abraham and Isaac. 'Tuning Up' translates the Latin term 'Exordium', which just means 'beginning'. In fact, we might identify at least three beginnings to *Fear and Trembling*: first the Preface; now 'Tuning Up'; and then the 'Preliminary Outpouring from the Heart', alternatively translated as 'Preamble from the Heart' or 'Preliminary Expectoration'. It is as if the author of the text is struggling to begin, and this is perhaps due to the difficulty of its subject-matter. How does one begin to speak about Abraham?

The story of Abraham

In fact, 'Tuning Up' seems to begin very directly, with a clear and concise summary, in just one sentence, of the story of Abraham: 'There was once a man who as a child had heard that beautiful story about how God tested Abraham and how he withstood the test, kept the faith, and received a son a second time contrary to expectation' [7]. Already, however, the subject-matter of the text is split in two: we have Abraham, and we have a man who hears the story of Abraham. It is the second figure who dominates this section of the text, but before we consider him more closely we should reflect on Johannes de silentio's terse summary of the story of Abraham.

The original story of Abraham's life is told over the course of fifteen chapters of Genesis, the first book of the Hebrew bible. Abraham is born in chapter 11, and he dies, 'an old man and full of years', in chapter 25. Genesis 12 tells how God singles out Abraham, telling him to leave his country, his father, and his brothers, and to travel to a new land 'that I will show you'. 'I will make of you a great nation, and I will bless you', promises God. Abraham and his wife Sarah set off for their destination, the land of Canaan, which God promises to give to their offspring. However, Sarah is unable to become pregnant; she suggests that Abraham have a child with her maid, Hagar – who is to be, in effect, a surrogate mother, since the child will be given to Sarah – and this child is named Ishmael. Chapter 17 describes God's covenant with Abraham, in which the promise that he will father 'a multitude of nations', who will have Canaan as their own land, is renewed; in return, all Abraham's descendants must be circumcised as a mark of their special relationship with God. Here, God promises that Sarah will have a son, Isaac, who will father future generations; Abraham laughs, because he is by now about one hundred years old, and Sarah is ninety. Sarah also laughs when she hears this news – but, in chapter 21, Isaac is born (and circumcised). At this time the family are living in a place called Beer-sheba. Seeing Ishmael as a rival to her son, Sarah tells Abraham to turn Hagar and Ishmael out of their home, into the desert. Chapter 22 narrates the episode in Abraham's life that is the focus of *Fear and Trembling*:

After these things God tested Abraham. He said to him, 'Abraham!' And he said, 'Here I am.' He said, 'Take your son, your only son Isaac, whom you love, and go to the land of Moriah, and offer him there as a burnt-offering on one of the mountains that I will show you.' So Abraham rose early in the morning, saddled his donkey, and took two of his young men with him, and his son Isaac; he cut the wood for the burnt-offering, and set out and went to the place in the distance that God had shown him. On the third day Abraham looked up and saw the place far away. Then Abraham said to his young men, 'Stay here with the donkey; the boy and I will go over there; we will worship, and then we will come back to you.' Abraham took the wood of the burnt-offering and laid it on his son Isaac, and he himself carried the fire and the knife. So the two of them walked on together. Isaac said to his father Abraham, 'Father!' And he said, 'Here I am, my son.' He said, 'The fire and the wood are here, but where is the lamb for a burnt-offering?' Abraham said, 'God himself will pro-vide the lamb for a burnt-offering, my son.' So the two of them walked on together.

When they came to the place that God had shown them, Abraham built an altar there and laid the wood in order. He bound his son Isaac and laid him on the altar, on top of the wood. Then Abraham reached out his hand and took the knife to kill his son. But the angel of the Lord called to him from heaven, and said, 'Abraham, Abraham!' And he said, 'Here I am.' He said, 'Do not lay your hand on the boy or do anything to him; for now I know that you fear God, since you have not withheld your son, your only son, from me.' And Abraham looked up and saw a ram, caught in a thicket by its horns. Abraham went and took the ram and offered it up as a burnt-offering instead of his son. So Abraham called that place 'The Lord will provide'; as it is said to this day, 'On the mount of the Lord it shall be provided.'

The angel of the Lord called to Abraham a second time from heaven, and said, 'By myself I have sworn, says the Lord: Because you have done this, and have not withheld your son, your only son, I will indeed bless you, and I will make your offspring as numerous as the stars of heaven and as the sand that is on the seashore. And your offspring shall possess the gate of their enemies, and by your offspring shall all the nations of the earth gain blessing for themselves, because you have obeyed my voice.' So Abraham returned to his young men, and they arose, and went together to Beer-sheba; and Abraham lived at Beer-sheba.[5]

In his brief introductory summary of this story, Johannes de silentio selects three key elements. First, 'God tested Abraham and . . . he withstood the test'. The Danish word translated here as 'the test' is *Fristelsen*, which means both spiritual trial – as we would ordinarily understand the 'test' that Abraham undergoes – and temptation, and both these sense are brought into play in the interpretation of the story of Abraham presented in *Fear and Trembling*. Abraham is *tested* insofar as he is challenged to demonstrate his obedience of God, but faced with the command to sacrifice Isaac he is also *tempted* to disobey. This temptation is particularly compelling because Abraham could easily justify his disobedience by invoking his moral duty to his son, and also by submitting to the will of his wife Sarah (as he does on other matters, such as the treatment of Hagar and Ishmael), who would surely have insisted on saving Isaac's life if she had known about God's command. So here, 'the temptation is the ethical itself' [52], as Johannes de silentio suggests further on in the text – and this is a strange situation, since normally a temptation would be understood as something that pulls one away from one's moral duty.

The second element of the story selected in the pseudonym's synopsis is that Abraham 'kept the faith'. What does this mean?

The question of faith is not discussed in 'Tuning Up', but post-poned until the following section of the book. The third element is that Abraham 'received a son a second time contrary to expectation.' By emphasizing this, Johannes de silentio reminds the reader that Isaac's birth was a gift from God, a kind of miracle, since Sarah was old and barren. When he is reprieved at the last minute on Mount Moriah, Abraham has his son restored to him: in a sense, Isaac is given as a gift a second time, since he seemed to have been lost, and, in light of God's command that he be killed, the gift is as 'contrary to expectation' as it was the first time. So, Isaac is given in the first place; lost – or at least apparently lost; and given again. This is a kind of repetition, and repetition is an important idea for Kierkegaard that, even though it is not discussed explicitly by Johannes de silentio, is pertinent to *Fear and Trembling*.

Understanding Abraham

Having familiarized ourselves with the story of Abraham, we can now return to the character who becomes obsessed with it. As this man grows older, he grows more fascinated by the story, and yet he understands it less and less. It is significant that his passion and his understanding are inversely related in this way: this man's inability to understand Abraham echoes Johannes de silentio's claim in the Preface not to understand Hegelian philosophy, and moreover his position is the opposite of that which Kierkegaard attributes to contemporary thinkers, who are accused of understanding everything, intellectually speaking, but lacking passion.[6] (This theme is discussed more explicitly in the Epilogue.) The pseudonym's remark that the man might have understood Abraham better if he had been able to read Hebrew is sarcastic, since – as will become more apparent in later sections of *Fear and Trembling* – the kind of understanding of Abraham that is called into question here is not to be gained by better knowledge of the bible. If Hegelian philosophy represents one aspect of nineteenth-century historicism, another aspect of this historical thinking was an increasingly critical approach to the scriptures, as the view that these are humanly-created texts written from a particular point of view, and in the service of a particular moral, cultural or political agenda, became more mainstream. Kierkegaard was not necessarily opposed to this modern approach to the bible, but he certainly wants to suggest that any knowledge of the scriptures that could be gained by exegetical expertise will not illuminate the story of Abraham, since what is most important in the narrative is Abraham's existential situation, and the questions this raises about the nature of faith. Such questions remain even if Abraham is regarded as just a fictional character who was created by an unknown author, and at an unspecified time. For Kierkegaard, the objective knowledge sought by historical study is of a different order than the subjective truth that is at stake in the story of Abraham.

The suggestion that 'life had separated what had been united in the child's simplicity' [7] is presented by Johannes de silentio as a reason for the man's increasing admiration for Abraham, and yet this supposed explanation is at this stage enigmatic: *what* 'had been united', and then became 'separated'? Only in the light of later sections of the book can we attempt to answer this question, for it concerns the relationship between religious belief and the world as we experience it. If as a child one believed that a loving God created the world, and that it is good and just, then as the years went by there would almost certainly emerge a disparity between this belief and the fact that the world is actually harsh and unfair. This theme of a conflict between religious belief and 'real life' experience – sometimes formulated in philosophical terms as a 'problem of evil', which undermines the case for the existence of God – is taken up in subsequent sections of *Fear and Trembling*.

'This man was not a thinker, he felt no need to go beyond faith,' writes Johannes de silentio, and moreover 'it seemed to him that it must be . . . an enviable lot to possess faith, even if no one knew it' [8]. As well as having no aspiration to go further than faith, the man, it is implied, has not even got as far as faith; indeed faith itself is an aspiration for him. This should be understood as a strategic manoeuvre on Kierkegaard's part, aimed at challenging the religious complacency that, as is hinted in the Preface, is widespread among his contemporaries: by looking at Abraham through the eyes of someone who recognizes his own lack of faith, Kierkegaard invites the reader to question her own assumption to possess faith. If the reader finds herself identifying with the pseudonym, or with the man who he describes as passionate about the story of Abraham (and perhaps this character *is* Johannes de silentio), then she may also come to identify with the view that faith is an aspiration rather than a possession.

On this point, Kierkegaard's approach can be compared with that of Socrates – a comparison that Kierkegaard himself draws attention to in some of his other works. In Plato's dialogues, Socrates is often presented as unsettling his contemporaries' assumptions that they possess knowledge, or wisdom: Socrates, at least as he is depicted by Plato, saw philosophy as a task with the ultimate aim of finding the truth, which was certainly difficult to achieve, and perhaps even impossible. If people assumed, mistakenly, that they already possessed the truth, then this assumption would prevent them from even embarking on the task of philosophy. Similarly, Kierkegaard thought that misguided complacency about faith would prevent people from undertaking the task of faith. Socrates certainly does seem to have thought that his Athenian acquaintances were ignorantly complacent, and his attempts to expose this and to guide his interlocutors in a more philosophical direction made him unpopular with some people, and revered by others. In Plato's *Republic*, for example, Socrates questions several different characters about the nature and value of justice, and over the course of the dialogue it becomes clear that those who thought they knew what justice is, and whether it is beneficial or detrimental, were mistaken in their assumptions.

Much of the discussion in the *Republic* turns on the distinction between reality and appearances, and one of the implications of this is the insistence on the more particular distinction between merely appearing to be just, and truly being just – that is to say, between having a reputation for justice, and actually living justly. Socrates suggests that most of the discussion in Athens on the question of justice focuses on external things: on the reputation for justice, and the rewards or sufferings that will follow from a good or bad reputation, and in order to reorient the debate in a more inward direction he poses the question of how one should behave when one is entirely unobserved. A similar question is in play in *Fear and Trembling*: notice that the man who admires Abraham thinks that it would be 'enviable' to have faith 'even if no one knew it'. Just as Socrates argues that genuine, inward justice is more important than the appearing to be just, so Kierkegaard suggests that it's not the appearance of faith that matters, but the individual's inward relationship to God.

This brings us back to the sphere of subjective truth that is the real location for the drama of Abraham and Isaac. The man who admires Abraham yet fails to comprehend him focuses his – and, consequently, the reader's – attention on a specific part of this drama. He is indifferent to the 'beautiful' ancient lands in which his hero lived, to Abraham's 'blessed' and 'venerable' status as a husband and patriarch, and to Isaac's 'vigorous' youthfulness. He only longs to accompany Abraham and Isaac on their three-day journey to Mount Moriah: he wants to be present in the moments leading up to the sacrifice – the first sight of Mount Moriah, the climb up the mountain – as with each step Abraham draws nearer to the time when he will kill his son. Rather than focusing on what we might call the aesthetic elements of the story, which are easy to admire, the man just cares about 'the shudder of the thought' [8].

Four faithless Abrahams

This characterization of Abraham's admirer is followed by four alternative versions of the story of the sacrifice, each one with a different deviation from the version according to which Abraham 'kept the faith, and received a son a second time', and each one emphasizing different elements of the Genesis narrative. Some details are added to this original version, suggesting that these alternative stories are produced in the imagination of the man who wishes to accompany Abraham to Mount Moriah. Indeed, these imaginings are the very substance of this accompaniment: the man goes on the journey with Abraham in his imagination. Reading them, one has the impression of a dream sequence: of a recurrent dream – or nightmare – that in being repeated betrays an underlying fear or anxiety. Perhaps the fact that these imagined or dreamed Abrahams never reach the outcome of faith conveys the man's inability to understand him; perhaps, even, this repeated failure to 'get the story right' indicates the difficulty or impossibility of attaining faith. In each version Abraham is tested, and passes the test insofar as he obeys God's command to sacrifice Isaac – but his response is not that of faith.

In the first alternative version of the story, Sarah watches her husband and son until they disappear from view. The introduction of her perspective, which is absent from the Genesis narrative, brings out a dimension of the story that will be important for its analysis further on in *Fear and Trembling*, particularly in Problem III. This version also adds some details about Isaac's role: the boy realizes what is happening and begs his father not to kill him. In response, Abraham pretends that it is his own wish to sacrifice Isaac, instead of God's command, in order to save Isaac's faith in God. The outcome of this story, then, is that although Abraham is prepared to kill his son, he takes this course of action in such a way as to prioritize Isaac's interest over his own: 'it is surely better for him to believe that I am a monster than to lose faith' in God [9]. However terrible the sacrifice, then, Abraham is still portrayed as a father who loves his son.

Like the first imagined version of the story, version II features Sarah, and adds that Isaac was 'her pride, her hope for all generations' [9]. This time, the events on Mount Moriah leave Abraham in despair, his relationship to God fundamentally changed. From that day on, 'he saw joy no more' [9].

The third version again accentuates Sarah's love for her son, but here Sarah has become a young mother, as if she has undergone a dream-like metamorphosis. As in the previous version, Abraham remains tormented by the attempted sacrifice, but here it is not his relationship to God that has changed, but his relationship to himself. After the briefest summary of the story – 'He climbed Mount Moriah, he drew the knife' [10] – the focus switches to its aftermath: several times Abraham repeats his journey, but in the evening, and begs God to forgive his sin of failing in his duty to his son. This is the first mention of duty, and the exact nature of the paternal duty that is in question is unclear. It seems, however, that the duty is to love his son, so that the duty is transgressed only if this love is absent or inadequate. This would mean that the possible breach of duty is not in Abraham's willingness to sacrifice Isaac, but in his inward relationship to his son. The sacrifice itself does not signify a failure to love; on the contrary, it is a sacrifice precisely because Abraham loves Isaac, and the value of the sacrifice is proportional to this love. Isaac is not required as a burnt offering because of his intrinsic value, but because he is 'the best' that Abraham has – many times better, far more highly valued, than Abraham's own life. This version of the story emphasizes the contradiction of

Abraham's situation. On the one hand, he cannot understand that it is a sin to have been 'willing to sacrifice to God the best he owned, that for which he himself would gladly have laid down his life many times' [10]. But on the other hand, if his action were sinful, which it would have been if it had not expressed his love for Isaac, then he cannot understand how this could ever be forgiven. Here we have an Abraham in anguish, because he cannot know whether his action was motivated by love; either way, he cannot understand its significance.

In version IV, the details are similar to those in the second version: Abraham is in despair. This time, however, he despairs at the moment of sacrifice, and in front of Isaac, instead of afterwards, in private. Whereas 'Isaac flourished as before' [9] according to version II, here the boy loses his faith as a result of seeing his father's despair.

These four alternative scenarios are presented as examples of the man's imagined journeys alongside Abraham, each one ending in a different failure to envisage a response of faith. At the end of the section we are told that these belong to a much larger series of virtual 'pilgrimages' to Mount Moriah. We need to pay attention not only to the specific details of the alternative accounts, but to the way in which these come together to provide a certain approach to interpreting the biblical text. The most striking difference between the Genesis account and the re-imagined versions is that the original text is a detached narrative described as if by an invisible spectator, which makes no mention of the protagonists' thoughts, feelings, gestures and body language: there are no signs of interiority. In Kierkegaard's text, however, the versions of the story attribute an inwardness to Abraham, and also to Isaac and to Sarah; taken together they invoke a world in which the family are bound together with emotional ties. One consequence of these attachments is that the suffering and anguish of the journey to Moriah become more immediate, more vivid. Of course, the Genesis narrative can be read with the same pathos, but Kierkegaard's concern is that the outcome of the story is so familiar that, since we know that Isaac will be spared, we forget about the 'fear and trembling' of the situation up to the point at which the knife is raised over Isaac.

This forgetfulness is linked to another effect of the re-tellings of the story in 'Tuning Up'. The repetitions of the story do not just encourage the reader to slow down, instead of rushing to the happy ending, and to reflect on Abraham's journey anew. They also emphasize that Abraham had to choose how to respond to God's command to sacrifice his son. This requirement to choose is an essential ingredient of the 'fear and trembling' to which the book's title refers: the anguish of Abraham lies not in the deed of sacrifice, but in the decision, and the burden of responsibility this entails. If he were compelled to kill his son, he would suffer grief, pain, sadness and anger; but the choice adds anguish to these other feelings. This interpretation of Abraham is a particular instance of a more general theme in Kierkegaard's thought: he emphasizes the importance of decision, especially in the religious life, and he also suggests that freedom is always attended by anxiety. This analysis of human freedom is formulated more explicitly in *The Concept of Anxiety* (1844), but it is certainly implicit in *Fear and Trembling*.

The sequence of imagined journeys also indicate that Abraham was not simply faced with the choice between obeying and disobeying, but that he had to decide *how* to obey or disobey. It seems that Abraham's faith does not consist merely in obedience to God – for even though he obeys in all the alternative versions, he still does not attain faith – but in the manner of his obedience. By presenting the different possibilities that Abraham could have chosen, the fact of his choice itself comes more to the foreground. And however harrowing the alternative possibilities are, these seem somehow more understandable, easier to relate to, than Abraham's actual response.

Of course, when we talk about Abraham's actual response we are not recounting historical fact, nor even offering a reading based on the biblical text, since as we have seen this text only describes what happens from an external point of view – and thus it is compatible with all the non-faith responses dramatized in the alternative versions. Abraham's actual response, then, is a reconstruction of his inward response to the test as it must have been if he truly was a man of faith.

If faith is not just a matter of obedience to God, but something inward, something about the 'how' of this obedience – then what is it? This section of the text gives us no positive account of this, but it does indicate what faith is not: the four alternative Abrahams do not differ in their external actions, but in each of

these scenarios the dynamic of the situation changes fundamentally. First, Isaac loses his father; second, Abraham is deprived of
joy; third, Abraham finds no peace of mind; fourth, Isaac loses
his faith in God. So even if 'Tuning Up' leaves us waiting for a
description of faith itself, it nevertheless accentuates the particularity of faith by comparing it to other responses. We will see
that this comparison between faith and its alternatives is repeated
in subsequent sections of the text: in 'A Preliminary Outpouring
from the Heart' faith is contrasted with resignation, and in
'Problem I' Abraham is compared with other fathers whose willingness to kill their offspring makes them 'tragic heroes', but not
men of faith.

The mother and her child

Each of the four descriptions of an imagined journey to Mount
Moriah is followed by a shorter paragraph about a mother weaning her child off breast milk. These passages are enigmatic, like
parables, but it is natural to suppose that they provide a feminine
counterpart to the relationship between Abraham and Isaac.
And indeed, the passage that follows version I of the journey
seems to correspond to it: just as Abraham pretends to his son
that he is 'a monster' in order to preserve Isaac's faith in God, so
the mother blackens her breast in order to make it unattractive
to the baby and so reduce its suffering at losing it. However,
the remaining passages about the mother and child are less
evidently in parallel with the stories they follow, and commentators have struggled to provide an interpretation that makes the
couplings coherent.[7] If the alternative versions of the story of the
sacrifice are like a sequence of recurrent dreams, or nightmares,
the little parables juxtaposed with them exhibit the disjunctive
logic of successive fragments of dream. But perhaps these apparent disjunctions mask an underlying train of thought.

Putting the Abraham stories to one side for the moment, and
looking just at the set of four parables about the mother weaning her baby, we can identify the theme of separation and loss.
This is an ambiguous transition for both mother and child: their
bond is less close than it once was, and yet this allows each of
them greater independence, more autonomy, and facilitates the
child's development. In each version of the parable, the mother's
love for the child is evident. In the first instance she blackens her

breast; in the second she conceals her breast; in the third the mother and child mourn their separation together, sharing this 'brief sorrow' [10]; and in the final version the mother makes sure she has food ready for the child. In a way, these are cosy scenes, but in each case they are darkened by an exclamation to the effect that either the mother or the child is fortunate to experience the process of weaning – the process of separation and loss – in this limited way. Hovering in the background of these parables is a figure who provides an interpretative context that helps to make sense of them.

The figure is Regine Olsen, and the context, at least on the face of it, is personal. Kierkegaard was engaged to Regine for a few months in 1841. He had gone to Berlin two weeks after breaking up with her, in October 1841, and while in Berlin he wrote *Either/Or*, a diverse anthology of philosophical writings on the theme of marriage. He travelled to Berlin a second time shortly after an encounter with Regine in church at Easter 1843, and during this visit he wrote *Repetition* and *Fear and Trembling*. The pseudonymous narrator of *Repetition* travels to Berlin a second time in order to try to repeat his first experience there; the other character in this text is a young fiancé who, after going through a crisis, breaks off his engagement and becomes a poet. On May 17th 1843, while working on *Fear and Trembling* in Berlin, Kierkegaard wrote in his journal: 'If I had had faith, I would have stayed with Regine.'[8] All of this makes it clear that, at the very least, Regine was on Kierkegaard's mind as he was writing *Fear and Trembling*. It seems that in his writing Kierkegaard worked through the obscure processes of his inner life, coming to an understanding of and with himself; furthermore, his writing, while concerned with philosophical and spiritual questions, also dramatized the relationship with Regine from his personal point of view. The broken engagement provided fuel – both in the sense of material, and in the sense of emotional energy – for his philosophical reflections.

The four parables about separation and loss can be read as possible ways of breaking not only the engagement, but also the profound bond that seems to have persisted between Kierkegaard and Regine even after they split up. As the mother blackens her breast, Kierkegaard might somehow make himself less attractive to Regine: this possibility is also considered in *Repetition*, where the pseudonym Constantin Constantius advises the young man to pretend to be unfaithful in order to free his fiancée from her attachment to him, and perhaps such a strategy was actually attempted by Kierkegaard in *Either/Or*, particularly by including the cynical and amoral 'Seducer's Diary' in that text. In his biography of Kierkegaard, Georg Brandes writes that 'certain features of unreasonableness or hardness towards his betrothed (which, insofar as they were the case, were all due to his efforts to make the young girl weary of him, to put himself in a bad light before her and thereby ease the break for her) were rumoured about [Copenhagen]'.[9] Alternatively, as the mother hides her breast, so might Kierkegaard conceal himself by staying out of Regine's way or leaving town, as when he went off to Berlin. In the third parable, the mother's own grief is emphasized, and she mourns the loss together with her child, but this is only a brief sorrow because they are still close; this possibility seems poignant when read as a comment on the break-up with Regine: 'how fortunate the one who kept the child so close and did not need to grieve any more!' The final way of accomplishing the separation is to have solid food ready for the child. What might this mean in relation to Regine? Might the 'stronger nourishment' he offers to her be his writings? In an 1849 journal entry that comments on his motivations for the 1843 works, Kierkegaard indicates that both *Either/Or* and *Two Upbuilding Discourses* (published in May 1843) were in a way written to, or for, Regine.[10] Or might he try to encourage her to marry someone else?

Of course, the parables about weaning could be read, more cynically, as an attempt by Kierkegaard to convince his readers – whether Regine and her family, or the gossipers who disapproved of his behaviour – that he was motivated by love for Regine, and was acting for her sake, whereas perhaps his reasons for breaking off the engagement were more prosaic and less noble than he suggested. But this would be a misunderstanding, for the question of motivation is precisely what is problematized in *Fear and Trembling*. If the parables seem to have a closer connection to Regine than to Abraham, in juxtaposing them with the alternative versions of the sacrifice story Kierkegaard posits a connection between his relationship with Regine and Abraham's relationship with Isaac. As we have seen, one element of the story of Abraham that is accentuated in the different readings is his choice, his freedom, understood as the source of his anguish – and this element, which is missing from the maternal parables, is pertinent to Kierkegaard's treatment of Regine. The third version of the journey to Mount Moriah is especially relevant here, since Abraham's inability to find peace of mind is due to the insoluble question of whether he truly loves his son. This indicates that Kierkegaard, anticipating the cynical reader, is dramatizing an inward struggle fuelled by doubts about his love for Regine. A passage written in the margin of a draft of this section of *Fear and Trembling* makes this issue more explicit:

> The point of the whole story lies in Abraham's being genu-inely assured that he loves Isaac more than himself. The doubt is dreadful; who decides it; assurances to the Cherethites and Pelethites [i.e. all kinds of people; an allusion to 2 Samuel] are of no use; here it is a question of the God-consciousness in an individual, since the outward manifestation, the deed, is in contradiction to it . . . if he is in error, what salvation is there for him?[11]

Having considered the parables about weaning independently of the story of Abraham, then, we have arrived at an interpretation that brings them back together again. If the imagined journeys to Mount Moriah describe failures of faith, then the sequence of parables, read as possible responses to the broken engagement, likewise indicate a lack of faith. 'If I had had faith, I would have stayed with Regine.'

There is a second interpretative context that may help us to see the significance of the parables of the mother and child, and their connection to the story of Abraham. The themes of separa-tion and loss are pertinent not only in the sphere of human relationships, but in the relationship between human beings and God that is the substance of the Judeo-Christian tradition (and also, of course, in other theistic traditions, although these are not Kierkegaard's concern). In the Hebrew bible this relation-ship is often represented in terms of a rift, perhaps a separation that follows from a more original oneness. We might think here of the rift between God and the first humans, Adam and Eve, in the garden of Eden, or of the angel Lucifer being cast out of heaven: both of these stories dramatize a fall from grace, in the original sense of this phrase. Just as the weaning of a child is equivocal, insofar as separation signifies both loss and freedom, so these religious separations are similarly ambivalent transitions. When we considered the Preface to *Fear and Trembling* in the previous section, we saw how it brings into question the issue of autonomy, understood historically and primarily in terms of the assertion of human self-sufficiency within the philosophical tradition – but the story of man's increasing independence from God is already being told in the scriptures.

How is this story taken up in the Christian tradition? We cannot consider this question without entering into a theological debate, for it depends on who Jesus is and how his teachings are to be understood. On the one hand, the incarnation of the divine in the human form of Christ effects a reconciliation between God and man; on the other hand, it might be argued that this event grants more autonomy to the human world since it liberates God's people from the legalistic covenant originally established between God and Abraham and places the 'kingdom of heaven' within the human heart. For Kierkegaard, I think, the issues of doubt and faith are evidently inter-personal, relational, and he regards the relationships both between Jesus and his disciples, and between Jesus and God, in terms of the *question* of faith. This is not merely an objective question about the nature of faith, but a subjective question: a question *about* faith – about whether I have it, or am able to attain it – but also a question *of* faith in the sense that faith is itself a question. We do not need to read *Fear and Trembling* to find in the story of Abraham and Isaac an anticipation of Jesus' death, both because the crucifixion is understood, theologically, as a sacrifice – a sort of reversal of Abraham's sacrifice, since instead of a human making a sacrifice for the sake of God, God makes a sacrifice for the sake of humanity – and because of Jesus' sense of being forsaken by God as he hangs on the cross. Just as in the Genesis story Isaac carries the fire-wood up Mount Moriah to the altar, so Jesus carries his wooden cross up the hill to the place of his execution. (Of course, these parallels may be attributed to the influence of the Hebrew bible on the New Testament texts: the narratives of Jesus' death may have been modelled on the story of Abraham and Isaac.) Johannes de silentio hints at such Christian resonances in his alternative accounts of the story of

Abraham in 'Tuning Up', especially in the first version where Isaac thinks that his father has forsaken him; and the Christian significance of Abraham's situation is indicated more explicitly in later sections of *Fear and Trembling*.

We seem to find in this enigmatic section of the text, then, parallels between Isaac and Jesus, between Isaac and Regine, between Kierkegaard and Abraham. And of course, as we have seen, the question of faith that is at stake in the stories of these characters is discussed by Johannes de silentio in response to concerns that nineteenth-century Christians are complacent about their faith; that 'the present age' is one in which faith has been devalued, and that the popularity of Hegelian philosophy is a symptom of this decline; that the assertion of human autonomy needs to be subjected to a genuine questioning, that is to say a form of questioning that is not itself an expression of this very assertion. If we attempt to disentangle all these threads, we soon find ourselves weaving them together again, for they constitute the material of Kierkegaard's thought.

It is often regarded as a mistake to 'psychologize' a philosophical text – that is, to interpret it with reference to psychological observations or suppositions based on biographical details about the author – and it would certainly be wrong to try to reduce *Fear and Trembling* to the story of his broken engagement (or, as is also sometimes attempted, to the story of his relationship with his father). However, it would also be wrong to exclude the relationship with Regine from our interpretation of the text, because this personal situation not only provided inspiration for Kierkegaard's philosophical work, but constituted a particular instantiation of philosophical questions that are pertinent to every existing individual: How can I know how to act? What is the basis of my decisions? What could it mean to live truthfully? Kierkegaard himself wrote that 'He who has explained this riddle [of Abraham] has explained my life.'[12] Moreover, keeping in view the broken engagement to Regine helps to clarify the fact that in *Fear and Trembling* faith is not just a religious category – or, at least, that it is not confined to the relationship to God, but concerns human relationships too.

Some readers might criticize a text like *Fear and Trembling* on the grounds that its strange conflation of personal, philosophical, theological, spiritual, aesthetic and cultural issues, and its sometimes baffling blend of theoretical reflection, lyrical description, introspection, polemic, literary allusion and biblical references do not amount to 'proper philosophy'. Other readers admire the way Kierkegaard's thought reflects his own life and responds to his immediate milieu, while also drawing on the intellectual, religious and literary traditions that he was heir to; they may even regard this irreducible synthesis of diverse elements as a sign of his philosophical talent and profundity.

A TRIBUTE TO ABRAHAM[13]

As its title suggests, Johannes de silentio's 'Tribute' to Abraham is written, like the preceding section, from the perspective of someone who admires the biblical hero. However, its literary style is very different from that of 'Tuning Up': it is a eulogy, self-consciously rhetorical, and whereas the sequence of stories and parables in the previous section seems to invite the reader into a private, quiet world of imagination and contemplation, 'A Tribute to Abraham' takes the form of a public address.

The emotional tone or register of this eulogy also differs from that of 'Tuning Up'. Here, as if rising to the occasion of a public performance, Johannes de silentio is up-beat: his speech is full of fine phrases and exclamation marks. Instead of grappling darkly with Abraham's anguish, he celebrates his faith. The pseudonym's mood is confident, joyful, exuberant, inspired.

One of the ideas in this section is that Abraham, insofar as he is a paradigm of faith, is an antidote to despair, 'a guiding star that rescues the anguished' [18]. The threat of despair is vividly described in the opening paragraph, where the pseudonym invokes the 'emptiness', 'thoughtlessness', 'hopelessness' and 'futility' [12] that must characterize all of life unless there is an 'eternal consciousness in a human being' and a 'sacred bond that tied humankind together' [12]. Here, then, the reader is presented with a clear contrast between a hopeful religious vision of reality, and a despairing secular worldview, and the pseudonym equally clearly espouses the former option. His reasoning on this point is strange: he seems to claim that the hopelessness of life without faith is itself an argument for – or, even more strongly, some kind of proof of – the falsity of the secular hypothesis. We have reason to question the remarkable conviction of Johannes de silentio's 'But that is why it is not so' [12], especially when we consider that this is coming from the person who, in the first two sections of the book, seemed to be preoccupied with doubt. Underlying this unlikely bravado, however, is an attempt to emphasize the significance of Abraham, to indicate that the stakes in the question of his faith could not be higher: it is a matter of the value of human life. According to the pseudonym, the story of Abraham 'testifies' not only to the latter's faith, but 'to God's grace' [19].

Poets and heroes

The question of the hopelessness or hopefulness of life with which Johannes de silentio begins his eulogy on Abraham leads, apparently seamlessly, into a discussion of the roles of 'hero' and 'poet or orator'. The pseudonym's discourse is reflexive here: as he, as poet or orator, pays tribute to Abraham as hero, he reflects on the reciprocal relationship between these two roles, which he compares to those of man and woman. He suggests that the hero and the poet were – quite literally, since he speaks of divine creation – made for one another. Thus it is not only Abraham whose significance lies in the question of life's meaning and value, for Johannes' interpretation of Abraham is essential to the latter's significance. Just as 'the hero is so to speak [the poet's] better nature' [12], so 'the poet is so to speak the hero's better nature' [13]. If people need heroes to rescue them from despair, they also need poets to facilitate this rescue by providing access to these heroes: by describing their deeds and qualities, and preserving these in the collective memory of a literary tradition. For example, figures such as Socrates, Jesus and the Buddha, who wrote nothing themselves, can only continue to guide and inspire people if there are sermons and texts – and orators and poets – to tell the stories of their lives and teachings. Without Plato, Paul, and the authors of the New Testament gospels and the Pali *suttas*, these wise and holy men would probably be long forgotten. Even though Johannes de silentio emphasizes the asymmetry between the hero and the poet, insofar as 'the latter can do nothing that the former does, he can only admire, love and rejoice in the hero', in fulfilling this task the poet 'remains true to his love' [13] – and it is significant that the pseudonym uses this phrase, since it is exactly the one employed to sum up Abraham's achievement near the end of the book [see 106].

This implies that being true to one's love may take many different forms.

This comparison between the roles of hero and poet signals a set of questions that we need to keep asking as we read *Fear and Trembling*: Who is Johannes de silentio? What is his point of view? How should we respond to him? Furthermore, we need to ask such questions in a double way, first from the perspective of Kierkegaard's contemporary reader, and second from our own individual perspectives. When we think about the pseudonym from the first perspective, we should remember that a nineteenth-century reader was likely to regard herself as a Christian, and to have a positive view of Abraham and his faith, and we should also keep in mind Johannes de silentio's suggestion – which is echoed by other Kierkegaardian pseudonyms – that his own times are characterized by religious complacency.

From this point of view, we have reason to call into question the sharp contrast drawn in this section of the text between the roles of hero and poet. It is easy to see that Johannes has the role of poet in relation to Abraham as hero, but might it also be possible to regard him as a hero – in which case, Kierkegaard himself takes the role of poet? Might the pseudonym be a hero precisely to the extent that he recognizes his own lack of faith and his own inability to understand Abraham, in contrast to the self-deceiving complacency that is attributed to his contemporaries? Just as Socrates could be regarded as the wisest man in Athens because he knows that he lacks wisdom, unlike his fellow citizens who misguidedly assume themselves to posses it, so Johannes de silentio can be considered the wisest or even the most religious man in Copenhagen because he is at least aware of his own spiritual limitations.

Moreover, this is a striking possibility insofar as an essential aspect of being a Christian is the acknowledgement of such limitations: from a specifically Christian point of view, it is precisely because human beings are unable to live good lives through their own efforts that God's grace is needed; it is precisely because human beings are unable to maintain a proper relationship to God that Christ's help is indispensable. If the task of becoming a Christian is nothing more than the task of faith, then the first step along the path is to see that one does not yet have faith and thus to recognize the task *as* a task – and so it would seem that

Johannes de silentio is at least one step closer to becoming a Christian than a deluded person who, assuming she has faith already, remains ignorant of her spiritual task. For such a reader, then, the pseudonym might himself become a hero, and the very process of coming to see him as a hero would be this reader's first step along her own path of faith.

'The one who loved God'

The rest of this section of *Fear and Trembling* is devoted to the greatness of Abraham. Here we receive the first positive indication of the nature of faith, for in previous sections we have only been told what faith is not, and confronted with the question of its value. 'Tuning Up', in presenting the different possible inward responses to God's command to sacrifice Isaac, suggested that faith consists not merely in obedience, nor in any other outward action, since all four of the imagined faithless Abrahams obey God and go through the motions of the sacrifice. Faith, then, lies in inwardness, and in his tribute to his hero Johannes de silentio identifies three modes or qualities of inwardness which pertain to Abraham's greatness: love, expectancy, struggle.

Although these might be described as qualities, here they must be recognized as activities. They are not static characteristics of a person, but dynamic processes occurring through time: loving, expecting, struggling. They are inward activities or movements, and the concept of such a movement is integral to Kierkegaard's thought as a whole. Usually when we think of movement, we think of locomotion – movement through space – but the kind of movements that constitute Abraham's greatness are spiritual, not physical, and temporal rather than spatio-temporal. Notice that the word 'inward' itself implies movement, since it indicates a direction – like 'towards', 'backwards', 'upwards' and so on. 'Inwardness' is a very important term for Kierkegaard, and it does not denote some kind of space 'inside' a person through which movement might occur, but instead signifies movement itself. Sometimes, when writing about this movement, Kierkegaard (or his pseudonyms) describes it as 'intensification', 'inward deepening', or 'movement on the spot'. In the case of Abraham, his external movements such as the journey to Mount Moriah and the raising of the knife are not his faith, nor even expressions of faith, but rather *symbolize* his inward movements of love, expectancy and struggle, which do not themselves have any outward expression or sign.

Kierkegaard's emphasis on inwardness is one aspect of his account of the religious life that we may well want to question. Although his emphasis on the interiority and incommunicability of faith does not necessarily amount to individualism – since it is accompanied by a concern for genuine relationships to other human beings as well as to God – it does seem to invoke a dubious idea of a pure, non-physical spirituality. What would Kierkegaard make of the suggestion that our embodiment is not an obstacle to faith but, on the contrary, allows a communion with others that can be at the heart of the religious life? Would he want to dismiss as spiritually irrelevant, perhaps as 'merely aesthetic', the fact that 'compassion' signifies a real, felt experience of another being's inner feeling, and that in this way we can 'touch' and be touched by others? If so, then the notion of receptivity that is so central to his philosophy lacks an important dimension.

The idea of a movement that takes place within a person, or which a person enacts inwardly, is also thematized in *Repetition*, and represents one of the important ways in which this text is a companion piece to *Fear and Trembling*. In *Repetition* the pseud-onymous author Constantin Constantius takes a second trip to Berlin in order to find out whether repetition is possible, but his journey, it is suggested, is an unwitting 'parody' of repetition, since this must be an inward movement. The behaviour of the book's other main character, the young fiancé, can be contrasted with Constantin's physical movement, for when he tries to resolve his existential crisis he stays 'inside' and 'does not stir from the spot'.[14] The message that emerges from *Repetition* is that, while there can be no genuine repetition in the physical world, repeti-tion is possible in the spiritual domain, where it signifies the restoration, return or recovery of something that has been lost. The character of the fiancé realizes that he has lost himself, or his freedom, by becoming engaged; when he regains himself, he states that a repetition has occurred. He also suggests that this repetition is something he receives from another, rather than something he accomplishes by himself, and this might indicate that an individual who loses her freedom is not in a position to recover it by herself – for if she were able to do this, then her freedom would never really have been lost.

The inward movement of repetition in Constantin Constantius's text mirrors the inward movement of faith attributed to Abraham. Constantin's 'confusion' about repetition 'consists in this: the most interior problem of the possibility of repetition is expressed externally, as if repetition, if it were possible, were to be found outside the individual when in fact it must be found within the individual, for which reason the young man does indeed do just the opposite . . . '.[15] In *Repetition* the idea of inward movement is also tied to the reading of a biblical text; here the hero is Job, rather than Abraham, but it is the similarities between these two figures that makes them the focus of the discussions of religious inwardness. We will return in later sections to the theme of movement, and to the significance of the concept of repetition.

Johannes de silentio claims that Abraham is great in proportion to the greatness of what he loved and struggled with, and in proportion to his expectation. '[T]he one who loved God became greater than everybody . . . the one who expected the impossible became greater than everybody . . . the one who struggled with God became greater than everybody' [13]. We will now consider each of these three inward movements in turn. It might seem easy to see why Abraham can be described as loving God, but in fact this is by no means evident from the Genesis account of his sacrifice of Isaac. In fact, when the angel intervenes to prevent him from killing his son, he says: 'now I know that you fear God, since you have not withheld your son, your only son, from me.' Acting out of fear is quite different from acting out of love. As we saw in the previous section, the interpretative work done in *Fear and Trembling* consists, in the first place, in attributing an inwardness to Abraham that is not there in the biblical text. We know from reading the Genesis narrative that Abraham obeys God's command, but the question is *how* he obeys it – whether he obeys lovingly or fearfully, in faith or in despair. Having said this, the reference to Abraham's fear of God in Genesis 22 might be taken as an indication of his inward motivation for carrying out the sacrifice, and in this case Johannes de silentio's reading would deviate from the original version of the story. However, there is reason to question this, and there is also reason to defend the claim that Abraham acted out of love rather than fear.

It is certainly possible to argue that in the biblical narrative the angel's reference to Abraham's fear concerns his outward behaviour rather than his inner attitude, both on the general grounds that this fits better with the text as a whole, which describes what people said and did rather than what they thought or felt, and on the more specific grounds that the blessing Abraham receives after the sacrifice is given 'because you have done this . . . because you have obeyed my voice.' If we accept this argument, this leaves open the question of Abraham's motivation. When we consider Abraham's situation, the view that he acted from fear of God is undermined by the fact that he has nothing to fear, because he has nothing to lose: if he gives up Isaac, his only son who contains the promise of future genera- tions, then the best is lost, and nothing worse can happen. It would not make sense to say that Abraham sacrifices Isaac because he is afraid that God will punish him, because no pun- ishment could equal the loss of his only son. This therefore supports Johannes de silentio's claim that Abraham's obedience can be attributed to his love of God.

Before we move on to consider the question of expectation, another important point to bear in mind here is that Abraham's love for God incorporates his love for Isaac. These two loves cannot be separated. This is not simply because Isaac is a gift from God. If the sacrifice of Isaac is motivated by love for God, then this is only because Abraham loves Isaac. The sacrifice would not have value – and thus would not be a genuine sacrifice – if Abraham did not love Isaac more than anything else. It is a symbol of Abraham's love for God precisely to the extent that it is a symbol of Abraham's love for Isaac. In this section of the text Johannes de silentio suggests that, as an alternative response to God's command, Abraham could have killed himself instead of Isaac, acknowledging as he did so that 'this sacrifice . . . is not the best I have' [17]. Of course, if Abraham had loved himself more than Isaac, the sacrifice of his son would have been lesser, and might well have been motivated out of fear of losing some- thing worse – his own life.

Expecting the impossible

The thought that Abraham expected 'the impossible' is central to the interpretation of his faith presented in *Fear and Trem- bling*. So what exactly did he expect, and how was this impossible? He expected the fulfilment of God's promise that he would become the father of many generations, of a great nation, and he expected this twice, each time in the face of an apparently insurmountable obstacle. First, he expected it even when he and Sarah were old and childless, and this hope was fulfilled when Isaac was born. Isaac is from the beginning an impossible child, a miracle, a gift from God. Then, second, he continues to expect it when God demands the sacrifice of Isaac. How can the promise to father a nation, with Sarah, be fulfilled if their only child is dead? This seems to be impossible. Of course, it might be objected that for God all things are possible, since God is all-powerful and can intervene in history to make anything happen, even in defiance of natural laws. And in fact in the following section of *Fear and Trembling* Johannes de silentio writes, quoting the gospels of Matthew, Mark and Luke, that 'for God everything is possible' [39].[16] This is an important idea for Kierkegaard: later, in *The Sickness Unto Death* (1849), his pseudonym Anti-Climacus transforms this from a claim about God to a *definition* of God, asserting that 'God *is* that all things are possible, and that all things are possible is God.'[17] So, the fulfilment of Abraham's expectation is only impossible humanly-speaking; it is impossible in a world without God. This seems to imply that a person who believes in God must expect the impossible, at all times, and indeed to say that God *is* 'that all things are possible' leads to the view that belief in God *is* the belief that all things are possible. In other words, if one accepts that a promise comes from God in the first place, then surely its fulfilment must be expected?

However, we need to be careful here. There is a difference between the belief that all things are possible, and the belief that a divine promise will be fulfilled. The first belief does not amount to expectation. Abraham could have believed that it was within God's power to fulfil the promise to give him a son without expecting that God would actually do so. God might have changed his mind and decided not to keep his promise; even though he demonstrated his power to give Abraham a son when Isaac was born to an aged Sarah, he could still take the child away – and indeed his command that Abraham should sacrifice Isaac might be interpreted as just such a change of mind. The difference between the two beliefs is the difference between believing merely that God exists, and believing something about God's nature. The belief that all things are possible follows from belief in the existence of God, but this does not entail that God will keep his promises. This requires the further belief that God is loving. But even this does not quite justify Abraham's expectation, for a loving God could change his mind and break his promise for the sake of some inscrutable 'greater good' which Abraham might not understand or be aware of. Abraham's expectation, then, is based on his belief that God loves *him*. This belief is personal; it is faith in his own particular relationship to God. By contrast, the belief that God is loving, or that 'God is love', lacks this element of particularity – and precisely this is crucial to Johannes de silentio's interpretation of Abraham's faith.

Of course, the suggestion that Abraham's expectation is based on his belief that God loves him raises the question of what this latter belief rests on. Is it grounded in previous experience of God's beneficence – such as, for example, the original gift of Isaac? No, because Abraham expected this first gift in faith, and even if he could recall other good things as signs of God's love, he could equally well recall painful things that might indicate that God did not favour him – for instance, his wife's barrenness. Moreover, God giving Isaac in the first place only to change his mind would be, as Johannes de silentio points out, 'even more frightful than if it had never happened!' [16], and such a God would be not merely capricious, but cruel. Abraham's belief that God loves him is not the result of a weighing-up of evidence; indeed, the interpretation of his faith in *Fear and Trembling* seems to suggest that his belief in God makes him receptive to God's gifts, rather than that the gifts provide a basis for his belief in God. So perhaps we will have to conclude that Abraham's belief that God loves him is based on *nothing*: that it is groundless, unjustified, and absurd. Johannes de silentio describes his belief as 'preposterous' [17]. This idea will be pursued further in subsequent sections of the text.

In his 'Tribute' Johannes de silentio mentions something important about the nature of Abraham's expectation that he will develop at much greater length when he turns to discuss three 'Problems' that are, he claims, implicit in the story of the sacrifice. He indicates that Abraham maintained his expectation that God's promise would be fulfilled 'after having given it up' [15]. The pseudonym adds here that 'it is great to lay hold of the eternal, but it is greater to stick doggedly to the temporal after having given it up' [15]. Abraham gives up his expectation precisely by obeying God's command to sacrifice Isaac, by raising his knife over his young son. But it is not as if he renounces the expectation and then, only afterwards, takes it up again: if this were the case then he would have been in despair as he prepared for the sacrifice. More remarkably, indeed unfathomably, Abraham *simultaneously* gives up hope of fathering a nation and believes that God will keep his promise; he gives Isaac up and *at the same time* expects to hold onto him. In one sense, then, it is misleading to claim that Abraham maintains his expectation 'after' relinquishing it, although it is nevertheless correct – at least, according to Johannes de silentio's interpretation of the story – to say that he maintains his expectation after receiving the order to sacrifice Isaac and deciding to obey it. In his 'Preliminary Outpouring from the Heart' which introduces the 'Problems' presented by the story of Abraham, Johannes describes faith as a 'double movement' [29]. This doubleness consists in the renunciation of expectation, on the one hand, and the preservation of expectation, on the other.

The pseudonym's remark about 'sticking to the temporal', which is connected with this last point about expectation, also anticipates a significant element of his analysis of Abraham in subsequent sections of the text. He contrasts the person who grasps 'the eternal' with one who holds on to the temporal, and he also contrasts the person who has faith 'only for a future life' – which he doubts is really faith at all – with Abraham who 'believed for this life' [17]. These are two versions of the same distinction: between a faith, or pseudo-faith, that focuses on another, eternal world, which might be a heaven in which dwells an eternal God and in which human souls live eternally after bodily death; and a faith that focuses on this life, this world in which we are now living. The first faith is oriented to eternity, the second to temporality and finitude, which are the conditions of the human situation in this world. Johannes de silentio admires Abraham because his faith was of this latter sort: 'Abraham believed precisely for this life, that he would grow old in the land, honoured by the people, blessed by posterity, forever remembered in Isaac, his dearest one in life . . .' [17].

Struggling with God

Let us turn now to the claim that Abraham was great because of his struggle with God. It is one thing to say that he struggled with himself, with doubt, with despair – but in what sense did he struggle with God? Surely his obedience expresses surrender rather than combat? One way of understanding this is to take 'with God' to mean 'alongside God' rather than 'against God'. However, the references to conflict and conquering here suggest that Abraham's struggle is at least some sort of confrontation with God, even though it is a paradoxical struggle, since his victory is gained, according to the pseudonym, by his 'powerlessness' [13]. The reversals of ordinary greatness in this passage allude to Christian texts: Abraham was 'great by that power whose strength is powerlessness [2 Corinthians 12: 9–10], great by that wisdom whose secret is folly [1 Corinthians 3: 18–19] . . . great by that love which is hatred of oneself [John 12: 25]' [14]. We have seen that the key to Abraham's faith, and thus to his greatness – if, that is, faith is valued highly – lies not in his obedience to God, but in his inward manner of obeying, and in the 'preposterous' expectancy he maintains while he is obeying. His struggle must lie here too, for if he simply obeyed God and gave up hope of keeping Isaac and fathering a nation then he would not be contending with God, but merely submitting to him. Of course, Abraham does not resist God antagonistically, and in a sense his obedience *is* absolute submission. However, in maintaining his expectation that the divine promise be fulfilled he tacitly holds God to the promise and thus, it might be said, struggles in a purely inward and non-violent way against the sacrifice. Perhaps this is what Johannes de silentio refers to when, in the following section, he praises Abraham's 'paradoxical and humble courage' [41].

Because Abraham's struggle is inward, it is not apparent to the observer. From the outside, the movement of faith looks effortless, but Johannes de silentio wants to ensure that the reader is not deceived by appearances. As we saw in the Preface, he suggests that faith is being devalued to the extent that people, assuming that faith is something easy, complacently suppose themselves to have faith as a matter of course. Part of his effort to raise the value of faith is to emphasize the difficulty, the struggle, the 'fear and trembling' contained within it. So, the fact that – according to the pseudonym – Abraham did not doubt should not be taken to mean that he did not struggle. The nature of this inward struggle is illustrated very nicely by the metaphor of a dancer presented in the following section of the text. The grace of a ballet dancer consists in her ability to make her movements and positions look easy, but this is only achieved by hard work, by years of vigorous and painful training to build up her muscles, refine her balance, and so on. Arduous struggle is concealed within the apparently effortless grace of the dance, just as it lies within Abraham's ready obedience to God and unwavering trust in him.

This metaphor of the dancer may prompt us to return to the question of Johannes de silentio's neglect – which is echoed elsewhere in Kierkegaard's corpus – of the practices that are integral to the religious life. Just as the dancer becomes a dancer through practising various physical exercises, so the Christian becomes a Christian at least in part through spiritual exercises such as prayer, confession, reading the New Testament, taking sacraments, and so on. And these practices, like the dancer's techniques, have to be learned from a more experienced practitioner, and are often acquired communally – within a family; at Sunday school; in church. Does Johannes de silentio's insistence on the inwardness of faith give too little weight, and accord too little value, to this more public aspect of religion? Should we understand his emphasis on the 'single individual' as a corrective to the defects of socially-embedded religiosity that Kierkegaard perceived in his own society, or is this emphasis supposed to indicate the essence of faith?

Inwardness and interpretation

In his 'Tribute', then, Johannes de silentio argues that Abraham is great by virtue of his love, expectation and struggle, considered as the inward movements of faith. But how does the pseudonym know that his hero loved, expected and struggled in the way he describes? The short answer to this question is that he does not know this – and cannot know it. If these movements are purely inward, they are inaccessible to others; perhaps they are even inaccessible to the individual within whom they occur, a possibility that is acknowledged by Johannes when he alludes, in 'Tuning Up', to Abraham's doubt about whether he really did love Isaac more than himself. In speaking of the nature of Abraham's faith, the pseudonym can only imagine and interpret; this is why his task is that of a poet. He is imaginatively reconstructing Abraham's inward movements *as they must have been if he had acted in faith*. This 'if' should not be forgotten, in spite of Johannes de silentio's apparent confidence in this section of *Fear and Trembling*: faith remains questionable, and a question. And we should also be aware that his imaginative, interpretative account of Abraham's inner life, insofar as this constitutes his faith, amounts to a decision about what is meant by faith itself. There is a circularity here that cannot be avoided: the pseudonym describes Abraham's faith in terms of unknowable inward movements that can only be deduced, so to speak, from a certain idea of faith that he attributes to Abraham. All we have in the 'Tribute to Abraham', in other words, is an interpretation of faith.

This interpretation has a decidedly Christian character, as is signalled by the various references to the gospels and the Pauline letters in this part of the text. Is Johannes attempting to smuggle a Christian conception of faith into the story of Abraham? If so, then Kierkegaard, who was a master of deception, would surely have covered his tracks more carefully. If *Fear and Trembling* were pretending to offer an historical, critical exegesis of Genesis 22: 1–19 then it would be difficult to defend it against scholars, but this is itself an indication that this is not Kierkegaard's intention. The 'Preface' announces, albeit obliquely, that Johannes de silentio's main concern is with the value of faith in the nineteenth century, and this means that one of the core questions posed by the text as a whole is whether and how it is possible for a contemporary reader, who is presumed to regard herself as a Christian and a person of faith, to admire Abraham for being the 'father of faith'. If Abraham's faith is interpreted in such a way as to bring it as close as possible to Christian faith, without actually contradicting the Genesis account, then this only makes this question more pertinent to *Fear and Trembling*'s intended reader.

As we have seen, Johannes de silentio's strategy is to attribute an inwardness to Abraham by interpreting the description of his external, physical actions that is supplied in the biblical account of the sacrifice. Since this subjective perspective is missing in the Hebrew text, or at least left to the imagination, this leaves the pseudonym free to develop his own interpretation without undermining the original narrative. On the other hand, the biblical narrative cannot provide support for the interpretation either. For example, the pseudonym interprets the statement that Abraham 'rose early in the morning' as indicating that, far from dragging his feet, he 'hurried as if going to a celebration'. But another interpretation, equally compatible with the biblical text, is that Abraham, in despair, wanted to get the sacrifice over with as quickly as possible. There is no objective way of deciding between these interpretations, and this means that there is no way of knowing whether Abraham really did have faith of the kind that Johannes de silentio attributes to him – or, indeed, of any other kind.

On the one hand, the pseudonym wants to accentuate the difficulty of Abraham's faith for the sake of a supposedly complacent reader. His vivid account in this section of his hero's courage in the face of the most challenging test imaginable, 'the hardest sacrifice that could be demanded of him' [18], represents an attempt to save Abraham from oblivion, in accordance with his poetic vocation. It is not Abraham's name that is in danger of being forgotten, nor his reputation as the 'father of faith', but rather the inward movements that lie hidden in the story of the sacrifice and make it truly a story about faith. The pseudonym suggests that while Abraham was able to raise his knife above Isaac while looking at his son, anyone watching him would become 'paralyzed' and 'blind'. However, this is not the effect that the story commonly has on modern listeners or readers, who forget Abraham's inward movements because they know the outcome of the story: 'We all know it – it was only a test' [19].

On the other hand, this emphasis on inwardness means that what matters most in the story of Abraham is not the extremity of his situation, which is certainly rare if not exceptional, but the basic elements of his faith: his love, his expectation, and his struggle. If faith means loving God, believing that he loves you and expecting him to behave in accordance with this, and struggling to maintain this belief in the face of certain obstacles (the general nature of which we will explore in the following section), then isn't Abraham's achievement actually the bare minimum that could be expected of a person of faith? Although his particular story involves the testing of this faith in extreme circumstances, is his faith itself exceptional? This is an important question, and I think it is one that is deliberately raised by *Fear and Trembling*.

It is significant that Johannes de silentio ends his effusive eulogy on Abraham by saying that 'in a hundred and thirty years you got no further than faith': this is what his hero's achievement amounts to. His tribute to Abraham is also a tribute to faith. If Abraham is an exception, it is because faith itself is exceptional; if Abraham is inexplicable, this is because faith itself cannot be understood. If the reader finds herself doubting that she would have responded as Abraham did to the command to sacrifice Isaac, then it follows that she must also doubt whether she has faith at all.

A PRELIMINARY OUTPOURING FROM THE HEART[18]

The title of this section contains a play on words that gives some indication of its key themes. An alternative translation of the Danish title is 'Preliminary Expectoration'. The word 'expectoration' comes from the Latin words *ex*, out of, and *pectus*, breast, so that it means coming out of the breast, or expelling from the chest. The term is commonly used, often in a medical context, to signify 'coughing up', clearing the throat or lungs. Johannes de silentio's 'preliminary expectoration', then, implies that he is coughing or clearing his throat prior to speaking. On the other hand, as the translation of the phrase in the Cambridge edition of *Fear and Trembling* indicates, it can be taken more figuratively to mean 'coming from the heart'.

Matters of the heart

This reference to the heart is important, since Johannes' discourse in this section is concerned with three activities or processes that are traditionally associated with the heart: love, suffering, and courage. (Notice that our word 'courage' comes from the Latin *cor*, which means heart: this etymology remains more apparent in the French words *coeur* and *courage*.) This shared association with the heart highlights the way in which love, suffering and courage are closely interlinked in Johannes de silentio's account of faith. All three might, in fact, be understood as forms of open-heartedness.

The idea that the pseudonym's words come from the heart also fits with the passionate nature of his discussion of religious faith. As I explained in my Overview of Themes, Kierkegaard wrote using several different pseudonyms, each of which has his own perspective – and one of the distinctive characteristics of Johannes de silentio is his passion. This is evident in 'Tuning Up', where he introduces the story of Abraham from the perspective of someone who has a 'desire' and 'longing' to understand Abraham *from the inside*, so to speak, and it is also evident in the passionate tone of his 'Tribute' to Abraham. In his 'Preliminary Outpouring from the Heart' the pseudonym emphasizes, in an important footnote, that passion is required in making what he calls 'the movement of infinity', and he suggests that 'our age lacks . . . passion' [35]. We will examine these claims later in this section. Here, though, we can note the general point that one of Kierkegaard's concerns, which is expressed in many of his works, is that modern intellectual life has lost the passion that in ancient Greece provided the impetus for philosophizing. In Kierkegaard's philosophy, the concept of passion means something similar to the concept of *eros* in Plato's philosophy, which signifies desire in general, but most particularly desire for eternal truth, goodness and beauty. In *Concluding Unscientific Postscript*, for example, the pseudonym Johannes Climacus makes a couple of important references to Plato's *Symposium*, the dialogue in which Socrates' desire for truth is discussed and dramatized most explicitly. While Socrates, in this dialogue, suggests that the desire for truth, goodness and spiritual beauty that motivate the philosopher are superior versions of the desire for sensual pleasure and physical beauty, Johannes Climacus argues that sensuous passion undermines spiritual or 'idealizing' passion.[19] We can detect in Johannes de silentio's writing an erotic relationship to his subject-matter that echoes Socratic passion.

One final point to be made about the title of this section is that the reference to the heart serves to accentuate Johannes de silentio's emphasis on inwardness, and at the same time raises the question of communication. The suggestion that his discussion of faith comes 'from the heart' provides a kind of mirror-image of a process of appropriation that Kierkegaard envisages, throughout his writing, as the way an individual makes a truth her own, incorporates it into her life. To illustrate this we can turn again to *Concluding Unscientific Postscript*, where Johannes Climacus distinguishes between objective truth, or knowledge, which is traditionally thought to lie in the correspondence between ideas or propositions and reality; and subjective or spiritual truth, which consists in 'a taking to heart' leads to 'the subject's transformation in himself'.[20] The Danish word translated here as 'taking to heart' is *Inderliggjørelse*, which means 'making inward' and is otherwise translated, in different editions of the *Postscript*, as 'inward deepening' and 'intensification of inwardness'.

The issue of communication is often problematized in Kierkegaard's works, not least in *Fear and Trembling*, where one of the three 'Problems' arising from the story of Abraham is the latter's inability to communicate his intention to sacrifice Isaac. Of course, this means that Johannes de silentio faces the challenge of talking about something – Abraham's faith – that in an important sense cannot be talked about; but on the other hand the idea of a discourse coming *from the heart* of the writer, to be *taken to heart* by the reader, implies a process of truly subjective communication. Perhaps this gives an indication of Kierkegaard's hope for how his ideal reader will take on and respond to the text. This is certainly not to suggest that the text attempts to bring about the transferral of a ready-made truth, in the form of a piece of knowledge, from one heart to another. Because each reader who takes to heart the pseudonym's discourse does so in her own way, we cannot say in advance exactly what the process of communication amounts to. But one strong possibility is that what passes between the two hearts is a question about faith: a question that is only properly meaningful when it is made inward; when it is posed by the individual in relation to her own existence.

The problem of evil

Just as the title 'A Preliminary Outpouring from the Heart' can be read in more than one sense, so the opening paragraph of this section also has a double significance. Most immediately, Johannes de silentio's discussion of the proverb 'only the one who works gets the bread' is concerned with the 'work' involved in faith – not only in having faith, but also in understanding faith, and thus also in understanding Abraham. The pseudonym argues that although the proverb does not apply in the 'external and visible world', in the 'world of spirit . . . it holds true that only the one who works gets the bread, only the one who was in anxiety finds rest, only the one who descends into the underworld rescues the beloved, only the one who draws the knife gets Isaac' [21]. This makes it clear that 'work' in this context refers to existential struggle, to an emotional investment, to a willingness to suffer. We can already see in this short passage hints of the themes of love, suffering and courage.

A little further below the surface, however, are intimations of another idea that is connected to this more immediate one, and which provides a sort of background or context for the discussion of faith throughout this section of the book. It is significant that Johannes de silentio introduces the notion of the 'work' of faith by making a comparison between the external world and the world of spirit, for he believes the question of faith to be concerned precisely with a contradiction between these two worlds. The fact that the individual has to live in both of them means that this contradiction has a deep existential significance – and this, as we shall see, is the substance of religious faith. Moreover, the pseudonym's contrast between the external and spiritual worlds picks out the issue of justice. He suggests that 'the external world is subject to the law of imperfection', or injust-ice, insofar as 'here it happens again and again that the one who does not work also gets the bread, and the one who sleeps gets it more abundantly than the one who works' [21]. In other words, in the external world rewards are not proportional to effort; happi-ness is 'indifferent' to striving or to conduct. In the world of spirit, by contrast, justice is always done: 'Here an eternal divine order prevails, here it does not rain on both the just and the unjust, here the sun does not shine on both good and evil' [21].

These two issues – the contrast between the external and spiri-tual worlds, and the evident injustice within the former world – are, so to speak, the essential ingredients of the traditional 'problem of evil' that is often invoked as an objection to religious belief. There are several versions of this problem, but the basic argu-ment identifies an incompatibility (or 'incommensurability', as Johannes de silentio puts it) between the religious person's belief that there is an all-powerful, just and loving God who created the world and continues to direct its course, and the fact that this world is often unjust in the way the pseudonym indicates here. In its crudest form the 'problem of evil' points to suffering and wrongdoing as evidence against religious belief, but the most compelling forms of the problem focus on the issue of justice:

human freedom might require the capacity to commit evil acts, and perhaps suffering is part of life – but surely a good God would not allow innocent or virtuous people to suffer more than those who behave cruelly or immorally? This question is not just an intellectual objection to beliefs about the nature of reality, but an existential question that confronts religious believers themselves. It is a deep question that faith must always contend with, and may frequently be tested by. As we will see, Johannes de silentio's discussion of faith in his 'Preliminary Outpouring from the Heart' does contend with this question, although he does not explicitly formulate and address the 'problem of evil'. He makes a distinction between two types of religious individual: the knight of resignation, and the knight of faith. Both resignation and faith are responses to the incommensurability between religious belief and the way the world is; between – to put the problem more subjectively or 'inwardly' – the individual's relationship to God, and her relationship to the world. The pseudonym's characterization of faith provides an implicit response to the classical 'problem of evil' that is quite different from the defences of religious belief offered by other philosophers and theologians.

Copycat killings

Before we examine in detail the positions of resignation and faith, however, we must consider Johannes de silentio's discussion of the spiritual 'work' of understanding Abraham that occupies the first few pages of 'A Preliminary Outpouring from the Heart'. He begins by offering a characterization of what he takes to be a typical way of responding to the story of Abraham's sacrifice, and he does so by imagining a parson who preaches about the story to a congregation who are so complacent and comfortable that they fall asleep. These people – including the parson – are not willing to do the work of understanding Abraham's situation; they say to themselves that 'The great thing was that he loved God so much that he was willing to sacrifice the best to him' [22], but here 'what is left out of Abraham's story is the anxiety' [23]. Johannes de silentio disrupts this cosy scene by introducing a character who listens to the sermon, and decides to go home and do what Abraham did: kill his own son. The parson, naturally, is outraged by his behaviour: 'You detestable person, you pariah of society, what devil has so possessed you that you want to murder your son?' – but what if, continues the pseudonym, the man replies, 'After all, that was what you yourself preached on last Sunday' [23]? Johannes suggests that the parson's simple mistake of not knowing what he was saying when he spoke of Abraham is, in its consequences, at once infinitely comic and infinitely tragic.

Of course, this scenario is a parody of religious complacency. However, it raises some serious questions: 'How does one explain such a contradiction as that speaker's? . . . The ethical expression for what Abraham did is that he intended to murder Isaac; the religious expression is that he intended to sacrifice Isaac. But in this contradiction lies precisely the anxiety that indeed can make a person sleepless, and yet Abraham is not who he is without this anxiety' [24]. Looked at from the outside, there is no difference between murder and sacrifice: in each case, Abraham climbs the mountain, binds his son, and raises the knife. The only difference between the two – if there is a difference at all, and this 'if' is one of the questions that Johannes de silentio is putting to the reader – lies in the purely inward movements of faith. This means that a 'copycat' killing, like that imagined by the pseudonym, always betrays a misunderstanding, a 'mental confusion', since 'it is only by faith that one acquires a resemblance to Abraham, not by murder' [25]. All that can be 'copied' are external movements, for only these can be observed, and this means that Abraham, insofar as he is a man of faith, cannot be copied at all. His faith is absolutely singular, and every person who makes the movement of faith does so in her own situation, in response to specific requirements.

Having said this, we need to consider more carefully the question of how to regard those who act in a way that resembles Abraham. As Johannes de silentio indicates, it is important that our response to Abraham isn't blinded by his reputation as a great man, the 'father of faith', and reflecting on cases that appear similar to his own will help us to detach our judgement from any preconceptions of Abraham's greatness. When I teach *Fear and Trembling*, students often make the comparison between Abraham and the Islamic terrorists who flew into the World Trade Center in New York on September 11th 2001, or those who detonated bombs on London tubes and buses on July 7th 2005.

Of course, the ethical expression for these terrorists' actions is murder – but are they to be admired from a religious perspective? There are no doubt some people who do admire them, and perhaps, like Abraham, these terrorists also have their poets who will preserve their names and deeds in memory for future generations; there are certainly many others who would be horrified at such a view. (Likewise, suggests Johannes de silentio, when we hear the story of Abraham we should 'learn to be horrified by the prodigious paradox that is the meaning of his life' [45].) Since they killed themselves as well as others in the name of a religious cause, were the Islamic terrorists, like Abraham, making sacrifices that earn them reputations as heroes of faith?

These questions should not be closed down too quickly: just as Johannes de silentio confesses his inability to understand Abraham, so we might perhaps pause before trying to settle the matter with political, sociological or psychological explanations of the terrorist attacks. On the other hand, there are some points that should be made in thinking through the comparison between Abraham and the terrorists. First, we can remind ourselves again that Johannes de silentio is concerned only with Abraham's inward movements, which he characterizes in his 'Tribute' as love, expectation and struggle, and in the present section as love, suffering and courage. The most important of these is love – which is perhaps why it figures prominently in both sections – and Johannes suggests that the interpretation of the sacrifice pivots on the question of whether Abraham loves Isaac more than himself [see 26]. Second, we should be absolutely clear that the contradiction or paradox of Abraham's situation is that his willingness to kill perfectly coincides with his love: it is Isaac who he loves, and Isaac who he is prepared to kill. This means that what condemns Abraham from an ethical point of view is precisely that which elevates him from a religious point of view. This is the paradox of his situation. When we consider the terrorist attacks, however, the situation is rather different. Insofar as the bombers committed suicide, it is possible to say that, as with Abraham, what they love coincides with what they kill. But it is not their acts of suicide that make them ethically reprehensible, but the fact that they killed many other people. And there is no indication that these acts of murder coincided with their love. Of course, since love is inward we cannot be absolutely sure that the terrorists did not love their victims, but it seems more likely that they killed with fear or hatred in their hearts rather than with love. If this is the case, the murders they committed cannot be regarded as sacrifices.

If we are to focus on the inward movements of Abraham's faith, then what is really in question here is love, expectation, struggle, suffering and courage. It is with regard to these things that Kierkegaard was able to see parallels between the story of Abraham and his own situation in relation to Regine Olsen. The common ground in this instance is not a willingness to commit murder in the name of religious belief, but the prospect of losing a loved one by virtue of a decision that is morally culpable – in Kierkegaard's case, by breaking his promise to marry Regine. Like Abraham, he harmed the person whom he loved. (And in fact, I suspect that it would be difficult to find a pair of lovers, whether partners, friends, or relatives, who have not hurt one another in some way: love and suffering seem to belong together, and this is why it requires courage to love and be loved.) The important point to grasp here is that Abraham's story is relevant to ordinary, domestic situations as much as to extreme ones. The extremity of Abraham's case only serves to accentuate the questions of faith that can play themselves out in the most humdrum, humble circumstances. Or, to look at this another way, the interpretation of Abraham's story that is presented in *Fear and Trembling* indicates that all these ordinary circumstances are, or at least can be, exceptional: that they can push a person to the edge of reason and into the abyss of despair just as the command to sacrifice Isaac tests Abraham – tests him not *to* his limit, but beyond any limitation, beyond finitude. Abraham's response to this test shows that his faith has no limit: is this a sign that he has extraordinary faith, or does it rather suggest that a faith that has limits is not really faith at all?

'By no means do I have faith'

Having raised the question of whether it is possible to 'speak candidly about Abraham without running the risk that an individual in mental confusion might go and do likewise' [25], and responded by describing how he would speak to an audience 'so they were really sensible of the dialectical struggles of faith and its gigantic passion' [26], Johannes de silentio raises the question of his own faith. He suggests that his audience may assume that he has faith to 'a high degree', and he immediately refutes this: 'By no means do I have faith' [26]. By identifying himself as someone who lacks faith, in contrast to Abraham, the pseudonym introduces the distinction between resignation and faith that is explicated in the rest of this section of the text.

Johannes de silentio says that he is 'a clever fellow', and that clever people 'always have great difficulties in making the movement of faith' [26]. Why would this be? Perhaps because intelligent people are more likely to be complacent than 'simpler' characters. Perhaps because cleverness is located (so to speak) in the head, while faith is located in the heart, and thus clever people may tend to ignore or neglect the heart-qualities of love, suffering, courage and so on that the pseudonym associates with faith. Johannes suggests that the clever person's difficulties in making the movement of faith are especially acute, or perhaps especially manifest, in modern intellectual life, where theology is subordinate to philosophy; where, to speak very generally, faith is subordinate to reason. In this sophisticated modern milieu, the difficulty – and, implicitly, the value – accorded to intellectual achievements is seen as greater than that of faith: 'It is said to be difficult to understand Hegel but to understand Abraham is a small matter. To go beyond Hegel is a miracle but to manage Abraham is the easiest thing of all' [27]. This reference to understanding Hegel's philosophy and 'going beyond' it is probably directed at Kierkegaard's contemporary Martensen, who was indeed influenced by Hegelian thought and sought to develop a philosophy that would overcome certain shortcomings he identified within it.

By presenting himself as a 'clever fellow' who nevertheless fails to understand Abraham, Johannes de silentio attempts to reverse the respective values accorded to philosophy and faith, against the grain of the contemporary intellectual scene he depicts. He states that he has 'easily, naturally' studied Hegelian philosophy and understood it quite well, whereas

> when I must think about Abraham, I am virtually annihilated. At every moment I am aware of that prodigious paradox which is the content of Abraham's life; at every moment I am repelled, and in spite of all its passion, my thought cannot

penetrate it, cannot make a hairs-breadth of headway. I strain every muscle to get a perspective, and at the same instant I become paralysed . . . I cannot think myself into Abraham. When I reach that height I fall down since what is offered to me is a paradox. Yet by no means do I therefore think that faith is something lowly but on the contrary that it is the highest, plus that it is dishonest of philosophy to proffer something else instead and to make light of faith. Philosophy cannot and must not bestow faith but must understand itself and know what it has to offer and take nothing away and least of all trick people out of something by making them think it is nothing [27].

This is an indirect challenge to the complacency that the pseudonym identifies. It is clear from passages like this one that *Fear and Trembling* was written primarily with an intellectual reader in mind, and, in being confronted by a character who understands Hegel but doesn't understand Abraham, this reader is invited to question her own imputed assumptions about the relative difficulties of faith and philosophy. The question that would naturally arise for such a reader is '*Why*? What's so difficult about faith?' – and this is precisely the question that this section of the text tries to address. In the passage quoted above, the word 'paradox' appears for the first time in *Fear and Trembling*.

Johannes de silentio's own admission that 'I cannot think myself into Abraham' performs, or exemplifies, the very movement that he wants philosophy to make. Philosophy should 'understand itself', he argues, instead of attempting to explain faith, and by this he means that part of the task of philosophy is to become aware of its own limitations – just as part of a person's spiritual task is to understand her limitations. This, of course, echoes the Socratic idea that the philosopher must come to know her own ignorance in order to make any progress along the path of wisdom. In Plato's dialogues, however, the question of the limit of philosophical thought is left open, and it certainly seems possible that after taking the preliminary step of understanding her lack of knowledge the philosopher may then go on to see things as they really are. Johannes de silentio seems to be more decisive about the limits of philosophy: he seems quite clear that faith is simply inaccessible to it. But when we think about this carefully, we see that he is not proposing a form of scepticism that would distinguish his position from that of Plato, because he is claiming that faith is not just beyond knowledge, but of a wholly different order. Faith is not a piece of reality that human beings happen to be unable to know, but an inward, existential movement that philosophical thinking cannot, of itself, initiate. Indeed, as we have just seen, Johannes de silentio thinks that purely intellectual reflection may hinder the movement of faith.

Infinite resignation

In a sense, then, Kierkegaard presents Johannes de silentio as an exemplary philosopher, just as the latter presents Abraham as a paradigm of faith. Having suggested that philosophy should come to terms with its own limits, the pseudonym embarks on an exploration of *his* own limits. He repeatedly insists that 'Abraham I cannot understand; in a certain sense I can learn nothing from him except to be amazed' [31]. But his limitations are existential as well as intellectual: they concern what he is able to *do* as well as what he is able to know or understand: 'For my part, I can very well describe the movements of faith, but I cannot make them' [31]. Johannes de silentio is, he tells us, acquainted with suffering, with 'life's hardships and dangers' [27]; and he is 'convinced that God is love'. However, he falls short of the faith of Abraham, because he lacks the courage of his hero: 'I have looked the frightful in the eye; I do not timidly flee from it but know very well that even if I approach it bravely my courage is still not the courage of faith and is nothing to be compared with that' [28]. Johannes de silentio's courage is the kind that belongs to what he calls 'infinite resignation'. The difference between resignation and faith turns on the question of courage: in order to make the movement of resignation, the individual has to face, come to terms with, and accept her suffering – but the courage of faith is something more. In clarifying what this 'something more' consists in, the true difficulty and value of faith's courage becomes evident.

Johannes de silentio confesses that 'to me God's love . . . is incommensurable with the whole of actuality' [28]. That is to say, he feels his suffering fully, and in so doing finds that this suffering is incompatible with the belief that God loves him; if he were unable to accept his painful 'actuality', then this would constitute an objection against the very idea of a loving God; in accepting his suffering, he makes it possible to accept God. He is 'convinced that God is love', but he also recognizes that 'I do not believe, this courage I lack' [28]. What does this mean? What is the difference between being 'convinced that God is love', and 'believing'? For Johannes, God's love is a 'thought', an idea that is sometimes present for him and sometimes absent; and it is impersonal insofar as it is an idea about the nature of God. The proposition that 'God is love', however fervently it is believed, is different from the belief that 'God loves me' – and, as I suggested in my commentary on the 'Tribute to Abraham', it is only this personal belief that could provide Abraham with a basis for his expectation that God would keep his promise to him. Johannes de silentio is unable to believe that God loves him: he can, perhaps, accept his suffering as part of the larger scheme of things and believe that there is a loving God, but he cannot feel that his painful existence is itself a sign of God's love for him. How could it be? So the pseudonym's relationship to God is in a sense set apart from his worldly existence, with all its suffering, and in this respect it is impersonal: 'I do not trouble God with my petty cares; the particular does not concern me, I gaze only at my love and keep its virginal flame pure and clear'. By contrast, 'faith is convinced that God is concerned about the smallest thing' [28]. This is the difference between resignation and faith. Resignation requires the courage to accept suffering, instead of trying to deny it or avoid it; faith requires the courage to be loved by God – and this is 'a paradoxical and humble courage' [41].

As we have seen, Johannes de silentio describes resignation as 'infinite', and it is important to try to understand what is meant by this term in *Fear and Trembling*. 'The infinite' signifies spiritual reality, both in relation to God and in relation to the human being. God can be thought of as infinite insofar as his being, his power and his love are unlimited and unending: the idea that for God 'all things are possible' expresses this infinity. From the point of view of an existing individual, 'the infinite' signifies his self insofar as it is related to, or grounded in, God's infinite reality; it also signifies the immortality of the self, or soul, that is part of Christian teaching. Resignation is 'infinite' because it is concerned with the spiritual domain – at the expense of the finite, temporal world. But it is also infinite in another, more subjective sense: the movement of resignation is without limit both insofar as it means giving up *everything*, and giving this up completely, and insofar as the movement has to be made 'continually', at every moment. Resignation is a task that is never completed, at least not until life itself is over; in this respect it is a limitless task, an endless striving that never finds a resting-place.

Johannes de silentio illustrates the contrast between faith and resignation by imagining himself in Abraham's position. He would have had the courage to obey God's command, and made the journey to Mount Moriah, but in doing so he would have told himself: 'Now all is lost; God demands Isaac, I sacrifice him and with him all my joy – yet God is love and continues to be that for me, for in temporality God and I cannot converse, we have no language in common' [29]. This remark about temporality is important: in this section of the text the pseudonym uses the terms 'temporality' and 'finitude' interchangeably to signify this world, this life, this human condition – this actuality which is characterized by suffering. As we have seen, at the beginning of 'A Preliminary Outpouring from the Heart' Johannes contrasts the external world and the world of spirit, suggesting that these two worlds are 'incommensurable'. And now a few pages later he echoes this by asserting that 'in temporality God and I cannot converse' since they share no language; again, this indicates that human, worldly actuality and God's spiritual being are separate and even incommensurable. Johannes de silentio's 'immense resignation' is renunciation of finite or temporal life for the sake of his relationship with God: since the two are irreconcilable, one must be given up if the other is to be preserved. This disjunction between finitude and spirituality reflects the logic of the traditional 'problem of evil': a person who saw the fact of undeserved suffering as an insurmountable objection to belief in a loving God would give up this belief, while Johannes holds onto the belief but at the expense of his concrete actuality.

But what does it mean to resign one's actuality or finitude? In this instance, it means sacrificing Isaac, but this sacrifice stands for a more inward movement, which would be the content of resignation in all the different situations in which it might occur. This inward movement is the giving up of one's expectation of happiness and justice in this life, for it is precisely this expectation that would cause a conflict between the pain of existence and belief in a loving God. In saying to himself 'Now all is lost,' Johannes de silentio enacts this renunciation of expectancy. We can remind ourselves here of the pseudonym's claim, in his 'Tribute', that Abraham was great by virtue of his expectation, and of the way in which this expectation was grounded in his belief that God loved him. Because Johannes cannot share this belief, he cannot share Abraham's expectation either.

It becomes clear in this section of *Fear and Trembling* that the difference between resignation and faith lies in a different relationship to temporal, finite existence: resignation gives up expectations of fulfilment within this life, while the movement of faith holds onto this expectation. In the story of Abraham, Isaac represents finitude, and thus the difference between Johannes de silentio and Abraham makes itself apparent in their relationship to Isaac. More specifically, they receive Isaac back differently, once the sacrifice has been called off:

> What came easiest for Abraham would have been difficult for me – once again to be joyful with Isaac! – for whoever has made the infinite movement [of resignation] with all the infinity of his soul, of his own accord and on his own responsibility, and cannot do more only keeps Isaac with pain. [29]

To have faith as Abraham did means to 'do more' than infinite resignation, and this extra movement is paradoxical because in a sense an individual can do nothing more than renounce everything. Johannes de silentio remarks that 'by my own strength I cannot get the least bit of what belongs to finitude, for I continually use all my strength to resign everything' [42]. And in fact, the movement of faith involves a special kind of 'doing' – which perhaps is not really 'doing' at all – for it requires receptivity rather than productive activity. Having faith means receiving Isaac – and, in more general terms, receiving one's finite existence – as a gift from God, that is to say as a sign or manifestation of God's love *for me* as a particular, existing individual.

The knight of faith

The religion of resignation is other-worldly, focused on God at the cost of one's own personal concerns; it might be described as a monastic form of life, or as a supernatural 'faith' whose expectation of happiness is oriented to an afterlife in which the sufferings of finite existence will be redressed. (This kind of religious belief is envisaged by the German philosopher Immanuel Kant, and in a sense it represents a response to the 'problem of evil'. Kant argues that because justice is lacking in this life, the moral project of striving for the highest good – which includes both virtue and happiness – is incoherent unless we postulate a just God and an immortal soul, which would facilitate a restoration of justice in the next world.) For true faith, by contrast, 'temporality, finitude is what it is all about' [42]; Abraham 'did not believe that he would be blessed one day in the hereafter but that he would become blissfully happy here in the world' [30].

Johannes de silentio explores faith's concern with this life – with 'temporality' and 'finitude' – by departing for several pages from the story of Abraham: first in offering an imaginative description of a modern 'knight of faith', and then by describing the movements of faith in a romantic situation.

The pseudonym's portrait of a contemporary knight of faith is interesting because as well as accentuating this figure's worldliness, he also emphasizes the way in which faith is necessarily undetectable. Of course, this issue has already been raised with regard to the story of Abraham, insofar as his faith consists wholly in inward movements, rather than in external, observable actions – and we have seen that this is why his faith is accessible only through the imagination. However, in the case of the contemporary knight of faith the idea that this character is incognito, unrecognizable from the outside, becomes more explicit:

> The knights of resignation are easy to recognize, their gait is airy, bold. However, those who carry the treasure of faith easily deceive because their external appearance bears a striking resemblance to that which both infinite resignation and faith deeply disdain – to bourgeois philistinism. [31–2]

This raises questions about Johannes de silentio's suggestion that few – if any – people in the modern era genuinely possess faith: if it is impossible to tell whether someone has faith or not, how can the pseudonym make such a claim? This brings us back to the idea that *Fear and Trembling* is concerned to pose a *question* of faith, and when we look carefully at Johannes' critique of the spirituality of his age we see that he does not, and cannot, simply state that his contemporaries lack faith. Instead, his critique takes the form of a question: 'I wonder, is anyone in my age actually capable of making the movement of faith?' [28]. Nevertheless, it is perhaps unavoidable that his account of faith as purely inward, and thus inaccessible to an observer, remains in tension with his suggestion that faith is a rare achievement.

So, when the pseudonym introduces his imagined knight of faith this tension is not far beneath the surface:

> I candidly admit that in my experience I have not found any authentic exemplar, although I do not for that reason deny that possibly every other person is such an exemplar. Nevertheless, I have sought in vain for several years to track one down . . . As I said, I have not found such a person; nevertheless, I can very well imagine him. [31]

It is precisely because the knight of faith is so comfortable in the finite, concrete world that he is incognito, indistinguishable from the 'bourgeois philistine' who lives wholly absorbed in worldly affairs and lacks any inward relationship to God:

> 'He looks just like a tax collector.' Nevertheless it really is him. I draw a little closer to him and pay attention to the slightest movement to see whether a little heterogeneous fraction of a signal from the infinite manifests itself – a glance, an air, a gesture, a sadness, a smile that betrayed the infinite in its heterogeneity with the finite. No! I examine his figure from head to foot to see if there might not be a crack through which the infinite peeped out. No! He is solid through and through. His footing? It is sturdy, belonging entirely to finitude. No dressed up citizen going out on a Sunday afternoon to Frederiksberg treads the ground more solidly. He belongs entirely to the world; no bourgeois philistine could belong to it more. Nothing is detectable of that foreign and noble nature by which the knight of infinite resignation is recognised. He enjoys and takes part in everything, and whenever one sees him participating in something particular, it is carried out with the persistence that characterises the worldly person

whose heart is attached to such things . . . No heavenly look or sign of the incommensurable betrays him [32–3].

This man might behave just like a 'bourgeois philistine', but inwardly the difference between these two could not be greater. The knight of faith has already confronted his suffering and made the movement of infinite resignation, and his relationship to finitude is lived upon the basis of this movement: he

> has made and at every moment is making the movement of infinity. He empties the deep sadness of existence in infinite resignation, he knows the blessedness of infinity, he has felt the pain of renouncing everything, the dearest thing he has in the world, and yet the finite tastes every bit as good to him as to someone who never knew anything higher. [34]

Having made the movement of resignation, the person of faith becomes, as a finite, worldly being, 'a new creation by virtue of the absurd' [34]. We will consider this notion of 'the absurd' shortly.

The account of faith that emerges from this section of the text identifies a dialectic between the finite and the infinite. Johannes de silentio uses the metaphor of a ballet dancer in order to illustrate this. Those who do not dance at all – the 'wallflowers' – represent the 'bourgeois philistines' described above. They remain on the ground, in finitude. The dancer's leap into the air symbolizes the movement of infinity; her descent symbolizes the return to finitude. The knight of resignation makes the leap upwards, but cannot land properly; by contrast, the knight of faith is as comfortable returning to the earth as one who has never leapt at all:

> It is supposed to be the most difficult task for a dancer to leap into a particular posture in such a way that there is no second when he grasps at the position but assumes it in the leap itself. Perhaps no dancer can do it – but that knight [of faith] does. The majority of people live absorbed in worldly sorrows and joy; they are wallflowers who do not join in the dance. The knights of infinity are dancers and have elevation. They make the upward movement and drop down again, and this too is not an unhappy pastime nor unlovely to behold. But every

time they drop down they cannot assume the posture at once; they hesitate an instant, and this hesitation shows that they are really strangers in the world . . . But to be able to land in such a way that it looks as though one were simultaneously standing and walking, to transform the leap of life into a gait, absolutely to express the sublime in the pedestrian – that only the knight of faith can do – and that is the only miracle [34].

'Wallflowers' or 'philistines' are wholly absorbed in finitude, in worldly concerns; it is this attachment to finite, particular things that is renounced in the movement of resignation: the knight of resignation exchanges the finite for the infinite, so to speak. Having made this movement, the knight of faith brings finitude and infinity together: 'after having made the movements of infinity, [faith] makes those of finitude' [31]. The task of faith is to maintain the synthesis of these apparently opposing terms, in living and enjoying each moment of life as a gift from God. This does not signify a lapse back into the form of life lived prior to resignation, for renouncing the finite world means that this is no longer in the individual's possession – and only because it is no longer her possession can it be received as a gift from God. The logic of the gift is different from the logic that governs relations of property and exchange: a gift is at once possessed and not possessed, for it is in transit, so to speak. Insofar as a gift is given to me it does become mine; but insofar as I continue to regard it as a gift, I continue to regard myself as someone who receives it – and receiving something is different from possessing it. Before resignation, a person is under the illusion that her life is her own, and more generally that the finite world is complete and self-sufficient; for the faith that follows after resignation, her life, and the whole of finitude in which it is lived, is grounded in God and only belongs to her insofar as it is given as a gift. From a subjective point of view, this means that the person's relationship to her life is thoroughly transformed, and since her relationship to her life is not just an aspect of her being but its very core, life is itself transfigured.

The upwards-downwards movement expressed in the metaphor of the dancer is also symbolized in Abraham's journey up and down Mount Moriah. It is not his ascent – his willingness to sacrifice Isaac – but his descent, his return to his home and to his family, that distinguishes him from a knight of resignation. While the latter 'keeps Isaac only with pain', Abraham's return to finitude is joyful.

Johannes de silentio's account of faith as a dialectic between finitude and infinity anticipates the discussions of these terms that we find in later Kierkegaardian texts, particularly *Concluding Unscientific Postscript* and *The Sickness Unto Death*. In the latter book, the pseudonym Anti-Climacus indicates that 'a self' is a spiritual being, defined as 'a relation that relates to itself', and he asserts that each human being has the task of becoming such a self. For this pseudonym, selfhood is an essentially religious category: the self has been established by God, and remains grounded in this divine power – and this means that its self-relating must be also at the same time a relating to God. Unlike other Kierkegaardian pseudonyms, Anti-Climacus ventures to offer a definition of God: 'God *is* that all things are possible'; and thus to claim that the self is grounded in God is to claim that the self is grounded in infinite possibility, in an infinite power. Integral to the conception of the self presented in *The Sickness Unto Death* is the relation, or synthesis, between the finite and the infinite: this synthesis relates to itself by becoming conscious of itself *as* at once finite and infinite, and thus as grounded in God. Anti-Climacus describes the failure to accomplish this task as despair, and suggests that perhaps every human being is to some extent in despair, to some extent falling short of becoming a self. Only in faith, he argues, is the synthesis between finitude and infinitude complete, and fully aware of itself in its relationship to God. Indeed, according to Anti-Climacus, faith is nothing other than this self-conscious relational movement – and because it is a dynamic process of becoming, it must be repeated constantly in order to maintain its continuity. The constancy of the self through time thus depends on the repetition of the movement of faith.

Young lovers: resignation and faith

Having described the knight of faith as an individual who moves continually between finitude and infinity – between the world and God – Johannes de silentio announces his intention to 'describe the movements in a particular instance which may illuminate their relation to actuality, for everything revolves around that' [34]. The 'particular instance' he discusses is a romantic relationship between a young man and a princess that 'cannot possibly be realized, cannot possibly be translated from ideality into reality' [35]. This is not an example chosen at random, for it is reminiscent of Kierkegaard's unrealized love for Regine Olsen, which, as we saw in the section on 'Tuning Up', influenced the writing of *Fear and Trembling*. We may recall that during the period when he was working on the text, Kierkegaard wrote in his journal: 'If I had had faith, I would have stayed with Regine.' This implies that just as Johannes de silentio identifies himself as capable of resignation but not of faith, so Kierkegaard saw himself as a knight of resignation in relation to Regine.

The young lover's renunciation of the princess does not amount to forgetting her, nor even to ceasing to desire her: he preserves his love and its attendant suffering in the form of an idea, a memory, but in renouncing his hope that he will actually be with her in a concrete sense he becomes 'reconciled with existence'. His finite, earthly love is spiritualized; exchanged, it seems, for a love for God:

The love for that princess became for him the expression of an eternal love, assumed a religious character, was transfigured into love for the eternal being, which to be sure denied the fulfilment of that love but still reconciled him once again in the eternal consciousness of its validity in an eternal form that no actuality can take from him. [36–7]

Having renounced his hope of sharing his life with his beloved, the young man gains peace and a kind of freedom – for he has nothing left to lose.

Johannes adds to his discussion of this knight of resignation a strange and important footnote, in which he raises the question of passion in contemporary philosophy. He emphasizes that passion is required in order to make 'the movement of infinity'; insists that 'no reflection can bring about a movement'; and claims that 'what our age lacks is not reflection but passion' [35]. All of a sudden the reader finds herself taken from a lyrical story about a doomed romance to a terse critique of Hegelian philosophy: 'This is the perpetual leap in existence that explains the movement, whereas mediation is a chimera which according to

Hegel is supposed to explain everything and which is also the one thing he has never tried to explain' [35]. This comment is enigmatic, but it expresses an idea that is explored more fully in some of Kierkegaard's other pseudonymous texts: that Hegel's philosophy does not do justice to the movement of becoming that characterizes human existence. One of the most important contributions of Hegel's thought is to accentuate process – to show that truth is not fixed and static, and to try to incorporate the processes of both thinking and historical development into a philosophical system. Kierkegaard agrees with Hegel that one of the fundamental tasks of philosophy is to understand movement, and particularly to understand truth in dynamic terms, but he often expresses the view that Hegel is wrong to attempt to conceptualize movement rationally. For Kierkegaard, real movement is existential, not intellectual: it is initiated by passion – that is, a kind of spiritual desire – rather than by thinking. He uses the term 'leap' to describe this existential movement, and we can see how Johannes de silentio's reference to a leap in this footnote echoes the metaphor of the dancer that he offers to illustrate the movements of resignation and faith.

The pseudonym describes how the young lover comes to make the movement of resignation after he has understood and accepted that his relationship with the princess is 'an impossibility' [35]. Just as the dialectic between finitude and infinity is at the heart of his characterization of the knight of faith, so the themes of possibility and impossibility are a key to this description of the movements of resignation and faith in a romantic situation. And in fact, when Johannes de silentio comes to consider how the knight of faith's response to the doomed love affair would have differed from that of the young man he envisages, we see that faith's synthesis of the finite and the infinite turns out to be mirrored in a synthesis of impossibility and possibility. In focusing on these terms, the pseudonym draws on one of Jesus' sayings that appears in all three of the synoptic gospels: following a discussion of the rich man's difficulty in entering the kingdom of God, Jesus is asked, 'Then who will be saved?', and he answers that 'For mortals it is impossible, but for God all things are possible' (Matthew 19:26, Mark 10:27); 'What is impossible for mortals is possible for God' (Luke 17.35).

For the knight of resignation, although his relationship with the princess is impossible in this world, in finitude, it remains possible 'spiritually speaking': in eternity, in some ideal realm, or in an afterlife, perhaps. 'Spiritually speaking, everything is possible, but in the finite world there is much that is not possible. The knight [of resignation] nevertheless makes this impossibility possible by expressing it spiritually, but he expresses it spiritually by renouncing it' [37]. Just as Johannes de silentio finds the finite and the infinite to be incommensurable, and accepts this rift by giving up on the finite, so this young knight of resignation sees that the spiritual possibility of love's fulfilment is at odds with its worldly impossibility, and accepts the latter for the sake of the former. The knight of faith, however, would make a further movement: 'He says: "I nevertheless believe that I shall get her, namely by virtue of the absurd, by virtue of the fact that for God everything is possible"' [39]. His belief in God is such that it brings the spiritual possibility into his finite existence, so that worldly impossibility is somehow, miraculously, transformed into possibility. Again, this transformation occurs only by virtue of a divine gift: the possibility that belongs to the spiritual realm is donated to the world, where the knight of faith receives it as a gift. Receiving this gift is, as we have seen, dependent on the prior movement of renunciation.

'By virtue of the absurd'

The way in which Johannes de silentio describes the knight of faith's movements in terms of believing the impossible to be possible leads to his claim that faith is 'absurd'. This means that faith is beyond reason, understanding and calculation: 'The absurd does not belong to the distinctions that lie within the proper compass of the understanding. It is not identical with the improbable, the unforeseen, the unexpected' [39]. In other words, if faith is absurd then it lies outside of the merely-human domain, although in the movement of faith the understanding continues to play an important role in recognizing that the impossible really *is* impossible:

The moment the knight resigned he assured himself of the impossibility, humanly speaking, that was the conclusion of the understanding, and he had energy enough to think it.

In an infinite sense, however, it was possible by resigning it, but this possessing [of possibility], you see, is also a relinquishing [of it]; yet this possessing is no absurdity to the understanding, for the understanding continued to be right in maintaining that in the world of finitude where it rules it was and remained an impossibility. The knight of faith is clearly conscious of this as well; consequently, the only thing that can save him is the absurd, and this he lays hold of by faith. He therefore acknowledges the impossibility and at the same moment believes the absurd, for if he imagines himself to have faith without acknowledging the impossibility with all the passion of his soul and with his whole heart, then he deceives himself and his testimony is neither here nor there since he has not even attained infinite resignation [39–40].

To describe faith as absurd, and to insist that its transfiguration of the finite is possible only as a gift from God, is to refuse to regard the merely-human domain as closed and self-sufficient. It is for this reason that, as we saw in the Preface to *Fear and Trembling*, Johannes de silentio regards the decline of faith in the modern age as intimately connected to the rise of the idea of human autonomy.

The difference between resignation and faith turns on this question of autonomy: resignation is a human movement, while faith involves an opening-up to God's power so that the whole finite domain is taken to rest upon its basis, in the form of a gift. In this section of the text the pseudonym emphasizes that in the movement of resignation the individual is sufficient unto himself: 'in infinite resignation there is peace and rest; every person who wills it . . . can discipline himself to make this movement, which in its pain reconciles one with existence' [38]. He repeatedly contrasts resignation with faith on this point:

> I can perceive that it takes strength and energy and spiritual freedom to make the infinite movement of resignation. I can also perceive that it can be done. The next movement amazes me; my brain whirls in my head, for after having made the movement of resignation, now by virtue of the absurd to get everything, to get the wish, whole, unabridged – that is beyond human powers, that is a miracle. [40]

By resignation I renounce everything; this movement I make by myself, and if I do not make it, then it is because I am cowardly . . . This movement I make by myself, and what I gain as a result is myself in my eternal consciousness in blessed harmony with my love for the eternal being. By faith I do not renounce anything; on the contrary, by faith I receive everything. [41]

I can resign everything by my own strength and then find peace and rest in the pain . . . But by my own strength I cannot get the least bit of what belongs to finitude, for I continually use my strength in resigning everything. [42]

Faith is paradoxical, 'by virtue of the absurd', insofar as it means living a contradiction between finite and infinite, between impossibility and possibility, that is irreconcilable in human terms. While the movement of resignation requires 'a purely human courage', an individual must have 'a paradoxical and humble courage next to grasp the whole of temporality by virtue of the absurd, and this is the courage of faith' [41].

It is important to reflect carefully on Johannes de silentio's claim that faith is absurd, for it is one of the central ideas of *Fear and Trembling*. Why exactly is Abraham's faith – his expectation that he will keep Isaac, or receive him back – absurd? After all, he does receive him back, not by a miracle but by an apparent change of mind on God's part. Two commentators who have discussed in some depth and detail the account of resignation and faith in this section of the text, Robert M. Adams and Sharon Krishek, have made illuminating remarks that will help us to think through this question. Adams points out that the idea that God will issue a new command to override the first one is not absurd, although such a turn of event may be improbable and unexpected – the very features that, as we have seen, Johannes de silentio takes care to distinguish from absurdity. Indeed, as Adams suggests, the fact that God's command to sacrifice Isaac contradicts his earlier promise to Abraham makes it more likely that this command might itself be contradicted. What Adams does recognize as absurd, however, is the 'double movement' within Abraham's heart, by which he takes Isaac back *at the same time* as giving him up: 'The absurd enters the picture because the movement of faith does not end the movement of resignation, but must be made simultaneously with it.'[21] This seems to be borne out by the fact that other commentators, who are unwilling to accept such a 'patently untenable', 'wildly implausible' and 'incoherent' position,[22] have engaged in debate about what exactly Abraham believes at the point of binding Isaac and raising the knife – does he believe that he will kill him, or that he will not kill him? – in an attempt to overcome what one such commentator, John Lippitt, describes as the 'contradictory beliefs problem'.[23]

Adams argues that the absurdity of Abraham's faith cannot be due to a contradiction between beliefs, since Abraham makes the 'double movement' of resignation and faith continually, even on the way home from Mount Moriah, when he no longer believes that the sacrifice of Isaac is demanded of him. The contradiction, then, is simply between resignation and faith: between renouncing one's expectations, in accordance with the nature of finite existence, and keeping hold of them, in accordance with the belief that one is loved by a God for whom all things are possible. It is not clear that this involves a contradiction between two opposing *beliefs*, although I suspect that it would be possible to formulate the positions reached through resignation and faith as propositional beliefs.

In her recent book *Kierkegaard on Faith and Love*, Sharon Krishek draws on and develops Adams's analysis, emphasizing that

> the dramatic moment of drawing the knife is only a manifestation – indeed, the most extreme and horrifying manifestation possible – of the movement that Abraham makes before the trial and continues to make after it . . . For Abraham the trial was only an expression of something he performed all the time.[24]

Krishek does not follow Adams in denying that Abraham holds contradictory beliefs, but she shows that the double movement of resignation and faith involves several different kinds of contradiction. Resignation, she suggests, already 'manifests a self-contradictory attitude', for

> it is clear that Abraham does not want to sacrifice his son – but in *resigning* he . . . is prepared to sacrifice his son willingly.

And yet, while doing this *willingly*, he still very passionately *wants* to keep hold of his son.[25]

And while resignation involves this 'paradox of wills', faith involves not just a paradox of beliefs, but also 'a paradox of emotions': 'Faith involves the paradoxical combination of being in a state of infinite pain (the pain of resignation) and an indescribable joy.'[26] Krishek concludes, then, that the knight of faith's life is 'a profound drama of holding harmoniously contradictory powers (of will, belief and emotion).'[27] This certainly accords with Johannes de silentio's description of faith as a way of existing in which 'my opposition to existence expresses itself at every moment as the most beautiful and most secure harmony with it' [42].

Adams's and Krishek's reflections on the nature of the absurdity and paradox that constitute the 'double movement' of resignation and faith help to demonstrate that this movement involves not just a theoretical contradiction, but a practical or existential contradiction. It is not simply a question of an opposition between two beliefs – for example, that Isaac will die and that he will live; or that Jesus was both human and divine; or that an unjust world was created by a just God – but a question of the individual's 'opposition to existence' being expressed 'as harmony with it'. It is a question of holding together 'at every moment' one's life in the world – the only life one has – with one's relationship to God. According to Johannes de silentio, this is a paradox of the heart as well as a paradox of the intellect. He can understand *what* such a 'double movement' entails, but he cannot understand *how* this movement can be made. This emphasis on the practical nature of faith's absurdity may help to explain why Kierkegaard, in a later journal entry reflecting on *Fear and Trembling*, suggests that faith is absurd only from the perspective of someone who does not have faith:

When I believe, then assuredly neither faith nor the content of faith is absurd . . . but . . . for the person who does not believe, then faith and the content of faith are absurd, and . . . as soon as I myself am not in the faith, am weak, when doubt begins to stir, then faith and the content of faith gradually begin to become absurd for me.[28]

Either/Or

The pseudonym's suggestion that true religious faith happens only 'by virtue of the absurd', as a 'miracle' that involves the overcoming of an impossibility, certainly points to the conclusion that it must be something very rare. And this, of course, is part of the text's strategy: Kierkegaard wants the reader to think about the difficulty of faith in order to appreciate its value, and to ask herself whether, if this is what faith actually entails, she can really claim to possess it. But, on the other hand, in a sense Johannes de silentio's account of faith only explicates, with the help of poetic language and some imaginative story-telling, the basis tenets of Christianity: the belief that God loves each individual in a personal way; the belief that for God all things are possible. His description of the inward movements made by Abraham and by the contemporary knight of faith does no more, it might be argued, than lay bare the implications of these Christian beliefs.

If the reader of *Fear and Trembling* accepts this interpretation of Christianity, then there are of course two alternative ways of responding to it. She may, like Johannes de silentio, be filled with admiration for faith, choose to recognize it as the highest spiritual task, and embark wholeheartedly on the path of becoming a Christian. Or she may reject faith as an ideal precisely because she sees its absurdity so clearly. What the pseudonym tries to exclude is a middle ground between these two extremes, in which faith can be regarded as comfortable and easy: it follows from his analysis of faith that it is 'no aesthetic emotion but something much higher, precisely because it presupposes resignation; it is not a spontaneous inclination of the heart but the paradox of existence' [40].

This account of faith presents the reader with a decision, and the idea of decision is itself an important element of Kierkegaard's philosophy: this is indicated by the title of his first pseudonymous work, *Either/Or* (1843), published a few months before *Fear and Trembling*. In the two texts written under the pseudonym Johannes Climacus, the theme of decision is developed further. In *Philosophical Fragments* (1844) Climacus focuses on the Christian doctrine of the incarnation and, arguing that this is an 'absolute paradox', presents the reader with a choice between responding to this with either offence or faith – that is to say, between rejecting or accepting the incarnation as a paradox. Just as Johannes de silentio suggests that 'the understanding' can see paradox or absurdity for what it is, but cannot penetrate it, so Johannes Climacus indicates that the role of reason is to recognize the paradox, but that the decision between offence and faith cannot be made on a rational basis. In offence, reason rejects the paradox; in faith, reason surrenders itself before it. In both *Philosophical Fragments* and *Concluding Unscientific Postscript*, Climacus suggests that the problem facing Christians in the modern age is that the decision that is integral to the movement of faith has been covered over, and thus the pseudonym sets himself the task of uncovering the decision and setting it before his reader. The situation of nineteenth-century Christians is, he argues, characterized by 'the *semblance* of a decision . . . if it looks as though it were decided, then if I am already a Christian (i.e., am baptized . . .), then there is nothing to help me to become properly aware of it.'[29] Climacus' analysis of Christianity can be regarded as an intervention that attempts to raise awareness of the decision that is essential to true faith, and *Fear and Trembling* seems to share this purpose.

This means that the text – if it is understood sufficiently well to accomplish this purpose – is, and must be, ambivalent to its core: it provides an account of the religious life that might halt and reverse the decline of faith hinted at in the Preface and Epilogue, or that might quicken and intensify this decline. Its effect depends on the reader's decision. In a sense, then, the text seeks to force its reader, and perhaps even to force Christianity itself, to a point of crisis. (Johannes de silentio's remarks about the declining value of faith indicate that he sees Christianity as already heading towards this crisis.) From this point onwards, faith becomes either the highest task of human life, or discredited as a ridiculous, dangerous and groundless venture. An important consequence of this crisis is that, in presenting readers with a decision, it addresses each one as a single individual who is responsible for her own spiritual life.

We can, then, read *Fear and Trembling* as intervening in the specifically modern form of religiosity, and attempting to bring the historical phenomenon of Christianity to the crisis-point that it seems to be destined for. But this may leave today's readers wondering what the text has to say to them, especially if they have no aspiration to live according to Christian categories – from an historical point of view, this may indicate that the decision to reject faith as absurd has already been taken, and become embedded in contemporary culture; that the question of human autonomy has thus been settled. However, insofar as Johannes de silentio's analysis of resignation and faith is concerned with love, suffering and courage, this communicates something about being human that is as relevant now as it was in the nineteenth century. Earlier in this section I suggested that love and suffering go together, and this is not a cynical observation but is based on the simple fact that our lives are impermanent, and in the process of change. This means that those whom we love will at some point be lost to us. This suffering is only escaped if we die first, but in this case the pain is felt by those who love us. Because we are mortal, every love relationship faces the prospect of loss and separation, and the suffering of this prospect is not a distant possibility but, insofar as we are aware of it and thus anticipate it, an ever-present fact that conditions life as it is lived.

This raises the question of how to respond courageously to the suffering of finitude, instead of attempting to flee from it. The response of resignation is a detachment from worldly relationships which, although painful, lessens the anxious anticipation of eventual loss. The response of faith involves the courage to love and be loved, and to find joy in this, in full awareness and acceptance of death – as Johannes de silentio puts it, 'to live joyfully and happily every moment by virtue of the absurd, every moment to see the sword hanging over the beloved's head and yet to find, not rest in the pain of resignation, but joy by virtue of the absurd' [43]. This joy in finitude is absurd because it knows that it is proportional to the suffering that will come when the beloved is lost: the more one loves, the more there is to lose, and therefore the decision to love cannot be the result of rational calculation. It is for this reason that the knight of faith's joy in life takes the form of a gift, and can be received not intellectually, but passionately – 'from the heart'.

PROBLEM I: IS THERE A TELEOLOGICAL SUSPENSION OF THE ETHICAL?

Here Johannes de silentio focuses on the idea that the story of Abraham contains a 'teleological suspension of the ethical'. It is revealing that Kierkegaard privately used this phrase to describe the breaking of his engagement to Regine Olsen:

> I am a poet. But long before I became a poet I was intended for the life of religious individuality. And the event whereby I became a poet was an ethical break or a teleological suspension of the ethical.[30]

This lends support to the view that Kierkegaard's relationship with Regine inspired the analysis of faith presented in *Fear and Trembling*. But in the text itself this connection is not made apparent, and indeed in the opening paragraphs of Problem I Johannes de silentio adopts a mode of discourse that is technical and rather abstract. Before we can examine his notion of a teleological suspension of the ethical, and consider how this applies to Abraham and to religious faith more generally, we need to clarify various terms that the pseudonym uses in this section of the text: 'the ethical', 'the universal', 'the particular', 'suspension', 'mediation', and '*telos*'.

The ethical: some key terms

Johannes de silentio's question 'Is there a teleological suspension of the ethical?' concerns the relationship between the individual and what he calls 'the ethical', defined as 'the universal' [46]. His discussion of the ethical engages directly with Hegel's *Elements of the Philosophy of Right* (1821), in which the German philosopher discusses the role of the individual within the community, beginning with an account of the will's freedom and concluding with an analysis of the state as 'the image and actuality of reason', in which 'self-consciousness finds in an organic development the actuality of its substantive knowing and willing'.[31] For Hegel, the 'system of right' – which encompasses civil law, morality, and the shared customs and practices of communal life – is 'the realm of freedom made actual, the world of mind (*Geist*) brought forth out of itself like a second nature'.[32]

In this section of *Fear and Trembling* Johannes de silentio takes up Hegel's analysis of the individual in terms of a distinction between the particular and the universal:

> Defined immediately as a sensuous and psychical being, the single individual is the particular that has its telos in the universal, and it is his ethical task constantly to express himself in this, to annul particularity in order to become the universal. [46]

'Universal' and 'particular' are relative terms: 'the universal' signifies all, everything, and it also denotes a level of generality, while 'particularity' denotes something specific. So, for example, the concept 'colour' is a universal category, insofar as it applies to all physical objects, while 'red' is a particular colour, a specific instance of the universal category; at another level of analysis, however, 'red' might be viewed as a universal or generic category, while a pillar-box is a particular red thing. One of the characteristics of Hegel's thought is that distinctions between terms are not rigid and static, but dynamic and relational, and in the case of the distinction between universal, particular and individual this means that, on the one hand, the universal is a category that encompasses particulars and individuals, while, on the other hand, the individual synthesizes within itself universality and particularity. For an individual human being, the universal could be regarded as the concept of humanness that constitutes the individual's essence, in common with other human individuals, while the particular consists of a person's specific features, such as her body, her thoughts, her habits, her experiences, her tastes, and so on. In the context of Johannes de silentio's discussion of the ethical, 'the universal' signifies the community, the whole of which the individual is a part.

Although Johannes de silentio's discussion of the ethical domain refers specifically to Hegelian philosophy, Hegel was not the first thinker to understand the ethical in terms of universality. Kant's moral theory is based on the view that morality is essentially universal, applying equally to everyone and at all times. His ethics focuses on the concepts of duty and obligation, and attempts to make sense of the moral force that is expressed in the idea that a person *ought* to do something; in the fact that moral judgements take the form of commands or imperatives. Kant argues that duties and obligations have the necessity of laws – not the physical, causal necessity of laws of nature, but a necessity that, because it is grounded in the rational capacities common to all fully-developed human beings, is not only compatible with, but a condition of, their freedom and dignity. For Kant, rationality is essentially connected to universality insofar as the faculty of reason is the same for everyone, and insofar as to rationally apprehend the force of a moral duty is to understand that it conforms to a principle, or maxim, that is valid for everyone all of the time. One of Kant's formulations of the moral law is: 'I ought never to act in such a way that I could not also will that my maxim should become a universal law.'[33] Johannes de silentio's assertion that 'as the universal [the ethical] applies to everyone . . . it is in force at every moment' reflects this Kantian view of ethics, and in fact seems to be closer to this than to Hegel's account of the ethical. Hegel criticizes Kant's moral theory for being too abstract; he regarded the universality that belongs to the ethical as concrete – as historically and culturally situated, embodied in the form of life of a particular community – rather than as atemporal and eternal, as Kant's conception of rationality implies. While Kant regards the universality of the moral law as, in a sense, entirely unrelated to particular actions, Hegel regards particularity as an essential element or 'moment' of the universal.

Johannes de silentio's assertion that the individual's ethical task is 'to annul particularity in order to become the universal' indicates that the universal is not outside a person, but an aspect of her own being, something that she can herself 'become'. The idea of 'annulling' particularity refers to a distinctive element of Hegelian philosophy, which is expressed by the German word *Aufhebung*. This term is ambiguous insofar as it signifies both cancellation and preservation: Hegel often uses *Aufhebung* to denote a movement of overcoming, or sublating, that contains both of these meanings. If particularity is 'annulled', it is not simply destroyed, but incorporated into a unity in which it becomes part of a larger whole, rather than something separate.

The Hegelian concept of *Aufhebung* is very important in the context of this section of *Fear and Trembling*, since it is echoed in Johannes de silentio's question about the possibility of 'suspending' the ethical. That is to say, suspending the ethical does not simply cancel it out, but overcomes it in such a way as to accord it a role within something greater. By this movement the ethical is not destroyed, but relativized within a new context. As the pseudonym puts it, 'whatever is suspended is not forfeited but on the contrary is preserved in the higher, which is its telos' [47]. Even if the ethical is suspended, it continues to have a claim upon the individual. As we have seen in the previous section of the text, 'the ethical expression for what Abraham did is that he intended to murder Isaac; the religious expression is that he intended to sacrifice Isaac' [24] – and the fact that Abraham's action has this ethical significance is precisely what makes it paradoxical, and what inspires the 'fear and trembling' of the onlooker as she tries in vain to make sense of Abraham's journey to Mount Moriah.

Having said this, Johannes de silentio puts distance between his idea of a suspension of the ethical and the Hegelian notion of *Aufhebung* by insisting that the standpoint of faith that follows from the suspension of the ethical 'cannot be mediated . . . and forever remains a paradox, inaccessible to thought' [48]. Again, this idea of mediation refers to a specifically Hegelian concept: Hegel distinguishes between what is immediate and what is mediated (although once more these should be regarded as relative terms), and in his philosophy 'mediation' denotes a process of reasoning that integrates two opposing terms into a higher unity. For example, Hegel's logic begins with the concept of 'being', which is opposed to the concept of 'nothing'; these opposites are brought together by a third concept, 'becoming', which denotes the transition between, or synthesis of, being and nothing, so that these opposing terms are grasped as moments of a movement that encompasses them both. Being and nothing are *mediated* in becoming. Because Hegel regards reason as concrete – as instantiated in the world, and in the processes of history – rather than as something abstract that floats above these, mediation can refer to social relationships as well as to the relations between concepts. For instance, it can be argued from an Hegelian point of view that a social institution such as the church mediates between individual people and God, by recognizing the difference between the human and the divine while also bringing them together in concrete forms of life such as communion and collective prayer. When Johannes de silentio claims that Abraham's faith cannot be mediated, he means both that it cannot be understood through rational reflection, and that it cannot be communicated to other people and thus that it breaks the social ties that depend upon a shared understanding.

One more term that needs to be explained is *telos*, from which 'teleological' is derived. *Telos* is a Greek word meaning end, goal or purpose: a *telos* is that towards which an action or a process tends, or aims. Johannes de silentio indicates that the ethical, regarded as the universal, 'has nothing outside itself that is its telos, but is itself the telos for everything outside itself' [46]. The process proper to the ethical is to 'assimilate' what is outside itself, which means constituting itself as the *telos* of, say, particular beings; while, correspondingly, the task of an 'immediate' particular being is to appropriate the ethical-as-universal as her *telos*. The 'teleological suspension of the ethical' proposed by Johannes de silentio would involve suspending, or relativizing, the ethical for the sake of a distinct, higher *telos* – higher because otherwise it could not require or merit the suspension. But this is paradoxical, according to the pseudonym, since the ethical is precisely that which 'has nothing outside itself that is its telos'. This is why faith cannot be mediated, or understood: mediation belongs to the ethical-as-universal itself, for this is the domain of language and concepts that make understanding and communication possible. Mediation can only take place within the ethical, but from within the ethical it is impossible to recognize a *telos* that is higher than the ethical itself, and therefore it is impossible to justify or explain a suspension of the ethical.

Does Abraham need a teleological suspension of the ethical?

Having acquainted ourselves with the philosophical vocabulary employed by Johannes de silentio in Problem I, we may now begin to assess the content and significance of the idea of a teleological suspension of the ethical. It should be noted that the question of Abraham's righteousness – the question of how he should be judged – concerns his inward intention to sacrifice Isaac, and that it is therefore the period of time leading up to the sacrifice, culminating in the raising of the knife over Isaac, that is under discussion. The outcome of the story means that Abraham is not in fact a murderer, but Johannes de silentio is anxious to emphasize that we should not judge Abraham according to this outcome, precisely because this would obscure the nature of his situation as he experienced it. When Abraham made his decision to obey God he did not know what the outcome of his journey would be, and thus the fact that he was not in the end required to kill Isaac is, claims the pseudonym, ethically irrelevant.

It is also important to notice that the idea of a teleological suspension of the ethical is introduced in the form of a question, rather than a statement. Johannes de silentio is presenting the reader with two alternatives to decide between: *either* there is nothing outside the ethical, no higher *telos* than the ethical itself, which means that Abraham can only be viewed from within the ethical, and thus must be condemned as sinful and a murderer; *or* Abraham's faith stands above the ethical as a paradox that cannot be understood. Only if the second alternative is chosen is it possible to admire Abraham, although such admiration cannot be justified in rational terms. In the case of Abraham, the higher *telos* for the sake of which the ethical is suspended would be his relationship with God. So the question about whether this situation involves a teleological suspension of the ethical is inseparable from the question of whether the individual's relationship to God lies outside the ethical, or is contained within it.

But is Johannes de silentio right to suggest that 'the story of Abraham contains a teleological suspension of the ethical' [49]? This claim rests on the view that Abraham's actions are ethically unacceptable – but this is not self-evident. Our judgement about the ethical status of Abraham's willingness to sacrifice Isaac depends on precisely how we understand the ethical. From a Kantian point of view, it does indeed seem to be the case that Abraham's actions are immoral, and in fact Kant himself argues that Abraham was wrong to obey God's command to kill his son. In his essay *The Conflict of the Faculties*, Kant does not actually challenge the authority of God, but points out that God's will can guide human actions towards the good only if we know this divine will accurately and with absolute certainty. Here Kant is referring specifically to the problem of authenticating the bible as the revealed word of God, but he indicates that the story of Abraham's sacrifice serves as an example of this problem. According to Kant, if God should really speak to man, man could still never know that it was God speaking . . . if the voice commands him to do something contrary to the moral law, then no matter how majestic the apparition may be, and no matter how it may seem to surpass the whole of nature, he must consider it an illusion.[34]

In other words, a human being must use her reason, through which she apprehends the moral law, to decide whether she really has received a divine command; if the command conflicts with the moral law, she must conclude that it cannot come from God, since God's will is perfectly in accord with morality. According to Kant,

Abraham should have replied to this supposedly divine voice: 'That I ought not to kill my good son is quite certain. But that you, this apparition, are God – of that I am not certain, and never can be, not even if this voice rings down to me from (visible) heaven.'

Johannes de silentio echoes Kant in pointing out that Abraham may have been mistaken about God's command to sacrifice Isaac, and that, more generally, faith always lacks certainty. For the pseudonym, this contributes to the questionable and paradoxical nature of faith: 'if . . . the individual made a mistake, what salvation is there for him? . . . if . . . the individual has misunderstood the deity, what salvation would there be for him?' [53].

Kant's response to Abraham's situation seems eminently sensible, but we should note that it accords to human reason the highest authority. Although reason is placed in judgement not over God, but over the individual's own experience (of an apparent divine revelation), this in effect renders it impossible to accept a divine command that one doesn't understand. If there *is* a God, and if this God really did require something that conflicts with the moral law, then Kant would be prescribing disobedience. There is in this account, then, potential for conflict between religion and ethics: from a religious point of view, it is a sin to disobey God, while from an ethical point of view it is a sin to transgress the moral law. Kant therefore emerges as an advocate of human autonomy: we know God's will on the basis of our rational knowledge of the good, rather than defining the good in terms of God's will; religion is not the source of ethics, but, on the contrary, is legitimate only insofar as it follows from ethics, and thus remains within the bounds of reason.

From a Kantian point of view, then, Abraham's actions certainly do contravene the ethical – and the only possible response to this is to condemn them as wrong. Kant recognizes no room outside the ethical for the individual's relationship to God: God's will is identical with the good, and we obey this will insofar as we obey the moral laws that we formulate and give to ourselves through reason. Our relationship to God is wholly contained within the ethical, and the nature of the ethical follows from reason alone. As Kant writes in *Religion Within the Boundaries of Mere Reason*, 'Apart from good life-conduct, anything which the human being supposes that he can do to become well-pleasing to God is mere religious delusion and counterfeit service of God.'[35] According to this Kantian account, then, the answer to Johannes de silentio's question, 'Is there a teleological suspension of the ethical?' has to be 'no'.

But how does Abraham fare in terms of the Hegelian view of the ethical? As we have seen, Hegel regards the universal as concrete and situated: as instantiated in the ethical life of a community and as codified in that community's values, institutions, ways of life and customs. Hegel calls this communal ethical life *Sittlichkeit*, and the German word *Sitte* means 'custom'; he distinguishes *Sittlichkeit* from *Moralität*, which denotes the kind of individual morality – whether based on reason, feelings or conscience – that is for Kant the domain of ethics. *Sittlichkeit* is specific to an historical period and a geographical location, so that Hegel can discuss, for example, the *Sittlichkeit* of the ancient Greeks, and contrast this with modern German ethical life. If we are to assess the ethical significance of Abraham's sacrifice from a Hegelian perspective, then, we should consider it in the context of ancient Hebrew *Sittlichkeit*.

In the world in which the story of Abraham takes place, child sacrifice was a common practice, and, more generally, the modern distinction between the religious and the ethical domains did not apply. Johannes de silentio's claim that 'the ethical expression for what Abraham did is that he intended to murder Isaac; the religious expression is that he intended to sacrifice Isaac' does not accurately reflect the significance of Abraham's actions in his own time, when the sacrifice would have been regarded as ethically legitimate as well as religiously legitimate – for these forms of legitimacy were one and the same. It could therefore be argued that from Abraham's point of view there was no conflict between an ethical requirement and God's command. This is not to say that he did not experience conflict, but this conflict would have been between his personal wish to keep Isaac, whom he loved, and God's order to sacrifice him. Johannes de silentio states that 'Abraham's relation to Isaac, ethically speaking, is quite simply this, that the father must love the son more than himself', but there is no reason to think that Abraham regarded his love for Isaac as an 'ethical duty' [49]. As the pseudonym himself has indicated in earlier sections of the text, Abraham's willingness to sacrifice his son does not imply that he did not love him – on the contrary, the sacrifice has value as a sacrifice precisely because Abraham loved Isaac more than anything else. Furthermore, Johannes has also indicated that the paradoxical and truly faithful element in Abraham's action was not the sacrifice itself, but the manner in which he received Isaac back, having continued to hope that God would keep his promise to make him the father of a nation.

It is not the case, then, that in Abraham's time a father's sacrifice of his son transgressed a specific law or moral code. However, in Abraham's case this action has damaging implications for the wider community. The Hegelian account of the individual's ethical task indicates that a person should overcome her own particular interests for the sake of the community, understood as 'the universal'. This requirement takes the form of fulfilment of roles – such as the role of a parent, the role of a teacher, the role of a street-cleaner, the role of a magistrate, and so on – which involve specific duties and responsibilities to others. It is this account of the ethical that Johannes de silentio reads back into the story of Abraham. In his analysis of the story, the pseudonym points out that although there can be distinct and even conflicting duties within the ethical sphere – for example, a father's duties to his son, on the one hand, and to the whole community, on the other – Abraham's duty to the universal is synonymous with his duty to Isaac. This is because the community in which Abraham participates is the nation of Israel, which is not yet actual but has rather been promised by God: the nation of Israel is composed of future generations, beginning with Isaac. If Isaac is dead, there will be no more generations, and therefore no nation of Israel . . .

> There is no higher expression for the ethical in Abraham's life than this, that the father must love the son. There can be no question of the ethical at all in the sense of the ethical life. Inso-far as the universal was present, it was still latent in Isaac, hidden so to speak in Isaac's loins, and must then cry out with Isaac's mouth: 'Do not do it, you are destroying everything.' [52]

In other words, the 'universal' ethical claim upon Abraham comes not from his own *Sittlichkeit*, the customary morality of his time – since this seems to amount to little more than obedience to God, and the claims of possessive personal relationships – but from the future: from the community promised by God, of which Abraham is to be the father. Isaac's claim to his life *is* the claim of the ethical, of the universal. So, in going through with the sacrifice, Abraham is setting his own relationship to God above this ethical claim. It is important to emphasize that what Abraham recognizes as higher than the ethical is not God as such, but his own relationship to God: he obeys the divine command 'for God's sake, and what is altogether identical with this, for his own sake. He does it for God's sake because God demands this proof of his faith; he does it for his own sake so that he can prove it' [52].

Whereas the individual's task within the ethical sphere is to annul her particularity, to overcome her self-interest for the sake of the whole community through the fulfilment of social duties, the teleological suspension of the ethical resurrects, so to speak, the individual's particularity over against the universal. From within the ethical-as-universal, this assertion of particularity is indistinguishable from sin, understood as the individual's failure to prioritize the common good over her own interests. Only if there is a teleological suspension of the ethical can there be a higher position from which to view the individual's transgression of the ethical, which would elevate the individual from being merely a sinner to being justified by her faith. Of course, there is always a tension in this movement, since the ethical is suspended rather than cancelled out entirely: the ethical judgement remains, so that in the eyes of the ethical the individual is nothing more than a sinner, for from within the ethical sphere the higher *telos* cannot be recognized as such. So, from the point of view of the ethical, the elevation of the individual is paradoxical and absurd:

> Faith is precisely this paradox, that the single individual as the particular is higher than the universal and is justified over against the latter not as subordinate but as superior to it . . . Abraham acts by virtue of the absurd, for the absurd is precisely that he as the single individual is higher than the universal. [48–9]

Just as in his 'Preliminary Outpouring from the Heart' Johannes de silentio clarifies the nature of religious faith by showing how it differs from infinite resignation, so in Problem I he contrasts Abraham's relationship to the ethical sphere with that of a 'tragic hero', whose situation appears to resemble Abraham's. Johannes offers three examples of a tragic hero: Agamemnon, from Euripides' tragic drama *Iphigenia in Aulis*; Jephthah, from the Book of Judges in the Hebrew bible; and Lucius Junius Brutus, who established Republican government in Rome. These three figures all find themselves required to kill their own children. When his fleets of soldiers cannot sail to battle in Troy because the sea is too calm, Agamemnon is told by a soothsayer to sacrifice his daughter Iphigenia to the goddess Artemis in return for a wind that would take the Greeks to Troy – and Agamemnon makes the sacrifice. Jephthah, having returned from a victorious battle with the Ammonites, vows to thank God by sacrificing the first creature who comes out of his house to greet him, who turns out to be his own daughter – and Jephthah keeps his promise. Brutus' sons were involved in a treacherous plot to restore the monarchy, and in accordance with the laws of the Roman state Brutus sentenced them to death.

In each of these three examples, the hero's situation is one of conflict between two distinct ethical duties: the duty to love his children, and the duty to pursue the welfare of the community or the state as a whole. Agamemnon, Jephthah and Brutus all choose to honour their duties to the community – by ensuring success in battle, or by upholding the laws of the state – at the expense of their more personal parental responsibilities. Johannes de silentio remarks that 'the ethical has within its scope several gradations' [49], and indicates that

> the tragic hero . . . lets an expression of the ethical have its telos in a higher expression of the ethical; he reduces the ethical relation between father and son or daughter to a sentiment that has its dialectic in its relation to the idea of the ethical life. Here, then, there can be no question of a teleological suspension of the ethical. [51–2]

The tragic hero remains within the ethical: his decision to transgress one ethical duty can be justified in relation to another ethical duty. For Abraham, as we have seen, there is no higher ethical duty that could legitimate his decision to sacrifice Isaac, because Isaac represents Abraham's duty to his nation as well as his duty to his son. 'While the tragic hero is therefore great by his ethical virtue, Abraham is great by a purely personal virtue' [52] – by virtue of his own relationship to God, which concerns no one but himself.

Agamemnon, Jephthah and Brutus all suffer grief at deciding to kill their own children – this is why they are *tragic* heroes – but they have the double consolation of knowing that they have done what is ethically right, and of being understood and admired by others. The tragic hero can communicate his distress and grief: he has at his disposal the common language that is proper to the ethical-as-universal. In contrast, 'Abraham cannot be mediated, which can also be expressed by saying that he cannot speak. As soon as I speak, I express the universal, and if I do not do that, then no one can understand me' [52].

Agamemnon, Jephthah and Brutus are different from Abraham not only because they remain within the ethical sphere, but also because their sacrifices do not involve the absurd belief that their children will nevertheless be returned to them. 'If at the decisive moment these three men were to add to the heroic courage with which they bore their pain the little phrase, "but it will not happen," who then would understand them?' [51], asks Johannes de silentio.

A normal ethical situation can be regarded as a trial insofar as the individual has to resist the temptation to do whatever would prevent her fulfilling her ethical duty: for example, a wife has to resist the temptation of infidelity in order to keep her promise to be faithful to her husband. However, for someone faced with a teleological suspension of the ethical, the ethical itself becomes the temptation, since this would prevent her from acting for the sake of the higher *telos*. The pseudonym suggests that Abraham was subjected by God to a spiritual trial, in which he was tempted by the ethical: tempted to behave in a way that he knew for certain to be ethically defensible, rationally justifiable, and thus understandable to others. He was tempted by the sympathy and admiration that is owed to the tragic hero. As we have seen, and as Johannes himself acknowledges, Abraham has no 'ethical life' that is clearly distinct from his relationship to God, but nevertheless his refusal to sacrifice Isaac would no doubt have won his wife Sarah's sympathy and understanding, and would also have been honoured by the successive generations that owed their lives to this decision.

From a religious perspective, on the other hand, one consequence of his decision to obey God's command is that future generations can see that they owe their existence not only to Abraham, but to God as well, insofar as it was God who decided to let Isaac live. Abraham's actions made it possible for God to give the gift of Isaac – and thus the gift of the community itself – a second time. In this way, then, Abraham is the father of faith, since his own relationship to God becomes a basis for the faith of his descendants.

From a Christian point of view

In Problem I, Johannes de silentio is not only considering the ethical significance of the story of Abraham in its original context, but is also trying to draw out its implications from a more modern point of view. The question is not just whether Abraham's willingness to kill Isaac was ethically reprehensible in its own time, but whether it is ethically reprehensible to a nineteenth-century Christian – and, indeed, whether it is reprehensible now. The question about a teleological suspension of the ethical for the sake of an individual's personal relation to God concerns the *Sittlichkeit* of modern northern European society, not the *Sittlichkeit* of an ancient Hebrew tribe, for today child sacrifice is regarded as murder. And this seems to be borne out by the fact that in his 'Preliminary Outpouring from the Heart' Johannes de silentio considers the story of Abraham from the perspective of a nineteenth-century preacher and his congregation, and describes a contemporary knight of faith whose inward movements are the same as those of Abraham.

Throughout Problem I there are hints that Johannes de silentio is considering the story of Abraham from a specifically Christian point of view, and this becomes more explicit at the end of the section. Abraham is renowned in the Christian tradition as the father of faith, and faith is at the heart of the Christian life. Johannes de silentio's contention that faith is a paradox that involves a teleological suspension of the ethical applies to a Christian's belief in God as much as to Abraham's, and indeed it is primarily Christian faith that is being brought into question in *Fear and Trembling*, since the envisaged reader is someone who assumes herself to be a Christian and to understand the nature of her faith.

Johannes de silentio's interest in the Christian significance of Abraham's situation is hinted at in the third paragraph of Problem I, where he suggests that the categories of Greek philosophy cannot allow us to admire Abraham:

> if the ethical, i.e. the ethical life, is the highest and nothing incommensurable remains in a human being in any way other than that incommensurability constituting evil, i.e. the particular that must be expressed in the universal, then one needs no other categories than what the Greek philosophers had or what can be deduced from them. [47–8]

This remark is immediately followed by a reference to the contrast, often discussed among his nineteenth-century contemporaries, between the pagan world and the Christian world: 'it is all right to say that paganism did not have faith, but if something is supposed to have been said by that, then one must be a little clearer about what one understands by faith' [48]. This makes it clear that the pseudonym is concerned with Christian faith, and when in the next paragraph he describes faith as the paradox by which the individual becomes higher than the universal, the reader will naturally understand this as a comment about Christianity. Having elaborated this account of faith by means of the comparison between Abraham and the tragic hero, Johannes de silentio states that 'the necessity for a new category for understanding Abraham becomes apparent', since 'such a relation to the divine is unknown to paganism' [52].

This attempt to demonstrate the differences between the pagan and Christian worldviews is developed at far greater length in Kierkegaard's book *Philosophical Fragments*, which was published several months after *Fear and Trembling*. In the 1844 text the pseudonym Johannes Climacus argues that the Christian account of the nature of the individual's relation to the truth, and of the relationship between the teacher and the learner through which truth comes into being, is fundamentally different from the Socratic account. For Climacus, Greek categories cannot accommodate Christian faith; more generally, this suggests that a purely philosophical approach – which Socrates is taken to exemplify – will not make sense of the kind of truth that is at stake in the Christian life. The Christian doctrine of the incarnation is, claims this pseudonym, a paradox that cannot be mediated. If, as Johannes de silentio suggests, a 'new category' is needed for understanding Abraham's faith, then this category will be specifically religious, insofar as it encompasses an absolute relation to God that is inaccessible to the understanding.

The Christian significance of Johannes de silentio's claim that faith involves a teleological suspension of the ethical becomes more apparent when he discusses the issue of sin and justification. From the point of view of the ethical, to transgress an ethical requirement (however this is understood) is to sin, and if this point of view is the highest then there can be no justification for the sinner: without a teleological suspension of the ethical, 'then Abraham is lost' [47], as Johannes puts it. The idea of justification can have a purely ethical meaning, in the sense that one is 'justified' in acting in a particular way if the course of action is reasonable and understandable in moral terms – but it also has the specifically theological meaning of becoming righteous in the eyes of God. From a Christian point of view, individuals cannot achieve this through their own efforts, but must rather be made righteous through divine grace, which is mediated through Jesus Christ and through practices of the Church such as the Eucharist.

This denial of human self-sufficiency and emphasis on the need for grace is particularly prominent in the Lutheran, Protestant form of Christianity that was practised in Kierkegaard's Denmark. In the sixteenth century, Martin Luther formulated the doctrine of 'justification by faith' through his despair at failing to keep the ethical law: his theological breakthrough consisted in the realization that grace was not, and could not be, earned through meritorious moral actions, but that it was a gift given by God, purely out of love, to those who had the faith to receive it. The influence of this way of thinking is evident in *Fear and Trembling*. We have already seen, in the previous section of the text, that Johannes de silentio regards faith as a form of receptivity, rather than something that is accomplished through the individual's will and effort. When we read the following passage in Problem I with the basic principles of Lutheran theology in mind, their Christian significance becomes apparent:

> How . . . does the single individual in whom [the ethical] is suspended exist? He exists as the particular in contrast to the universal. Does he then sin? For this is the form of sin . . . If one denies that this form [i.e. the particular standing against the universal] can be repeated in such a way that it is not sin, then judgement has fallen upon Abraham. How then did Abraham exist? He believed. This is the paradox by which he remains at the apex and which he cannot make clear to anyone else, for the paradox is that he as the single individual places himself in absolute relation to the absolute. Is he justified? His justification is again the paradox, for if he is justified it is not by virtue of being something universal but by virtue of being the particular. [54]

Interpreted theologically, this echoes the idea – which as we have seen is implicit in Johannes de silentio's analysis of faith's expectation in his 'Tribute to Abraham' – that Abraham believes that God loves him personally, as a particular individual. If faith means receiving God's grace, and thus to become justified in relation to God, then this is a process that happens to the believer *as an individual*, as a singular, particular being. Again, we can see that Johannes de silentio is using the example of Abraham to draw out and clarify the basic elements of Christian doctrine, at least in its Lutheran form.

The last few paragraphs of Problem I focus more explicitly on the Christian significance of Johannes de silentio's analysis of faith. It is significant that the pseudonym here warns against considering the issue of justification in terms of 'the outcome' of the situation or event in question. His point seems to be a general one: any actions that are to be judged – in the case of Abraham, his willingness to sacrifice Isaac – necessarily take place before their outcome, and in ignorance of it. As Johannes puts it,

> If the one who is to act wants to judge himself by the outcome, then he will never begin. Even though the outcome may delight the whole world, it cannot help the hero, for he only came to know the outcome when the whole thing was over, and he did not become a hero by that but by the fact that he began. [55]

When this point is applied to Christianity, it becomes clear that according to Johannes de silentio the tendency to judge by the outcome, and thereby to forget 'the anxiety, the distress, the paradox' [56] that characterizes the situation of the person who has not yet reached an outcome, contributes to the mistaken view that faith is something easy.

Johannes de silentio applies this reasoning to the situation of Jesus' mother, Mary, and of the disciples: a modern Christian might think it wonderful to be so close to Jesus, but this attitude is conditioned by the 'outcome' of Jesus' life – in the first place, by the resurrection, and secondly, by the success of the Christian religion over many centuries. Of course, the resurrection is not a certainty that gives security to Christian believers, but nevertheless it now stands in the tradition as the outcome of Jesus' story and as a sign of his divine status. Moreover, the fact that by the nineteenth-century Christianity had become the dominant religion in Europe gave a sense of 'safety in numbers', whereas the earliest followers of Jesus were in a tiny minority, and very vulnerable. Thinking now about the apostles, suggests the pseudonym,

> One forgets the anxiety, the distress, the paradox. Was it so easy a matter not to make a mistake? Was it not appalling

that this person who walked among others was God? Was it not terrifying to sit down and eat with him? Was it so easy a matter to become an apostle? But the outcome, the eighteen centuries, it helps . . . . [58]

In fact, for Johannes de silentio the effect of knowing the 'outcome' of Jesus' life 'helps' only in an illusory sense, and in fact it promotes a 'self-deception' that hinders modern people in the task of Christianity because it conceals the paradox of faith.

It is worth pausing at this point to note that Kierkegaard is hostile to the Hegelian idea that 'mind' or 'spirit'[36] becomes 'naturalized' as it is embedded in concrete forms of communal life, for considering this issue clarifies the divergence between Kierkegaard's philosophy and Hegel's, and also illuminates the connection between Kierkegaard's critique of Hegelian thought and his diagnosis of spiritual decline in the modern age. For Kierkegaard, each existing individual should be most concerned with her own freedom, which is singular (specific to each person) and purely inward, since it is this inner personal freedom that faces the decision of faith, and is thus responsible for the receptivity to God's grace which constitutes the Christian's highest task. As we saw at the beginning of this section, Hegel in the *Philosophy of Right* suggests that communal ethical life, understood in the broadest sense, is 'the realm of freedom made actual': when 'mind' or 'spirit' becomes a 'second nature', its freedom is actualized, expressed concretely out in the world. The Danish theologian Hans Lassen Martensen articulates an explicitly Christian version of this Hegelian view when he claims that in later phases of the history of Christianity, 'when the Church had put out its firm roots in the world', the form of the religious life changed insofar as 'God's kingdom had become just like nature'.[37]

In *Philosophical Fragments*, the pseudonym Johannes Climacus argues that this 'naturalization' of Christian teachings is an effect of the worldly, historical 'outcome' of the original Christian event – the Incarnation – and that it contributes to the illusion that faith is not a task but something people are born into, and perhaps even born with.[38] Properly understood, a second nature must be an acquired nature, and for Johannes Climacus this means that it is acquired by the individual through the course of her life, rather than acquired through history and somehow transmitted through successive generations to those born into a Christian culture. According to Climacus, the latter kind of 'naturalization' or 'domestication' has the effect of neutralizing the paradox of Christianity: just as sense-experiences that are initially striking and intense become, through the process of habituation, normalized and weakened so that they may eventually occur unnoticed, so the process through which Christian teaching embeds itself in culture and becomes customary has the effect of dulling the spiritual senses, so to speak, to the strange and radical character of this teaching. For Climacus, this means that his contemporary Christians face the challenge of uncovering the paradox of their faith from beneath the layers of custom or naturalization that have accumulated around it through centuries of Christian culture. His own writings, in which he attempts to 'de-naturalize' the paradox of faith by accentuating its absurdity and difficulty, are directed towards this work of unconcealment – and we can regard the interpretation of Abraham presented in *Fear and Trembling* as having the same purpose.

Johannes de silentio ends Problem I by returning briefly to Abraham, and repeating the ultimatum that he offered to the reader at the beginning of the section: 'During the time before the outcome, Abraham was either at every moment a murderer or we are at the paradox that is higher than all mediations' [58]. He goes on to summarize his interpretation of faith as 'inexplicable', a 'miracle' that 'no one can understand' [58–9]. According to Johannes de silentio, faith lies not in reason nor in ethical conduct, but in 'passion'. Although this term is not defined in *Fear and Trembling*, we should understand it to signify spiritual passion rather than physical, sensual passion. In Kierkegaard's philosophy, the concept of passion is similar to that of *eros* in Platonic thought, where the pre-eminent form of *eros* is desire for truth, rather than for sensual pleasure. Johannes de silentio goes on to argue that even though faith is inaccessible to the understanding, it is available to everyone, 'for that which unites all human life is passion' [59]. The idea that no one is excluded from faith seems to restore to it the universality that the pseudonym, following Kant and Hegel, earlier attributed to the ethical realm, in contrast to the particularity of the religious life. But this is a different kind of universality: while Kant and Hegel would no doubt want to claim that it is reason which 'unites all human life', for Johannes it is passion that has this all-encompassing character – and, in his view, passion belongs to a paradox that, in its resistance to knowledge, ruptures the common understanding which provides the basis for communal life. So, if passion unites all people, it does so only by individuating them as singular beings who, standing before God, are each accountable above all to this personal religious relationship.

Suspending the ethical – without God

In the next section of *Fear and Trembling*, Johannes de silentio will analyse Abraham's situation specifically with reference to the question of his relationship to God. The concept of God is not essential to his reflections on the teleological suspension of the ethical, although of course in the case of Abraham ethical requirements are suspended in response to God's command. Before we move on to the pseudonym's discussion of whether or not there is an absolute duty to God, we might pause to consider other possible examples of a teleological suspension of the ethical that do not involve God.

One example is the story of Siddhartha Gotama, the man who became the Buddha in India, around the fifth or sixth century BCE. At the age of 29, Gotama decides to leave his wife and newborn son to go out into the forest and live the life of an ascetic, in order to seek enlightenment – release from his suffering and ignorance. According to the Buddhist scriptures, he leaves early in the morning while his wife is still asleep, without telling her he is going; like Abraham, he does not communicate his intentions to his family. A second example is the story of the nineteenth-century French artist Paul Gauguin, who left his wife and five children in Paris in order to devote himself to painting, first in Brittany and later in Tahiti. (A version of Gauguin's story is told in W. Somerset Maugham's 1919 novel *The Moon and Sixpence*.) And then, of course, there is the example of Kierkegaard's breaking his engagement to Regine Olsen, in part, it seems, in order to devote himself to his writing.

In each of these cases, our assessment of the hero's decision to transgress his duties to his wife (or fiancée) and children is likely to be influenced by what we know about the outcome of this decision. Gotama did attain enlightenment, and devoted the next 50 years to teaching others what he had learned; his *dhamma* (teaching) spread around the world and is practised by many people today. Gauguin became one of the most renowned artists of his time, and his interest in primitive painting and sculpture had a great influence on twentieth-century art. Kierkegaard became the best-known philosopher in Denmark, and wrote numerous influential philosophical and religious works that have been translated into many languages, and which continue to be read. Regine, for her part, married quite soon after her engagement to Kierkegaard came to an end, and seems to have enjoyed a long and happy marriage to her husband. The way these stories turn out might lead us to conclude that Gotama, Gauguin and Kierkegaard were right to do what they did. But from Johannes de silentio's perspective, this will not do: the outcomes of decisions have no ethical significance, because decisions are of course taken before the outcome, and to some extent in ignorance of it. This means that if we are assessing a person's decision then all we should focus on is the moment of choice itself: what matters is the decision to break a promise, or to neglect a duty.

Alternatively, the pseudonym might suggest, if we do reflect on the outcome of a decision, then we should do so from the point of view of the moment of choice – that is, we should consider the various possible outcomes. Gotama might succeed in gaining enlightenment – but what if he didn't? What if he met another woman on the way into the forest and went off with her? Gauguin might flourish as an artist – but what if he was wrong to believe he had more than a mediocre talent? What would happen to the children if his wife fell ill? What if he died on the journey to Tahiti? Kierkegaard might find his vocation as an author – but what if he failed to write anything of any value? And what if Regine never recovered from the broken engagement and grew old alone, or died young of a broken heart?

It seems that in all three examples, the hero of the story is faced with a claim on his life that seems higher, more important, than his family obligations. Let us assume that these men love the women, and children, whom they decide to leave, just as Johannes de silentio assumes that Abraham loves Isaac. The consequences of the decisions they took certainly include benefits to many other people, but this does not imply that Gotama,

Gauguin and Kierkegaard made their decisions for the sake of others – for the 'greater good'. Of course, we cannot know their motivations, but it seems likely that they acted for their own sakes, in spite of the anguish of their decisions, the distress at causing suffering to others, and the grief of losing those they loved. According to Johannes de silentio, from an ethical point of view their decisions must be condemned. If he is right (and we will return to this question in the final chapter), then we can admire the decisions taken by our three heroes only if we recognize the possibility of a *telos* that ethics does not recognize, but which is higher than ethical requirements.

PROBLEM II: IS THERE AN ABSOLUTE DUTY TO GOD?

Problem II is very similar in both its form and its content to Problem I. Here, Johannes de silentio repeats the claim, made in the previous section, that if faith has any meaning at all then it is a paradox that cannot be mediated, and that the person of faith is therefore incommensurable with, and unintelligible to, the ethical community. And, again as in Problem I, he develops his interpretation of Abraham against the background of modern philosophy; brings out the specifically Christian implications of his own account of faith; and thus presents his supposedly Christian reader with a stark decision: *either* there is an absolute duty to God, *or* else Abraham is lost. Although Johannes de silentio names Hegel as his target, his focus in this section on the concept of duty indicates that his analysis is at least as relevant to Kantian ethics.

God and the ethical

Each of the three 'Problems' discussed by Johannes de silentio has the same starting-point: the proposition that the ethical is the universal. In Problem I this universality is considered in terms of the way in which the ethical applies equally to everyone and is 'in force at every moment'; Problem II begins with the claim that the ethical, as the universal, is 'the divine' [59]. Johannes de silentio begins Problem II, as he began Problem I, by characterizing the ethical from within, so to speak: from a purely ethical perspective that recognizes nothing beyond itself. Understood in this way, the ethical-as-universal is identical with God, since God *is* the highest good that, as such, concerns everyone, and at all times. Insofar as ethical duties are defined in terms of the highest good, then every duty can be regarded as a duty to God. In other words, God is implicit in the concept of duty as such. However, this means that there is nothing special about a duty to God, since to say that a duty is 'to God' is in effect to say no more than that it is a duty. If *every* duty is a duty to God, then *no* duty is *specifically* to God. The 'absolute duty to God' that Johannes de silentio enquires about in Problem II denotes, on the contrary, a duty that is meaningfully, and specifically, to God.

What is at issue in this section of the text, then, is the nature of the individual's relationship to God. In the opening paragraph, Johannes de silentio suggests that the conception of God that belongs to the ethical is impersonal and abstract: God is simply 'the universal', the highest good, and so on. The pseudonym illustrates this with the example of the duty to love one's neighbour – which, we should note, is a basic Christian teaching. From the point of view of the ethical, this

> is a duty by its being referred to God, but in the duty I do not enter into a relation to God but to the neighbour I love. If I say then in this connection that it is my duty to love God, I am really only stating a tautology insofar as "God" here is understood in an entirely abstract sense as the divine, i.e. the universal, i.e. the duty. [59]

In other words, according to this ethical view an individual expresses her love for God solely through loving her neighbour; more generally, she expresses her relationship to God solely through her relationship to the ethical-as-universal. If she fulfils her ethical duty, then she fulfils her duty to God; if she sins against the ethical, then she sins against God. Another way of putting this is to say that the ethical sphere mediates between the individual and God: instead of relating directly to God, an individual relates to him through her ethical activities. And if this is the case, then there is no absolute duty to God, and no direct, unmediated relationship with him.

One of the consequences of understanding the relationship to God in this way is that God becomes quite easily dispensable. The ethical sphere appears to express the greatest respect for God by identifying him with the highest good, but in fact it makes very little practical difference if we drop the idea of God and define the individual's duty – her moral *telos* – simply in terms of the highest, universal good. Once God becomes a function of the ethical – as he does, in different ways, in both Kantian and Hegelian philosophy – then he in effect becomes absorbed into the ethical to the point that he disappears entirely. And this is perhaps what Kierkegaard foresaw: that the ethical theories of the modern period, although they nominally accord to God the highest place, are in fact already implicitly secular: they are signs of an assertion of human autonomy, and thus of a loss of God, that had not yet become explicit. The task of Kierkegaard's pseudonyms is to read these signs and thus to warn of an impending spiritual crisis. As Johannes de silentio puts it,

> The whole existence of the human race rounds itself off in itself as a perfect sphere and the ethical is at once its limit and its completion. God becomes an invisible vanishing point, an impotent thought, his power being only in the ethical. [59]

For Kierkegaard, moreover, this loss of God also means the loss of the individual who, as a spiritual being, is constituted by her relationship to God, and is therefore nothing without this relationship.

In Problem II, then, Johannes de silentio is concerned to accentuate the contrast between an abstract conception of God as nothing more than the ethical-as-universal, and the personal God with whom the 'knight of faith' has an intimate and particular relationship. He states that the knight of faith attains a 'wondrous glory . . . in becoming God's confidant, the Lord's friend, and, to speak very humanly, in saying "You" to God in heaven' [68]. The second-person form of address – saying 'you' rather than saying 'he' or 'she' – represents the individual's direct, personal relationship to God which is the content of religious faith, whereas 'even the tragic hero only addresses [God] in the third person' [68]. Here the pseudonym is repeating, in a different way, the comparison that he made in 'A Preliminary Outpouring from the Heart' between his own belief 'that God is love' [28], and Abraham's belief that God loves *him* as a particular individual. The belief that 'God is love' is abstract insofar as it says something about God that is, at least in principle, separate from one's own being, whereas the belief that 'God loves me' involves oneself in one's understanding of God. Similarly, to address God as 'you' is already implicitly to say 'I': to bring oneself into relation to God, and to conceive of God in relation to oneself.

Johannes de silentio himself, while putting forward these distinctions between an abstract, universal God and a personal God, occupies an ambiguous position with regard to them: he seems to be prepared to see beyond the boundaries of the ethical sphere, since he does not simply condemn Abraham as a murderer; on the other hand, although he can admire Abraham's personal relationship to God, he cannot himself move beyond the abstract, impersonal conception of God that he identifies with the ethical. The pseudonym is a transitional figure, hovering between the ethical sphere and the sphere of faith. He can describe the transition to faith but is unable to make this movement himself. By assuming this particular position, the pseudonym holds up a mirror to the reader: *this* is what faith would look like – and are these the movements that you make? *Could* you make such movements?

What happens to the ethical?

In Problem I, Johannes de silentio presents his critique of Hegelian thought by taking up the German philosopher's concepts of the particular and the universal, and applying these to the story of Abraham. In Problem II his analysis of the philosophical implications of Abraham's situation follows a similar pattern, but instead of employing the concepts of particularity and universality, he here focuses on interiority and exteriority: 'the inner', *das Innere*, and 'the outer', *das Äussere*. Johannes does not offer an explanation of these terms, but the fact that he uses them in a way that echoes his discussion in Problem I suggests that 'the inner' corresponds to particularity, while 'the outer' corresponds to universality. 'In Hegelian philosophy the outer (the externalization) is higher than the inner' [60], writes the pseudonym. Just as a person is ethically required to 'annul' her particularity through her participation in the universal, so 'the single individual's [ethical] task is to divest himself of the qualification of inwardness and to express this in an outward form. Whenever the single individual shrinks from doing so, whenever he wants to stay within or slip down again into the inward qualification of feeling, mood, etc. he commits an offense and stands in temptation' [60]. Ethics demands the overcoming of 'inward' feelings, desires, moods and inclinations since these are private and non-rational: to act morally is to act for the sake of the universal good that can be recognized by reason, and agreed upon by everyone irrespective of their personal feelings. The pseudonym's thought is that only when such feelings are externalized – that is to say, explained, rationalized and made intelligible – can they be taken up into ethical discourse, but through the process of this externalization they take on a different character: they lose their particularity, become generalized.

Just as the paradox of faith is defined in Problem I as the elevation of the particular above the universal, so in this section faith is described as a 'new inwardness' that transcends the ethical requirement for outward expression: 'The paradox of faith is this, that there is an inwardness that is incommensurable with the outer, an inwardness that, mind you, is not identical with the first one but is a new inwardness' [60]. The inwardness of faith is not the pure 'immediacy' of feelings, moods and inclinations which, from an ethical point of view, constitute the particularity that needs to be set aside for the sake of the universal. But faith cannot be assimilated into the ethical sphere either; and another way of putting this is to say that it cannot be mediated. So if faith is a 'new inwardness', it is also a new immediacy, which is to say a direct relationship to God that does not precede the individual's participation in the ethical, but rather follows after this.

This raises the question of the status of the ethical sphere from the point of view of faith. If the individual is elevated above the ethical by virtue of her relationship to God, what then happens to the ethical? How is the single individual related it to? We have already considered this question in the last section, but in Problem II Johannes de silentio addresses it more directly than he has done previously. If the individual's duty to God is absolute, 'then the ethical is reduced to the relative', but the pseudonym is careful to emphasize that

it does not follow from this that the ethical should be abolished, but it receives a different expression, a paradoxical expression, in such a way, for example, that love for God can cause the knight of faith to give his love for the neighbour the opposite expression of what duty is ethically speaking. [61]

This remark is interesting, because whereas at the beginning of this section Johannes de silentio referred only to the ethical duty to love one's neighbour, he now implies that it is possible to distinguish between this duty itself, and the way in which it is expressed. We should note that this is not a distinction between an action's intention and its consequences: the 'expression' of the duty is still in the domain of intentions (and thus still within the sphere of morality as understood by Kant). So, for example, Abraham's duty is to love his son, and the expression of his duty is his willingness – his intention – to sacrifice him. The 'expression' of a duty is not so much an action, but a *decision*.

An important consequence of this distinction between a duty and its expression is that it allows Johannes to argue that 'the absolute duty may bring one to do what ethics would forbid, but it can never make the knight of faith stop loving' [65]. In faith, the duty to love one's neighbour – that is to say, to love another human being – is always upheld, but the expression of this love may not conform to ethical standards. We can see how this might apply to the story of Abraham. From an ethical point of view it is impossible to understand how his decision to obey God's command to kill Isaac can be an expression of his love for his son. From a religious point of view, however, the decision to kill becomes a decision to sacrifice, which far from contradicting Abraham's love for Isaac gives this the highest possible expression. Again, I have discussed this idea in previous sections, but here it is articulated more clearly and explicitly by the pseudonym:

[Abraham] must love Isaac with all his heart; inasmuch as God demands Isaac, Abraham must love him, if possible, even more dearly, and only then can he *sacrifice* him, for it is indeed this love for Isaac which by its paradoxical opposition to his love for God makes his act a sacrifice. [65]

The sacrifice has value as a sacrifice precisely because of Abraham's love for Isaac. The fact that Abraham loves Isaac constitutes the content, the substance, of his decision to kill him, in the sense that it is this love that gives the decision its particular character: this is why it is possible to claim that the decision *expresses* his love for Isaac at the same time as it expresses his faith in God. We can see that the same logic is at work in the other example of faith that is discussed in this section of *Fear and Trembling*: the disciples' decision to leave their families in order to follow Jesus. This decision expresses the disciples' love for their families, for it is their love that makes their decision what it is: a decision to become disciples, that is to say, to make a genuine commitment to Jesus that demonstrates their faith. If they did not love their families, then leaving home would have little significance, and would therefore demonstrate nothing more than their indifference.

Of course, it is always possible to challenge this logic by appealing on behalf of the victim of the sacrifice. What good to Isaac is a father's love that expresses itself in a decision to kill him? What good to the disciples' families is a love that expresses itself in a decision to leave them? This is precisely the claim of the ethical, and it rings loud and clear throughout *Fear and Trembling*. In the case of the tragic heroes discussed in Problem I, these appeals can be answered with reference to a higher ethical claim. But the situation of a knight of faith is different in this respect: her decision is not made by weighing up conflicting ethical demands, but by existing in the conflict between the ethical sphere as such, and the requirement of faith. According to Johannes de silentio, it is not really possible to weigh up these alternatives, since they are of a wholly different order from one another: they are incommensurable, and there is no common ground between them that could provide a basis for making the choice; there are no criteria that could be recognized by both sides. This is what Kierkegaard's pseudonyms mean when they describe the ethical and the religious as distinct 'spheres'. Within Kierkegaard's philosophy, the inability to weigh up and calculate is the mark of a genuine decision. The only criterion for a decision is one's own inwardness, one's own subjectivity: as soon as the individual starts to look for reasons or criteria according to which her decision can be explained and justified to others, she has in fact avoided the decision, stepped back from the abyss of freedom that revealed itself in the moment of choice.

'A hard saying'

Johannes de silentio considers the Christian implications of Problem II by focusing on a passage from the gospel of Luke, which, he suggests, offers 'a remarkable teaching on the absolute duty to God' [63]. The author of this gospel reports Jesus as saying that 'If anyone comes to me and does not hate his own father and mother and wife and children and brothers and sisters, yes, even his own life, he cannot be my disciple' (Luke 14:26). Johannes de silentio suggests that people either ignore this 'hard saying', or try to modify it to make it more palatable, less offensive from an ethical point of view. Theologians may attempt to offer a 'tasteful explanation' for Jesus' exhortation to hate one's family by 'weakening it' so that 'to hate' is interpreted as 'to love less, esteem less, honour not, value as nothing' [63]. According to the pseudonym, this hermeneutic strategy is unacceptable, for two reasons. The first reason is that avoiding the full force of the teaching diminishes the difficulty of the task of faith, whereas in fact it is precisely this difficulty that is conveyed by Jesus' reference to hatred. 'The words should be taken as frightfully as possible in order that each person may examine himself' [63]: they constitute a test – analogous to the test of Abraham's faith through God's command to sacrifice Isaac – and thus they should be used by the individual to test her own willingness and ability to take up the task of following Jesus, the task of becoming a Christian.

The second reason for Johannes de silentio's insistence that this passage from Luke should be taken absolutely literally is that re-interpreting 'to hate' as 'to love less' and so on, implies that a person demonstrates her love for God by caring less about other people. On the contrary, argues the pseudonym, it is one's love for what one sacrifices that proves one's love for God. He illustrates this using the example of a man who requires his beloved to leave her parents in order to marry him:

> if he were to regard it as a proof of her extraordinary love for him that for his sake she became a lukewarm, indifferent daughter, etc., then he is more foolish than the greatest fool. If he has any idea what love is, he would then wish to discover that as a daughter and sister she were perfect in love and see in that an assurance that his wife would love him as she does nobody else. [64]

It is in this Christian context that Johannes de silentio insists that 'the absolute duty [to God] may bring one to do what ethics would forbid, but it can never make the knight of faith stop loving'.

In the case of the passage from Luke, Johannes' point seems to be that those who become Jesus' disciples are not required to stop loving their families, but are required to express this love in a way that cannot be understood. So, for example, by becoming disciples they not only leave their families behind, but also bring dishonour upon them and perhaps put them in danger, for Jesus was, of course, a controversial figure who broke with the ethical codes of his own community. This decision would be interpreted as an expression of hatred, and the disciples are unable to challenge this interpretation. They are acting purely on the basis of their own faith, and they cannot provide any justification for this: there are no objective signs they can point to in order to demonstrate that Jesus really is the son of God or the Messiah. From an ethical point of view, their decision to become disciples appears to be selfish:

> the paradox of faith . . . is the expression for the highest egoism (doing the frightful deed for one's own sake); on the other hand, it is the expression for the most absolute devotion (doing it for God's sake). Faith itself cannot be mediated into the universal, for it is thereby annulled. [62]

Love and solitude

One more issue that we have already considered, and which is revisited in this section of *Fear and Trembling*, is how Johannes de silentio's analysis of faith might apply to violent terrorist attacks that are carried out in the name of religious doctrines or ideals. As we have seen, and as Johannes has himself already pointed out, the idea that individuals can be elevated above the ethical sphere is a dangerous one, since it might appear to legitimate all kinds of immoral behaviour. However, several elements of the pseudonym's discussion of the absolute duty to God go against this view. First, there is no question of legitimizing the movements of faith, for the very concept of legitimacy belongs to the ethical sphere. Second, as we have seen, Johannes de silentio insists that the knight of faith always acts out of love, even if she expresses this love in a way that cannot be understood. To be sure, this does leave open the possibility that a terrorist who decides to blow up a bus or a train is sacrificing her victims, rather than just killing them, but her actions can only be regarded as a religious act – as a sacrifice – if she loves her victims more than herself, and is pained to see them die. Even though the behaviour of Abraham towards Isaac, and of Jesus' disciples towards their families, cannot be understood in ethical terms, Johannes' emphasis on love does allow us to distinguish, at least in principle, between these 'knights of faith' and terrorists.

Johannes himself seems to maintain a precarious balance between insisting that faith is unintelligible, and offering criteria that would allow us to recognize the difference between faith and sin:

> whether the single individual is actually situated in a state of temptation or is a knight of faith, only the individual himself can determine. Nevertheless it is surely possible to construct out of the paradox some distinguishing characteristic that one not in it can also understand. [69]

Love is precisely such a 'distinguishing characteristic'; and another is the 'absolute isolation' of the knight of faith, 'who in the loneliness of the universe never hears another human voice but walks alone with his frightful responsibility' [70]. On this point, Johannes de silentio accentuates the difference between the true knight of faith and the 'counterfeit', who is 'sectarian' [69]. Even if the latter belongs to a very small group, these 'comrades' still 'represent the universal' insofar as they share a common language, common values, can understand one another, and can assure one another of the rightness of their beliefs and actions.

This is not to say that the knight of faith must always be alone. Indeed, as we have seen Johannes de silentio emphasizes that faith is a way of living in the world, whereas resignation involves withdrawing from the world. And in this section of the text, the example he gives of Jesus' disciples also indicates that knights of faith are not actually solitary. The disciples shared their faith. However, the movement of faith can only be made inwardly: one disciple cannot give another a reason to follow Jesus, since then the second disciple would become a follower of the first, which would itself be a subjective decision. The individual always falls back on her own freedom, her own responsibility, and if she attempts to avoid this by joining in with the crowd then she is not relating directly and absolutely to God, and is therefore not a knight of faith. It is the moment of decision that Johannes de silentio refers to when he writes that 'the knight of faith has simply and solely himself' [69]; decision is the inwardness that makes each person a single individual. But decisions must be lived out with others, and of course they often involve others, have ethical implications. It is this tension between the inner and the outer aspects of human life that constitutes the difficulty of the task of faith, for if there were only inwardness then the stakes would not be so high, nor the risks so great. This brings us back to the need for courage, which Johannes de silentio emphasizes in his 'Preliminary Outpouring from the Heart', and to which he returns repeatedly throughout this section of the text.

PROBLEM III: WAS IT ETHICALLY DEFENSIBLE FOR ABRAHAM TO CONCEAL HIS UNDERTAKING FROM SARAH, FROM ELIEZER, FROM ISAAC?

In Problem III Johannes de silentio considers the significance of Abraham's faith in terms of the issue of concealment and disclosure. This is the most complex section of *Fear and Trembling*, as well as the longest. And it is at once the most boring and the most interesting part of the book: it repeats material from earlier sections, but in this repetition something new emerges.

Problem III has the same structure as Problems I and II insofar as it begins by outlining a certain characterization of the ethical, from the point of view of the ethical sphere; by attributing this characterization of the ethical to Hegelian philosophy; and by presenting the reader with a dilemma: a choice between remaining with the ethical, or transcending this position in order to admire Abraham. Johannes de silentio reiterates this dilemma at the end of the section. However, in the intervening portion of Problem III the pseudonym embarks on a lengthy discussion of the theme of concealment and disclosure with reference first to aesthetics in general, and then to a series of particular literary figures whose situations contrast with that of Abraham. As in previous sections of the text, these comparisons illuminate the exceptional and paradoxical nature of Abraham's faith. Here, though, they also point beyond the case of Abraham to facilitate a reflection on the specifically Christian issue of sin and redemption. But at the same time, the fact that these alternative situations concern romantic relationships indicates that the questions raised by the biblical narrative are not confined to a religious context, and suggests once again that Kierkegaard's broken engagement to Regine Olsen lurks behind Johannes de silentio's philosophical interpretation of the story of Abraham.

Luther's interpretation of Abraham's silence

Before we consider Johannes de silentio's lengthy discussion of Abraham's concealment of his intentions from Isaac, Sarah and Eliezer, it will be instructive to look briefly at Martin Luther's interpretation of this aspect of the Genesis narrative. As we will see, this is very different from Johannes de silentio's reading. At Genesis 22: 7–8, Isaac asks his father, 'where is the lamb for a burnt-offering?', and Abraham replies that 'God himself will provide the lamb for the burnt-offering, my son.' Commenting on these verses in his Lectures on Genesis, Luther suggests that 'Abraham does not want to torment his son with a long torture and trial. Therefore he does not yet disclose that Isaac himself must die.'[39] This implies that Abraham's response to Isaac's question is simply evasive, and that it is designed to protect Isaac from knowing the truth. Johannes de silentio, however, will argue that from an ethical point of view this cannot count as a justification for Abraham's failure to disclose God's command and his intention to obey it.

Luther goes on to speculate that, once the altar has been built and the wood laid upon it, 'some conversation between the father and the son must have occurred – a conversation through which Isaac was told of the will of God', and he expresses his surprise that the author of Genesis did not record this conversation. Filling in the gaps in the biblical narrative, Luther imagines Abraham's explanation of his actions as follows:

> He probably said: 'God has given a command; therefore we must obey Him, and, since He is almighty, He can keep His promise even when you are dead and have been reduced to ashes.' . . . Thus it was the father's address to the son which reconciled these two contradictory propositions: Isaac will be

the seed and father of kings and of peoples; Isaac will die and will not be the father of peoples. Those contradictory statements cannot be reconciled by any human reason or philosophy. But the Word reconciles these two, namely, that he who is dead lives, and that he who lives dies. Thus we live, and yet we die; for even though we are now living, we are reckoned as dead because of sin, and although we have died, we are reckoned as living. On this occasion these statements were treated and discussed between the father and the son, and they were believed not only by Abraham but also by Isaac.[40]

Here, Luther uses more poetic licence than Johannes de silentio in his reconstruction of the story of the sacrifice – and his version of the discussion that 'must have occurred' between Abraham and Isaac is clearly shaped by Paul's Christian theology. His assertion that Abraham's imagined explanation holds together two contradictory claims, which cannot be reconciled by reason or philosophy, seems to be very close to Johannes de silentio's insistence on the paradoxical nature of Abraham's faith. But the pseudonym's view is that Abraham could not make this faith intelligible to anyone and that therefore he was unable to explain himself to Isaac.

'Faith is not the aesthetic'

Problem III begins with the assertion that the ethical-as-universal requires the individual to disclose herself – that is to say, to articulate, explain and justify her actions. 'Defined immediately as a sensuous and psychical being, the single individual is the concealed. His ethical task, then, is to extricate himself from his concealment and to become disclosed in the universal' [71]. This is another variation of the movement from particularity to the universal, from self-interest to duty, from immediacy to mediation, and from inwardness to externalization that, as is claimed in the two preceding sections of *Fear and Trembling*, accomplishes the individual's participation in the ethical-as-universal. Here, then, Johannes de silentio presents a third formulation of the dilemma presented by the story of Abraham:

If there is no concealment that has its rationale in the single individual as the particular being higher than the universal, then Abraham's conduct is indefensible . . . If there is such a concealment, however, then we are at the paradox, which cannot be mediated because it is due precisely to the single individual as the particular being higher than the universal, but the universal is precisely the mediation [of the particular] [71].

Having thus reiterated the 'either/or' presented in Problems I and II, Johannes de silentio ends this paragraph by contrasting faith with 'the aesthetic': 'faith is not the first immediacy, but a later one. The first immediacy is the aesthetic . . . But faith is not the aesthetic' [71–2]. Here he echoes his earlier claims that 'faith is . . . no aesthetic emotion but something much higher, precisely because it presupposes recollection; it is not a spontaneous inclination of the heart but the paradox of existence' [40], and that this paradox of faith involves 'a new inwardness' [60] which is different from, and higher than, the inwardness of the person who has not yet fulfilled the requirements of ethics.

But what exactly does Johannes de silentio mean by the term 'aesthetic'? It is important to clarify this now, because the category of the aesthetic is employed throughout Problem III. In fact, 'the aesthetic' has two distinct meanings in *Fear and Trembling*: on the one hand, it signifies the domain of art, considered from a philosophical point of view – and Johannes de silentio's discussion of various literary figures is 'aesthetic' in this sense – but on the other hand it is used to refer to a certain kind of existence, a certain attitude to life. It is this second sense that is in play when the pseudonym insists that 'faith is not the aesthetic', and this way of using the term is peculiar to Kierkegaard's philosophy. The reader may wish to look back to the Overview of Themes, where I outlined the distinction between three spheres of existence – the aesthetic, the ethical, and the religious – that operates in many of Kierkegaard's texts, including *Fear and Trembling*.

Although Johannes de silentio does not explicitly discuss the three spheres of existence, his analysis of Abraham in the opening paragraphs of each of the three 'Problems' can perhaps be mapped onto this tripartite framework. Johannes distinguishes Abraham's faith both from the 'particularity' and 'immediacy' that characterize a person considered 'as a sensuous and psychical being', and from the 'universality' and 'mediation' that characterize ethical conduct. The first form of life corresponds roughly to the aesthetic sphere, the second to the ethical sphere. (Actually, this is debatable, since it might be argued that the 'immediacy' of a 'sensuous, psychic' being is opposed to the reflexivity – the self-consciousness and self-relatedness – that constitutes all three of the spheres. The fluidity of many of Kierkegaard's concepts and categories allows for this kind of ambiguity. But nevertheless it may be useful to consider the connections between the different sets of distinctions that structure Johannes de silentio's discussion of faith.) It is especially important for the pseudonym to clarify the difference between the aesthetic and religious spheres, since these share a view of the individual as particular, as immediate, and as in some way outside the universal. And this brings us back to his claim that 'faith is not the first immediacy but a later one. The first immediacy is the aesthetic . . . But faith is not the aesthetic'. More specifically, in this section of the text Johannes de silentio wants to claim that both the aesthetic and the religious forms of life require the individual to conceal herself – in contrast to the ethical sphere, which requires disclosure – but he also wants to argue that the concealment proper to the religious sphere is completely different from aesthetic concealment.

Having stated that 'faith is not the aesthetic', Johannes de silentio announces his intention 'to consider the whole matter purely aesthetically and for that purpose to embark upon an aesthetic deliberation' [72]. Here, the two senses of the term 'aesthetic' are brought together: on the one hand, the pseudonym is going to explore the issue of concealment and disclosure from the point of view of the aesthetic sphere, while on the other hand his method of doing this will involve a discussion of certain literary texts, and of the general principles that determine the structure of these fictional narratives. Of course, although it is possible to distinguish between these two senses of 'the aesthetic', they are related to each other insofar as they are both detached from actuality, from 'real life'. Johannes de silentio suggests here that 'the aesthetic' is characterized by the category of 'the interesting' [72], and again this applies to both senses of the term. The effects of art (and particularly of the art-form of dramatic literature that the pseudonym focuses on here) include being interesting, amusing, thought-provoking, entertaining; arousing emotions, invoking a mood – and these are all elements which motivate, and thus give form to, the aesthetic way of life.

Having said this, the pseudonym's discussion of the aesthetic significance of concealment also touches on ethical issues. This is natural, since literary texts usually deal with ethical themes: with deception, betrayal, justice, revenge, family ties, moral dilemmas, and so on. As Johannes de silentio puts it, 'the interesting is a border category, a common boundary between aesthetics and ethics' [72]. On the one hand, 'the interesting' implies the detachment of the aesthetic sphere; on the other hand, it implies the personal concern and involvement, the sense of something mattering and being meaningful, that characterizes the ethical sphere. To say that something is interesting implies that one is regarding it from a detached perspective, from outside the situation: for example, one might be interested in the news, or it might be interesting to follow the breakdown of an acquaintance's marriage after she discovers that her partner has been unfaithful to her; however, this woman would probably not herself describe her own situation as 'interesting'. (This does not imply that being interested in someone else's situation is necessarily callous: one may sympathize with a friend's misfortune, but still be curious to know the details and even enjoy gossiping about them with a mutual acquaintance.) If the betrayed wife did regard her situation as interesting then this would indicate a certain detachment, which in Kierkegaardian terms would mean that she has an aesthetic relation to her own life. As we have seen, 'the interesting' – alongside the pleasant, the amusing and so on – is a value within the aesthetic sphere; but actions and events are interesting precisely insofar as they touch upon actuality, and for this reason ethical situations are interesting from an aesthetic point of view. 'The interesting' is thus a category that relates to both the aesthetic and ethical spheres, although it has a different status within each: it is an aesthetic value, but not an ethical value, since a vicious action can be just as interesting as a virtuous action; it thrives on ethical content, but it is a product of looking at the ethical from the outside, or in a detached way – that is to say, from an aesthetic point of view.

Before we turn to Johannes de silentio's 'aesthetic deliberation' concerning the question of concealment and disclosure, we may at this point pause to consider how the Kierkegaardian account of the three spheres of existence applies to *Fear and Trembling* itself. What kind of a text is this? Is it aesthetic, ethical, or religious – or perhaps, ironically, all three at once? Johannes' discussion of 'the interesting' certainly applies to his own interpretation of Abraham's story: the biblical narrative has an ethical content that, viewed from the outside, is both interesting and emotionally engaging. Furthermore, the ethical situation of Abraham provides the pseudonym with an occasion for philosophical reflection on the nature of faith. According to Kierkegaard's schema, this intellectual reflection belongs to the aesthetic sphere, since it expresses the detached perspective of a spectator; it is quite foreign to those involved in the situation itself, and for this reason it is difficult to imagine Abraham and Isaac having a philosophical discussion about the significance of faith during their journey to Mount Moriah. But it could also be argued that *Fear and Trembling* is not simply aesthetic, since it seeks to make contact with the reader and to prompt her to make a decision about her own existence (an ethical movement), and perhaps to take up the task of faith. If this is the case, then the text – considered as a communication between writer and reader – is not merely imaginative or ideal, but has an actuality that brings it into the ethical sphere. And if the source of the book is Kierkegaard's own inward relationship to God, then it might even be regarded as belonging to the religious sphere too. There is an irony to Johannes de silentio's aesthetic approach to the question of faith, for like other Kierkegaardian pseudonyms he criticizes aestheticism – particularly as it is exemplified in contemporary philosophy and cultural commentary – at the same time as he exhibits it himself. This kind of irony is integral to Kierkegaard's writing as a whole, and especially his pseudonymous texts.

Johannes de silentio himself raises the question of 'whether faith and the whole life of faith can become . . . a subject for aesthetic treatment' [77], although he indicates that he will leave this issue 'undecided'. The pseudonym's comments about his own method in this section of the text are important. In his 'Tribute to Abraham' he compared the roles of hero and poet, and seemed himself to take up the role of poet in relation to Abraham, but here in Problem III he remarks that 'I am not a poet and go about things only dialectically' [79]. Although poetry and dialectics both belong to the aesthetic sphere, they are two different forms of writing. Poetry in this context means literature: a form of communication that uses narrative, character, metaphor and so on, and which seeks to engage the reader on an emotional and imaginative level. Dialectics, on the other hand, is a form of philosophical thinking: it involves reasoning – elucidation of the distinctions and connections between concepts, points of view or positions – and it appeals to the intellect rather than the imagination. Johannes de silentio's approach to the story of Abraham is, in fact, at once poetic and dialectical, or rather he alternates between these two forms. (This is why *Fear and Trembling* has the subtitle 'A Dialectical Lyric'.) When in this section of the book he indicates that his approach is dialectical rather than poetic, he is simply stating that he is not constructing a narrative, but is moving between different situations and ethical positions, as represented in various literary texts, in order to reflect on them philosophically. So, for example, he tells us that 'I shall call forward a few poetic personages. By the power of dialectic I shall hold them on end . . . so that through their anxiety they might be able to bring something or other to light' [77]. In other words, the characters he sketches are summoned to play a role in a philosophical discussion, not in a dramatic story.

Aesthetic and ethical concealment

Before he begins his reflections on the series of 'poetic personages' who may illuminate the particular kind of concealment that belongs to religious faith, Johannes de silentio offers some general remarks about the role of concealment and disclosure in the aesthetic and ethical spheres. He begins by referring to Aristotle's analysis of drama, suggesting that 'just as recognition is the resolving, relaxing element in the dramatic life, so concealment is the element of tension' [73]. Contemporary illustrations of this point include the way in which a TV crime drama is structured around the concealment and disclosure of a murderer's identity and motives; or a soap opera plot involves clandestine affairs and secret paternity that eventually come to light – often on Christmas day, or at a wedding. Sometimes the secret is known by the audience; sometimes it is concealed from them as well as from the characters in the drama.

Echoing Hegelian aesthetics, Johannes de silentio makes a comparison between this dialectic of concealment and disclosure within ancient and modern drama. In ancient drama – and the pseudonym is concerned with Greek tragedy in particular – the plot is governed by a fate that is initially concealed from the hero, and then disclosed; the tragedy consists in the fact that this disclosure comes too late, as, for instance, when 'a son murders his father, but only afterwards learns that it is his father' [73]. In modern drama, by contrast, actions and events are the product of the protagonists' free choices: 'modern drama has given up the idea of fate, has emancipated itself dramatically, is sighted, introspective, assimilates fate into its dramatic consciousness. Concealment and disclosure are then the hero's free act for which he is responsible' [73]. This emphasis on freedom and responsibility suggests that concealment and disclosure have greater ethical significance within modern drama than in ancient drama: the modern hero's decision to conceal or reveal something can be subjected to the audience's or reader's moral judgement, as well as functioning as a device that structures the plot of the play or novel, to either tragic or comic effect.

Johannes de silentio announces that 'the path I have to take is to carry concealment dialectically through aesthetics and ethics, for the point is to let aesthetic concealment and the paradox [proper to the religious sphere] emerge in their absolute dissimilarity' [74], and he begins by describing a hypothetical situation in which a protagonist chooses to conceal something for what might be regarded as an ethical reason: in order to prevent another person from suffering. In fact, Johannes wants to argue that this is not a genuinely ethical motive, but an aesthetic one, since it concerns a particular individual rather than 'the universal'. We are invited to imagine a young girl who is secretly in love with someone, without his knowledge; her parents want her to marry another man; she chooses to conceal her feelings from the man she loves so as not to hurt him. (Johannes also sketches an alternative version of this situation in which the protagonist is a young man instead of a girl.) In this instance, the girl's concealment creates a tension that is the basis of the dramatic plot. In the fictional domain of aesthetics, this tension can be resolved, and thus the story developed, by means of some kind of coincidence that brings to light the concealed love and facilitates a

happy ending: on the one hand, the girl has demonstrated courage and selflessness by hiding her feelings; on the other hand,
without compromising this proof of her virtue, her love is nevertheless brought out into the open, enabling her to get the
happiness she has earned by keeping silent.

This example shows how aesthetics 'demands' concealment in
order to create a plot; in order to make the situation interesting;
in order to make the girl a heroine with whom we can sympathize. Johannes de silentio contrasts this with the ethical requirement
for disclosure. Within the ethical sphere, the concern is not to
construct an interesting and moving story, but to do what is
right. And whereas the aesthetic sphere is concerned with feelings, and thus the girl acts in order to spare the feelings of those
she loves, the ethical sphere is concerned with freedom, with
each individual's autonomy, for it is this that grounds their own
ethical actions. From an ethical point of view, one has a duty to
be open with other people, because one has a duty to preserve
their freedom, which enables them to be moral. Concealing from
another person something that concerns her deprives her of
autonomy, takes away her power of deciding how to respond to
the situation. In the story of the girl's secret love, the right outcome is in fact brought about: her parents, the man they want
her to marry, and the man she loves are all made aware of her
feelings, and this gives them the opportunity to respond in the
way they judge to be right. But this happens accidentally, by a
coincidence, and not by the girl's own decision: ethically speaking, her attempt to conceal her feelings is wrong, even though it
appears to be motivated by concern for another's happiness.
(The ethical point here is that she should be more concerned to
preserve the other's freedom than to prevent him from suffering
– because freedom is the ground of ethics itself, and is thus the
most fundamental ethical requirement.) Ethics deals with actuality, and in actuality we cannot trust that a coincidence will
bring about the right outcome; we have to take responsibility for
this ourselves, and then live with the consequences of our actions.
According to Johannes de silentio, 'the aesthetic idea contradicts
itself as soon as it must be carried out in actuality. Ethics therefore demands disclosure' [76].

Johannes here returns to the figure of the 'tragic hero', who
was first introduced in 'A Preliminary Outpouring from the

Heart', and then discussed more extensively in Problem I, in relation to the question of a teleological suspension of the ethical. Johannes now suggests that a tragic hero has to be subjected to the emotional responses of those who will be affected by his actions, since this is part of the ethical trial that makes him a tragic hero. For example, Agamemnon is 'tempted' away from doing his duty to the state, which means sacrificing his daughter Iphigenia, by her tears and those of his wife, Clytemnestra. Having to carry out his higher ethical duty in the face of their distress heightens his suffering, and this intensifies both his tragedy and his heroism. In Euripides' play *Iphigenia in Aulis*, the 'aesthetic' demand that Agamemnon conceal his situation 'out of solicitude for the women' remains in place, and so it is an old servant who, having found out accidentally that Iphigenia will be sacrificed for the sake of the nation, informs Clytemnestra of this. However, 'ethics has no coincidence and no old servant standing by' [76]: ethically speaking, Agamemnon has to tell Iphigenia and Clytemnestra of his plans himself.

As we have seen, this disclosure is necessary in order to preserve the freedom of others; but it is also important because concealment may be self-interested. Agamemnon, or the girl who loves the man she isn't supposed to marry, may tell themselves that they will conceal their situation from those involved in order to minimize their suffering – but what if their real motivation is to save *themselves* from having to deal with these others' distress? Because the human psyche is adept at self-deception, it is very difficult to be clear about one's own motivations, and since it is precisely these motivations that determine the ethical status of one's actions (at least according to the view of ethics that is in play in *Fear and Trembling*), then this tendency to self-deception presents a threat to moral life. Thus the real tragic hero, as distinct from the fictional, 'aesthetic' depiction of this figure, has to be open, because this guarantees that she is acting for the sake of others, and not simply for her own sake.

In fact, Johannes de silentio's discussion of this issue seems to expose a certain tension not just between the aesthetic and ethical spheres, but within the ethical life itself. On the one hand, ethics requires the individual to disclose her intentions, both in order to preserve the freedom of others, and in order to ensure that she is not, even unwittingly, keeping a secret for her own sake rather than to spare another's feelings. But on the other hand, this disclosure can be a way of avoiding one's own responsibility. Johannes remarks that 'if [the tragic hero] keeps silent, he assumes a responsibility as the single individual inasmuch as he disregards any argument that may come from outside' [76]; in concealing his intentions, he can be certain that the decision he makes is wholly his own, and thus that he is fully responsible for it. This responsibility is an essential aspect of ethical life. It seems to be clear to the pseudonym that the former consideration is, from an ethical point of view, more important than the latter, but still the tension seems to remain: 'Despite the rigour with which ethics demands disclosure, it cannot be denied that secrecy and silence actually make for greatness in a person precisely because they are qualifications of inwardness' [77]. If concealment is morally ambiguous insofar as it might be motivated by self-interest rather than concern for another person's feelings, then surely disclosure can also be ambiguous – ostensibly motivated by duty, but possibly motivated by a flight from responsibility? One may disclose one's situation to another in order to put the decision in their hands, or at least to make them complicit in one's own decision. We could imagine an Agamemnon, for example, who tells Clytemnestra about his intention to sacrifice Iphigenia precisely because he does not want to carry out what he knows to be his duty: when his wife cries and begs him not to kill their daughter, he declares that he is 'unable' to make the sacrifice, perhaps even that Clytemnestra's response 'leaves him with no choice' but to put his family before the interests of the state. This would amount to a dishonest attempt to deny his own freedom. The twentieth-century French philosopher Jean-Paul Sartre – whose 'existentialism' was indebted to certain aspects of Kierkegaard's thought, such as the latter's emphasis on decision and responsibility – uses the term 'bad faith' to describe this kind of evasiveness in the face of freedom. According to Sartre, bad faith is a universal human tendency that haunts the ethical life.[41]

More recently, Jacques Derrida has accentuated the issue of responsibility and secrecy in his reading of *Fear and Trembling*, suggesting that Johannes de silentio's discussion of Abraham's silence shows the very concept of responsibility to be paradoxical. 'The ethical,' Derrida argues, can end up making us irresponsible. It is a temptation, a tendency, or a facility that would sometimes have to be refused in the name of a responsibility that doesn't keep account or give an account . . . Such a responsibility keeps its secret, it cannot and need not present itself.[42]

Because responsibility is paradoxical in this way, 'Abraham is thus at the same time the most moral and the most immoral, the most responsible and the most irresponsible of men.'[43] Derrida's reading departs from Johannes de silentio's in making this claim that Abraham can be considered moral as well as immoral. For the pseudonym, Abraham's silence takes him out of the ethical, and marks a contradiction between the ethical and religious spheres, while Derrida identifies a paradox of responsibility *within* the ethical sphere.

Does Johannes de silentio's claim that secrecy is the mark of an 'inwardness' which 'makes for greatness in a person' mean that this inwardness cannot be accommodated within the ethical sphere? Johannes appears to think so: 'The tragic hero, who is the favourite of ethics, is the purely human; him I can also understand, and all his undertakings are in the open as well. If I go further, I always stumble upon the paradox . . . ' [77]. One way of interpreting the pseudonym's position is as suggesting that the 'purely human' ethical sphere harbours a tension that points beyond itself, signalling its own incompletion. This is the tension between disclosure and concealment; between the requirement for mediation in the community, on the one hand, and the requirement to take full responsibility for one's own actions, on the other. As we have just seen, the human tendency to self-deception introduces complication and ambiguity into both concealment and disclosure, since the motives for either decision can always be called into question. Concealment threatens the other's freedom and responsibility; disclosure threatens one's own freedom and responsibility. On this view, the ethical sphere's claim to be self-contained, self-sufficient, would be misguided: the ethical would *not* in fact constitute a perfect sphere, but would rather open itself out to something other, something higher – something that transcends it and calls it into question. This is, perhaps, integral to the logic of Kierkegaard's existential spheres. Just the portrayal of the aesthete in Part I of *Either/Or*

suggests that the pursuit of pleasure and stimulation that constitutes the aesthetic form of life leads, ironically, to melancholy
and boredom, so Johannes de silentio's discussion of concealment and disclosure suggests that the pursuit of an ethically
good life is undermined by internal tensions which frustrate the
preservation of freedom that is the condition of such a life.

The religious sphere: sin, despair, and anxiety

This inadequacy of the aesthetic and ethical spheres, within
Kierkegaard's schema, is not surprising if we regard the religious
sphere as not just the 'highest' or 'best' form of human life, but
as the *grounding* form of human life. The religious sphere is constituted by the individual's relationship to God – by faith – and
from the religious point of view this God-relationship is the
basis of the individual's entire existence: the ground of her relationship to herself, to others, to the world. The possibility of a
religious life is exemplified by Abraham, at least as he is portrayed in *Fear and Trembling*, but this possibility is elucidated in
a more theoretical way in Kierkegaard's later text *The Sickness
Unto Death*, where the pseudonym Anti-Climacus defines the
human self as a spiritual being that is established by and endur-
ingly grounded in God. Invoking the Aristotelian distinction
between potentiality and actuality, Anti-Climacus asserts that
the self *is*, potentially, a relationship to God, but that each individual has the task of becoming such a self – the task of
actualizing her potential. It could thus be said that the aesthetic
and ethical forms of existence represent two ways in which
human beings fail to achieve this self-actualization. However,
this way of putting it is not entirely accurate. The failure to relate
properly and fully to God, even though one essentially *is* this
relation, is what the pseudonym Anti-Climacus, and probably
Kierkegaard too, understands as sin, and according to Christian
teaching every person is a sinner. Living religiously does not
mean that one is not a sinner – or, to put it another way, that one
relates properly and fully to God – but rather that one recognizes
this sinfulness and takes on the task of actualizing the God-relationship, and thus actualizing oneself, with the understanding
that this task cannot be accomplished without divine assistance.
The aesthetic and ethical forms of life are not, then, merely ways
of failing to relate to God and to oneself; rather, they are ways

of avoiding this task: they are ways of attempting to live without God. From a religious point of view, these ways of existing are bound to fail, because the self *is* a relation to God.

The category of sin plays a quiet yet important role in *Fear and Trembling*'s Problem III, and for this reason it is worth attempting to clarify it here. Sin is at once a failure to relate to God, and a failure to realize one's human potential. Sin is possible only because the human being is a spiritual being; only because the human being is constituted by its relationship to God. This means that sin is only intelligible within the religious sphere; it is no coincidence that of all Kierkegaard's pseudonyms it is Anti-Climacus, an overtly Christian writer, who goes furthest in employing the category of sin. The distinction between three spheres of existence that pervades Kierkegaard's pseudonymous writings is ingenious, because on the one hand it brings to light the limitations of the aesthetic and ethical spheres from a religious perspective, while on the other hand it acknowledges that many people do not live in the religious sphere and allows a variety of voices outside this sphere to be heard, thus avoiding the dogmatism of much Christian literature.

When Johannes de silentio announces his intention to consider a series of 'poetic personages' in order to illuminate Abraham's faith, he indicates that he will 'brandish the discipline of despair over them' [77]. This reference to despair is important: Johannes uses the term without explaining it, but again we may turn briefly to *The Sickness Unto Death* in order to clarify its religious significance. Despair is the suffering that attends the failure to be, or to become, oneself: 'Insofar as the self does not become itself, it is not itself; but not to be itself is precisely despair.'[44] According to the religious view of the self as constituted by its relation to God, despair can be regarded as the subjective aspect of sin, as the way in which the condition of sin affects the individual. Anti-Climacus suggests that despair is universal (just as, from a Christian perspective, sin is universal): 'anyone who really knows mankind might say that there is not one single living human being who does not despair a little.'[45] In order to make this claim, the pseudonym has to acknowledge that many people are in despair without being aware of it, but in fact this is a sign not simply of innocence, but of a wilful if unacknowledged attempt to ignore one's own existence, and one's relationship to God. To say that despair is universal is not to imply that everyone despairs in the same way; several different forms of despair are described in *The Sickness Unto Death*. According to Anti-Climacus, the opposite of despair is faith, which is defined as a state in which the self 'rests transparently in the power that established it' – that is to say, in God.

At this point in *Fear and Trembling* Johannes de silentio invokes the concept of anxiety as well as despair, indicating that the literary figures he is about to discuss have in common the experience of anxiety. In Kierkegaard's thought anxiety, like despair, is connected to sin: in 1844 Kierkegaard published, under the pseudonym Vigilius Haufniensis, *The Concept of Anxiety*, which offers a psychological (as opposed to a theological or dogmatic) exploration of the Christian doctrine of sin. According to Vigilius Haufniensis, human beings feel anxious when they become aware of their freedom; and it is this awareness of freedom that makes sin possible in the first place. This means that sinful actions are always performed in a state of anxiety, and, in a sense, it is anxiety that gives rise to each new sin. In *Concluding Unscientific Postscript*, the pseudonym Johannes Climacus offers some remarks about anxiety that indicate its role in *Fear and Trembling*:

> Just as 'fear and trembling' is the state of the teleologically suspended person when God tempts him, so also is anxiety the teleologically suspended person's state of mind in that desperate exemption from fulfilling the ethical. When truth is subjectivity, the inwardness of sin as anxiety in the existing individuality is the greatest possible distance and the most painful distance from the truth.[46]

So, for Kierkegaard's pseudonyms, sin is always accompanied by both anxiety and despair. These two can be distinguished insofar as anxiety is a felt experience, whereas one can be in despair without being conscious of it, which means that it cannot really be described as an experience. One way of explaining the difference between anxiety and despair would be to say that the former is psychological, while the latter is existential. Despair is a state that one is in; it is the subjective corollary of the state of sin, which an individual might be said to be 'in' objectively. Anxiety is an experience that attends each new sin as it freely comes into being. Despair is the suffering that comes from being a sinner, from not being oneself; anxiety is the suffering that accompanies the committing of particular sins.

In Problem III Johannes de silentio indicates that both faith and sin belong to the religious sphere, for these both rest on the idea that each individual is constituted by her relationship to God. Sin is the brokenness of this relationship; faith is the healing of the relationship. That the two are mirror images of one another is implied by the pseudonym's claim that sin 'is not the first immediacy, but a later immediacy' [86], which echoes his assertion earlier in this section that 'faith is not the first immediacy but a later one'. This characterization of faith and sin can be traced back to Paul's Letter to the Romans, where Paul writes that knowledge of sin follows from knowledge of the ethical law: 'sin was indeed in the world before the law, but sin is not reckoned when there is no law' (5: 13); 'What then should we say? That the law is sin? By no means! Yet, if it had not been for the law, I would not have known sin. I would not have known what it is to covet if the law had not said, 'You shall not covet'. But sin, seizing an opportunity in the commandment, produced in me all kinds of covetousness. Apart from the law sin lies dead' (7: 7–8). In this Pauline theology lies one of sources for Kierkegaard's distinction between the three spheres of existence. Ethical demands lift a person out of aesthetic categories, while the religious life involves a response to the failure to live up to the requirements of ethics, by appealing to a power beyond the ethical sphere for help and forgiveness.

When Johannes writes that silence is a paradox that may be 'divine' or 'demonic', he is suggesting that silence, and concealment, belong to both sin and faith. The pseudonym wants to argue that the individual's relationship to God – whether this is lived in the mode of sin, or in the mode of faith – is beyond the ethical sphere, since it is incommensurable with the ethical demand of disclosure.

Five stories – and some Christian teachings

We will now consider in turn the series of literary figures that Johannes de silentio discusses before returning, in the last few pages of Problem III, to Abraham. Most of these characters are couples who are faced with the question of marriage. This suggests parallels with Kierkegaard's relationship to Regine Olsen, and the reader might like to reflect on this possibility as she reads this section of the text. We should also note at this point Johannes de silentio's remark that he carries out his 'investigation' into the issue of concealment and disclosure as it is raised in various literary scenarios 'not so Abraham might become more intelligible by [this investigation], but so that the unintelligibility might become more explicit' [99]. The 'poetic personages' he discusses may exhibit some similarities to Abraham, but unlike Abraham they can all be understood, even if they choose to conceal themselves.

(i) The bridegroom and the bride at Delphi

This story is taken from Aristotle's *Politics*, and Johannes de silentio considers it in order to clarify the difference between ancient and modern forms of concealment. In light of the issue of sin that is brought into play in Problem III, this distinction between the ancient and the modern facilitates a comparison not just between two forms of dramatic art, but between the Greek and the Christian worldviews. This comparison is one that is often made in Kierkegaard's texts, and it reflects the sense of historical development that shapes much nineteenth-century thinking, beginning with Hegelian philosophy.

The bridegroom in this story receives an omen which predicts that he will suffer a misfortune brought about by his marriage; at the last minute he decides not to marry his would-be bride, leaving her waiting in her bridal gown. Johannes de silentio considers several possible responses to the situation in which the bridegroom finds himself: should he remain silent and get married anyway? should he remain silent and not get married? or should he speak? Ethics, for reasons we have already considered, requires the latter decision. The significance of this story is that it serves to highlight the fact that 'everything depends on how the hero stands in relation to the augurs' pronouncement, which in one way or another will be decisive for his life. Is this pronouncement in the public domain or is it a private matter?' [81]. Here, in the ancient Greek milieu, the life-changing pronouncement is public: it is 'not only intelligible to the hero but to everybody, and no private relation to the divine results from it' [81]. Johannes de silentio's point here is that this makes the bridegroom's situation completely different from Abraham's, which does involve a private and incommunicable relationship to God – and that, in this respect as in others, Abraham's story stands as a paradigm for Christian faith. The pseudonym summarizes his analysis as follows: 'If [the bridegroom] wants to speak, then, he can very well do so, for he can make himself intelligible'; by contrast,

> if heaven's will had . . . been brought to his knowledge quite privately, if it had placed itself in an altogether private relationship to him, then we are at the paradox, if, that is, it exists (for my deliberation takes the form of a dilemma); then he could not speak even if he wanted to ever so much. [81]

This anticipates Johannes' repeated claim, later in this section, that 'Abraham *cannot* speak' [100, 101]. God's command to Abraham is private: it is disclosed to Abraham alone, and it is not intelligible to anyone else. In a sense, it is not even intelligible to Abraham. If the bridegroom does not speak, then this is because 'by virtue of being the single individual he wants to be higher than the universal, wants to delude himself with all sorts of fantastic notions about how she will soon forget this sorrow, etc.' [81], and this makes him condemnable from an ethical perspective. In the case of Abraham, however, ethics may condemn him, but it does so without understanding him.

(ii) Agnes and the merman
Unlike the situation of the bridegroom, which stops short of the paradox that characterizes the religious sphere, Johannes de silentio's retelling of the Danish folk legend of Agnes and the merman 'follows along the lines of the demonic' [82]. According to the traditional fable, the merman rises from the sea and lustfully snatches Agnes against her will. The pseudonym, however, 'makes a change' that consists in attributing a will, and an inwardness, to Agnes: she is waiting to be seduced; the merman's seduction elicits her own desire; she willingly follows him to the sea (which, in its wild surging movement, represents sexuality). But when Agnes looks trustingly at the merman, the sea becomes calm, and his sexual power deserts him: 'the merman

collapses . . . he cannot seduce Agnes' [83]. It is at this point that the question of concealment or disclosure is raised: does he explain to Agnes that he was trying to seduce her, which would allow her to forgive him? Then he can marry Agnes. Or does he remain concealed, so that Agnes thinks he does not want her, and let his passion continue to rage, alone and in despair of satisfaction?

Johannes de silentio suggests giving the merman 'a human consciousness' and letting his being a merman 'denote a human pre-existence in whose consequences his life was ensnared' [84]. This signifies, rather opaquely, a Christian gloss on the story: the state of being a merman – that is to say, a seducer 'who cannot faithfully belong to any girl' [83] – represents the state of sin. We have seen that sin can be defined as the failure to relate properly and truthfully to God, and the merman's situation is analogous to this insofar as he cannot relate properly and truthfully to a woman. (This rather obscure characterization of impotence, and of the guilt associated with sexual desire, may provide hints about Kierkegaard's decision not to marry Regine Olsen.) But Agnes's trust in the merman alters him: 'the seducer is crushed, he has submitted to the power of innocence, he can never seduce again'. There is now a choice between 'two forces' which fight within him: 'repentance, and Agnes and repentance' [84].

The term 'repentance' has a specifically Christian significance: according to Matthew's gospel, both John the Baptist and Jesus urged people to 'Repent, for the kingdom of heaven has come near' (Matthew 3: 2 and 4: 17). The Greek word that is translated here as repentance is *metanoia*, which means a change of mind, a change of heart. In this Christian context, it signifies a profound existential reorientation. In the case of the merman, once he has 'repented' of his sin of desire, he 'can never seduce again'. But will he let his desire turn inward, and remain alone (and celibate)? Johannes de silentio indicates that this option of mere repentance is akin to the 'monastic movement' [88] of infinite resignation. Or will the merman repent *and* stay with Agnes, allowing his desire to come into the open within their marriage, and thus allowing it to be transformed into an expression of love and fidelity?

Whichever choice the merman makes, he is, according to Johannes de silentio, beyond the ethical sphere: 'in sin the single individual is already higher, in the direction of the demonic paradox, than the universal, because it is a contradiction for the universal to want to require itself of one who lacks the necessary condition' [86]. In the case of the merman, he 'lacks the necessary condition' to enter into the ethical commitment of marriage since, as a merman, 'he cannot faithfully belong to any girl'. We can perhaps see a little more clearly here how the merman's condition represents the condition of sin, for according to traditional Christian theology – in particular, that formulated by Augustine, to some extent under the influence of Platonic philosophy – sin takes the form of a bondage to selfish desires that prevents the individual from doing what is ethically right. This puts the sinner outside the ethical sphere. However, this does not mean that sin has no ethical consequences; on the contrary, according to Johannes de silentio, sin is beyond the ethical precisely because it renders a person incapable of fulfilling ethical requirements. As we have seen, sin belongs to the religious sphere insofar as it is a rupture of the God-relationship, but it manifests itself in the ethical sphere as immoral conduct. This is because the individual's relationship to God is inseparable from her relationship to herself (since the former is the ground of the latter), and thus a defect in her God-relationship will also be a defect in her self-relationship – that is to say, in her self. In the case of the merman, his inability to be faithful, coupled with his sexual desire, leads him to deceive Agnes. Johannes de silentio calls into question the view that the seduction attempt itself hurts Agnes – in his version of the story, she desires the merman too – but the merman's deception is less morally ambiguous, for as we have seen it is always wrong, from the ethical point of view, to deceive another person.

The pseudonym's discussion of the sinful individual's relationship to the ethical sphere at this point in the text is important and illuminating. When we considered his reflections on the possibility of a teleological suspension of the ethical in Problem I, we saw that this did not involve the rejection or invalidation of the ethical sphere, but a refusal of its autonomy and thus a shift that puts the ethical in relation to something higher than itself. Now we can see more clearly that, from a Christian point of view, it is sin that undermines the autonomy of the ethical sphere. When Johannes de silentio discusses the situation of the merman, he indicates that it is possible for him to return to the ethical sphere – by repenting, and then marrying Agnes – and he describes this movement in terms that echo his earlier descriptions of the 'double movement' of resignation and faith:

> the merman cannot then belong to Agnes without, after having made the infinite movement of repentance, making one more movement, the movement by virtue of the absurd. He can make the movement of repentance by his own strength, but he also uses absolutely all his strength for that and therefore cannot possibly come back and grasp actuality again by his own strength. [87]

The 'infinite movement of repentance', like the infinite movement of resignation, can be performed by the individual on her own, but 'to come back and grasp actuality again' – that is to say, to return to the ethical sphere – is, like the movement of faith, more than she is capable of doing by herself. Here the pseudonym suggests, more explicitly than he has done previously, that faith can actually consist in a return to the ethical sphere, where the individual lives happily and openly among others. But this return to the ethical sphere is possible only after leaving it behind, and recognizing something higher: if the merman marries Agnes, 'nevertheless, he must have recourse to the paradox. For when the single individual by his guilt has come outside the universal, he can only return to it by virtue of having come as the single individual into an absolute relation to the absolute' [86].

But if the individual cannot return to the ethical sphere by her own efforts – if repenting is not enough to accomplish this movement – then how can it happen at all? Johannes de silentio does not provide a direct answer to this question, but perhaps we can construct one on the basis of his retelling of the story of Agnes and the merman. He tells us that the merman is 'saved' by Agnes: he is forgiven, accepted and loved by her. There are Christian overtones here: this forgiveness, acceptance and love in response to human sin is integral to the saving power of Jesus, according to Christian teaching. It is probably not a coincidence that the name Agnes is a form of the Latin word *agnus*, which means lamb; in John's gospel Jesus is described as 'the Lamb of God who takes away the sin of the world', and the phrase 'lamb of

God' (*Agnus Dei*) is often included in the Christian liturgy. But surely the merman must first disclose himself to Agnes in order to receive her love and forgiveness? And isn't this disclosure precisely the return to the ethical sphere? Yet if so, this would suggest that the merman accomplishes this movement by himself, by virtue of his own act of disclosure. This is where faith comes in: the merman 'becomes disclosed and lets himself be saved by Agnes', and this act of disclosure is ventured in the faith that Agnes will accept him as he is. We should note the way activity and passivity belong together in this movement: on the one hand faith involves decision and action on the part of the individual, but on the other hand this is based on her anticipation that salvation will be bestowed by another. As Johannes de silentio suggested in his 'Tribute to Abraham', expectancy is an essential element of faith. Although he does not actually state that the merman needs to have faith in order to disclose himself, the fact that the pseudonym is willing to regard a merman who acts in this way as 'the greatest person I can imagine', and a 'heroic figure', suggests that this merman fits his earlier description of the 'knight of faith'.

Johannes adds in a footnote to his discussion of sin that 'As soon as sin is introduced, ethics runs aground precisely upon repentance, for repentance is the highest ethical expression but precisely as such is the deepest ethical self-contradiction' [86]. Repentance might be regarded as belonging to the ethical sphere – as 'the highest ethical expression' – because the individual can repent by her own efforts, and this is the most she can do. The merman, for example, can restrain his desires and abstain from seducing young girls. But repentance is a response to sin, and as we have seen sin already removes the individual from the ethical sphere insofar as it prevents her from fulfilling its requirements. Furthermore, repentance brings the individual back to the ethical sphere by virtue of something higher than ethics: by virtue of faith in the forgiveness of another. This, it seems, is why repentance is also 'the deepest ethical self-contradiction'. Faith and forgiveness are both beyond ethics because they are beyond reason and justice. The basic principle of justice is that people should be happy in proportion to their moral conduct: this is why, in what is called 'the judicial system', illegal actions are punished in proportion to their severity. Although in practice this judicial system can be complex and ambiguous, in theory it operates according to rational calculations that determine what is fair in relation to each particular crime's causes, context, consequences and precedents. Forgiveness, however, responds to ethical transgression with love instead of punishment; rather than weighing up the severity of the deed and metering out an appropriate response, it responds in an absolute, unconditional way that cannot be the result of rational calculation, and perhaps cannot be rationally defended and justified. For this reason, Johannes de silentio claims that the merman's return to the ethical sphere would occur 'through the paradox' [86], 'by virtue of the absurd' [87].

One more element of the discussion of the story of Agnes and the merman that is worth reflecting on is the pseudonym's attitude towards the monastic life, on the one hand, and the modern age, on the other. In his short discussion of these issues we find both an affirmation of the value of self-knowledge, and a repeated expression of his concern about nineteenth-century attitudes towards the religious life. As we have seen, the decision to repent and remain concealed, as opposed to marrying Agnes, is likened to infinite resignation and described as a 'monastic movement'. Johannes de silentio suggests that in the nineteenth century 'no one enters the monastery', and that this reclusive way of life is held in little regard by his contemporaries. Since withdrawal from the world in order to concentrate on one's relationship with God is, according to Johannes' existential schema, 'lower' than the faith which accomplishes a return to the finite world, he agrees with his contemporaries that 'to enter the monastery is not the highest' form of human life. However, because faith is preceded by a movement of resignation – which is exemplified concretely in the decision to become a monk or nun – Johannes is keen to emphasize the difficulty, and thus the value, of the monastic movement, and to point out that this is beyond the spiritual attainment of his contemporaries, while faith is something even more remote: 'what higher movement has the age discovered since the day it gave up entering the monastery? Is it not a wretched worldly wisdom, prudence, cowardice that sits in the place of honour, cravenly dupes people into thinking they have attained the highest, and slyly prevents them from even attempting lesser things?' [88]. Here, the pseudonym identifies a self-deceptive arrogance as typical of the modern age: people's misguided belief that they have 'attained the highest' prevents them from even taking on the task of resignation, which is not yet faith. This worldly self-deception is contrasted with the rigorous and profound pursuit of self-knowledge that is integral to the monastic life – at least in its ideal form:

> The very idea of taking time upon one's conscience in this way, of giving it time in its sleepless perseverance to explore every single secret thought, so that if the movement is not made every moment by virtue of what is noblest and holiest in a human being, one may with anxiety and horror discover and call forth, if in no other way than through anxiety itself, the dark emotions that still lie concealed in every human life . . . . [88]

In a footnote Johannes de silentio locates this spiritual practice of vigilant self-examination within the Greek philosophical tradition of self-knowledge: he points out that ancient thinkers such as Pythagoras and Socrates took the maxim 'know yourself' as the impetus for their way of life. This indicates that their philosophizing was practical, ethical, rather than just intellectual.

What is interesting about the pseudonym's discussion of the 'monastic movement' is that it brings the theme of concealment and disclosure into the inward, subjective domain. From an ethical point of view, the requirement is to disclose oneself to others; but part of the work of resignation is to overcome the human tendency to self-deception, and to see oneself more clearly. And how can one disclose oneself to others before one has come to know oneself? This suggests that the 'ethical' view that Johannes de silentio attributes to his contemporaries is hypocritical: on the one hand these people regard disclosure as a moral imperative, but on the other hand they are unwilling to look honestly and openly at themselves.

(iii) Sarah and Tobias

Sarah, a character in the apocryphal Book of Tobit, resembles the merman insofar as she is unable to marry. However, whereas the merman, as Johannes de silentio imagines him, sins against Agnes by deceitfully trying to seduce her, and then enters the ethical sphere only after repenting of this sin, Sarah is wholly innocent. An evil demon who loves her will kill any man she marries on the night of their wedding, and so she believes that she is excluded from the happiness of marriage – and thus from the ethical life.

In the original story in the Hebrew bible, Sarah is saved by the angel Raphael. Tobias, who loves Sarah and whose parents want him to marry her, is afraid of doing so, but Raphael advises him to burn the heart and liver of a fish in the bridal chamber on their wedding night in order to repel the demon, and also to pray to God for protection. Tobias takes this advice, and the young couple marry and survive their first night together. Johannes de silentio doesn't mention the use of the smelly fish liver, presumably because this detail, as well as being rather prosaic, detracts from the story's demonstration of faith in God.

The pseudonym remarks that while many poets writing versions of this story would be inclined to focus on Tobias's courage, he thinks that Sarah is the most heroic figure:

> For what love of God it surely takes to let oneself be healed when one is impaired in this way from the beginning without guilt, from the beginning a shipwrecked specimen of a human being! What ethical maturity to take upon oneself the responsibility of permitting the beloved such a daring venture! What humility before another human being! What faith in God that the next moment she would not hate the man to whom she owed everything! [91]

Tobias risks death for the sake of his beloved, but Sarah's achievement is to let herself be healed. As in the story of Agnes and the merman, we can see here the Christian significance of this tale: Tobias displays an active, assertive, human courage, but Sarah has the humble, spiritual courage to allow herself to be acted upon, to receive salvation. Johannes de silentio suggests that Sarah is heroic by virtue of 'the great mystery that it is far more difficult to receive than to give, that is, if one has had courage to do without and did not prove a coward in the hour of need' [91]. That Sarah had the 'courage to do without' suggests that she makes the movement of resignation – giving up on ever being able to marry – before making the further movement of faith, which returns her to the ethical sphere.

Johannes says little of concealment and disclosure in relation to Sarah, although his discussion throughout the rest of Problem III indicates that being married is a form of disclosure. However, he suggests that if a man were in Sarah's position then 'the demonic [and its concealment] is immediately at hand' [91], since it would be harder for a man to endure the pity with which others would view an innocent person in such a situation. In order to avoid the 'humiliation' of being pitied, a man might 'choose the demonic, shut himself up in himself, and speak in the way a demonic nature speaks in secret' [92], preferring to see a succession of young wives die on their wedding night rather than open himself to the salvation that Sarah receives. Johannes' point appears to be that men find it more difficult than women to bear pity, presumably because this places them in a position of weakness that is opposed to the traditionally masculine virtue of strength. But of course, the ability to endure pity and humiliation is a sign of strength and courage – a 'humble courage' that, in light of Jesus' endurance of the humiliation of being crucified, and the disciples' endurance of persecution, might be regarded as a specifically Christian virtue. Johannes de silentio seems to think that this kind of courage comes more naturally to women than to men, although of course he suggests that Abraham exemplifies the 'paradoxical and humble courage' [41] of faith.

(iv) Gloucester

In discussing the character of Gloucester from Shakespeare's *Richard III*, Johannes de silentio continues his reflection on this theme of pity. Gloucester is physically deformed after being born prematurely (like Kierkegaard, who had a curved spine and a limp), and this makes him feel unable to attract a woman: 'I, that am rudely stamp'd and want love's majesty / To strut before a wanton ambling nymph'.[47] Gloucester's nature is twisted by his resentment at being humiliated, so that his response to his physical defect manifests itself as a moral or spiritual defect: 'I, that am curtail'd of this fair proportion, / Cheated of feature by dissembling Nature, / Deform'd, unfinish'd, sent before my time / Into this breathing world scarce half made up – / And that so lamely and unfashionable / That dogs bark at me as I halt by them.'[48] Again, the character of Gloucester is invoked in order to make the point that he is beyond the universal, incapable of

entering into the community on account of a defect that is
beyond his control:

> Natures like Gloucester's cannot be saved by mediating them
> into an idea of society. Ethics really only makes a fool of
> them, just as it would be a mockery of Sarah if it were to say
> to her: 'Why do you not express the universal and get mar-
> ried?' Such natures are thoroughly in the paradox, and they
> are by no means less perfect than other human beings, only
> either lost in the demonic paradox or saved in the divine para-
> dox . . . The fact of originally being placed outside the
> universal by nature or historical circumstance is the begin-
> ning of the demonic, for which the individual, however, is not
> personally to blame. [93]

It is important to note that Johannes de silentio states that
Gloucester is 'by no means less perfect than other human beings',
implying that those who are physically normal share Gloucester's moral deformity. This suggests that his discussion of
Gloucester – and of Sarah – alludes to a condition of sin that all
human beings share.

Even more important, however, is the pseudonym's remark
here that these characters are 'not personally to blame' for their
condition. Is he suggesting here that, analogously, from a Christian point of view people are not personally to blame for their
sin? This would go against the traditional theological position,
according to which individuals *are* personally culpable for their
sinful condition – even though they are born into it – since they
are free, and thus that they are in need of the personal liberation
from sin offered through Jesus Christ. In fact, Johannes de silentio has no intention of challenging this conventional Christian
teaching; on the contrary, he is attempting to reinforce it. All the
literary figures considered in Problem III are different in some
way from Abraham, and in the case of Sarah and Gloucester
this difference lies precisely in the fact that they are prevented
from entering the ethical by circumstances for which they are
not responsible (although actually there is more ambiguity in
Gloucester's case, since he is responsible for his own reaction to
his deformity), while Abraham puts himself beyond the ethical
by means of his own actions. And it is on this basis that

Abraham's faith – his ability to return to family life, to resume his ethical duties – is unintelligible, whereas figures such as Sarah and the merman have a faith that is great, absurd, paradoxical and so on, yet still more accessible than that of Abraham. It is thus Abraham's situation that anticipates the Christian's situation, and it is thus *his* faith that, according to Johannes de silentio's analysis, offers a paradigm for specifically Christian faith.

(v) Faust and Margaret

According to the legend of Faust – which has been the basis of several literary works, including a tragic drama by the German poet and thinker Goethe – the hero sells his soul to the devil, Mephistopheles, in return for youth, knowledge and pleasure. We might expect Johannes de silentio to use this story to depict a wilful flight from the religious sphere to the aesthetic sphere, but in fact he changes the traditional narrative so that Faust becomes 'the doubter par excellence' who has 'a sympathetic nature' [95]. This Faust does not make a pact with the devil, but continues to struggle with the doubts – about the immortality of his soul, about the salvation promised by God – that underlie the legendary figure's decision to sell his soul. Johannes de silentio's Faust conceals his doubt for the sake of 'the universal', in order not to alarm others and undermine their beliefs: 'He keeps silent . . . he tries as much as possible to walk in step with other people, but what goes on inside him is consumed internally, and in this way he makes himself a sacrifice to the universal' [96]. This emphasis on the inwardness of Faust's doubt indicates that he presents another example of an interiority that is higher than the ethical sphere. As a doubter, Faust 'hungers just as much for the daily bread of life as for the nourishment of the spirit' [96]: that is to say, he wants to belong to the ethical, to marry, to fit in with other people, but is unable to do so, just as he is unable to maintain a faithful relationship to God. In the traditional legend, Faust seduces Margaret, an innocent young girl; in Johannes de silentio's version he falls in love with Margaret, and although he wishes to marry her he conceals his love from her.

From an ethical point of view, Faust is wrong to conceal his doubt, even though he does this for the sake of other people: 'If he keeps silent, then ethics condemns him, for it says: "You must acknowledge the universal, and you acknowledge it precisely by speaking, and you dare not pity the universal."' [97]. Here we find the same ethical reasoning as was presented earlier in this section: because motivations are difficult or even impossible to establish with certainty, there is always the possibility that a decision to remain concealed is really for one's own sake, and not for the sake of others. In the case of Faust, it may be that he is too proud to admit his doubts:

> If he keeps silent on his own responsibility, then he may well act magnanimously, but he will add a little temptation to his other pain, for the universal will constantly torment him and say: 'You should have spoken. How will you find out for certain that it was not after all a hidden pride that prompted your resolve?' [98]

Having articulated this ethical side of his dilemma, Johannes de silentio presents the other, religious side: 'However, if the doubter can become the single individual who as the particular stands in an absolute relation to the absolute, then he can receive an authorization for his silence' [98].

The pseudonym's main purpose in discussing Faust seems to be to give himself an opportunity to return to the theme of doubt that he introduced in the Preface to *Fear and Trembling*, and in particular to his critique of certain contemporary thinkers who profess to have doubted everything. In his Preface, we may recall, Johannes de silentio targets the Danish theologian Martensen, who repeatedly used the Latin phrase *de omnibus dubitandum est* ('everything should be doubted') in his writings and lectures, and who is associated not only with the view that philosophy should begin with doubt, but with the aspiration to 'go further' than this doubt. In the present section of the text, the pseudonym remarks that 'my Faust . . . does not belong with those scholarly doubters who doubt one hour every semester at the lectern but otherwise can do everything else, which in fact they do without the assistance of spirit or by virtue of spirit' [97]: as in his Preface, he is suggesting here that the doubt professed by Martensen is inauthentic, shallow, merely verbal, or at best merely theoretical, and he contrasts this with Faust's doubt, which affects his whole life, even preventing him from marrying the woman he loves. For Johannes de silentio, doubt and faith belong together, for they both concern the individual's relationship to God. If faith is genuine and meaningful, then it must have contended with doubt, and continually contend with it. This means that the value and significance of faith is tied to the depth and intensity of the spiritual trial brought about by the experience of doubt. For this reason, the pseudonym's emphasis on the greatness of Faust's doubt is part of his attempt to raise the value of faith in the face of those modern thinkers – particularly Hegelians such as Martensen – who, he suggests, belittle the task of religious faith by regarding it as easier and less important than the philosophical pursuit of knowledge.

As a transition between discussing these various literary figures and returning to the story of Abraham, Johannes de silentio offers a few remarks about the New Testament, indicating that the Christian scriptures contain passages that commend silence. The pseudonym may have in mind here occasions where Jesus, having healed sick people, tells them not to speak of what has happened (see, for example, Matthew 8:4, 9:30, and Mark 1:34, 1:44). However, he focuses on Jesus' instruction that religious practices should remain private, concealed from others:

> The Sermon on the Mount says: 'When you fast, anoint your head and wash your face, so that people will not see you fasting.' This passage testifies directly to the fact that subjectivity is incommensurable with actuality, even that it has a right to deceive. [98]

For Johannes de silentio, this religious teaching suggests that the ethical sphere may be disrupted by a concealment that is higher than that which belongs to the aesthetic sphere. He claims that this presents a challenge to contemporary Christians, since 'people in our age do not want to know anything about [a movement] that has its rationale in subjectivity being higher than actuality' [98] – that is to say, in the particular individual being elevated above the ethical-as-universal. Again, the pseudonym is here identifying and criticizing a specifically modern insistence on the autonomy and completeness of a rational, merely-human ethical domain, and he is suggesting that even though this ethical sphere is thought to be synonymous with the Christian community, it in fact implicitly signals a rejection of Christian teaching. The general form of the dilemma that Johannes de silentio has been presenting to his readers throughout the three 'Problems' here takes on a specifically Christian expression: *either* recognize nothing higher than the ethical demand for disclosure, and thus refuse Jesus' teaching; *or* recognize a higher form of inwardness that can be religiously justified in keeping silent, and thus remain true to the Christian gospel.

'Abraham cannot speak'

As we have seen, Johannes de silentio undertakes his aesthetic, dialectical discussion of the issue of concealment and disclosure in order to illuminate the singular 'unintelligibility' of Abraham's decision to keep silent about his sacrifice of Isaac. Returning at the end of Problem III to the story of Abraham, the pseudonym repeats his earlier insistence that he cannot understand Abraham, but can only admire him, and he asserts that

> none of the stages described [through the examples of literary figures] contained an analogy to Abraham; they were only developed in order that, while being shown within their own spheres, they could indicate . . . the boundary of the unknown region at the point of variation. [99]

In other words, Abraham cannot be understood, but clarifying the difference between his situation and those of other characters helps to show us precisely where the mystery lies. It is clear that Abraham is neither an aesthetic hero, who keeps silent to prevent another individual from suffering, nor an ethical 'tragic hero', who openly sacrifices himself for the sake of the universal. Abraham acts 'for his own sake and for God's sake' – neither for Isaac, nor for the universal, which in any case turn out to coincide since Isaac, as the progenitor of the future generations of Israel, represents the whole community.

Johannes de silentio suggests that the closest approximation to an analogy to Abraham would be 'the paradox of sin' [99], which as we have seen is dramatized in his version of the story of Agnes and the merman. There, the pseudonym argued that sin puts the individual outside the ethical sphere, since it renders her incapable of fulfilling the requirements of ethics; he also suggested that such an individual could return to the ethical sphere once she had repented and been forgiven. But in the case of Abraham, unlike in that of the merman, there is no defect in his nature that prevents him from fulfilling his ethical duty to another person: his willingness to kill Isaac in obedience to God is simply a matter of choice. Whereas the merman seems to be in a kind of bondage to sin, from which he cannot be released without Agnes, Abraham is free. According to the pseudonym, 'the paradox of sin . . . cannot explain Abraham and is itself far easier to explain than Abraham' [99].

So, Abraham's silence is not aesthetically defensible, and no silence is ethically defensible. He is not excluded from the ethical sphere by an original sinful condition for which he is not responsible; he is capable of responding to God's command in any way he chooses. In sacrificing Isaac, he chooses to put himself outside the ethical – not aesthetically, for another's sake, but for his own sake. The essential point at which the entire analysis of Problem III culminates is the claim that Abraham '*cannot* speak' [100, 101], in the sense that he cannot make himself intelligible to another person. He cannot *explain* his intention to sacrifice Isaac. Of course, he might tell Sarah, Eliezer or Isaac that he intends to obey God's command 'because it is a spiritual trial' – a test of his faith; he might then try to console them in their distress by saying that he loves Isaac more than anything else, more than himself. But then they could respond by asking, 'Why do you want to do this then? After all, you can let it be'. Why can't Abraham decide to fail the spiritual trial, when no consequence of this could be worse than the death of Isaac by his own hand? The fact that there is no intelligible answer to this question would expose the unintelligibility of Abraham's earlier utterances. Abraham cannot explain how his sacrifice of Isaac can be an expression of his love for his son:

> Speak he cannot; he speaks no human language. Even if he understood all the languages of the world, even if those loved ones also understood them, he still cannot speak – he speaks in a divine language, he speaks in tongues . . . At any moment Abraham can stop, he can repent the whole thing as a temptation; then he can speak, then everybody can understand him [this is the movement that the merman makes when he repents and returns to the ethical] – but then he is no longer Abraham. Abraham *cannot* speak, for he cannot say that

which would explain everything (i.e. so that it is intelligible), that it is a trial, of a sort, mind you, in which the ethical is the temptation. Anyone so situated is an emigrant from the sphere of the universal [101].

Johannes de silentio emphasizes the 'distress and anxiety' of Abraham's situation, cut off from the universal and from those he loves. Whereas the tragic hero has the double consolation of knowing that she has given others the opportunity to dissuade her from her actions, and of being able to explain her choice in terms of the ethical-as-universal and then weep along with those she loves, sharing their distress, Abraham has to bear 'the frightful responsibility of solitude' [101].

More than this, however, Abraham's decision to sacrifice Isaac is only one aspect of his 'double movement'; he also makes the movement of faith, believing that 'surely it will not happen, or if it does the Lord will give me a new Isaac, namely by virtue of the absurd' [101]. This, argues the pseudonym, is as unintelligible as his renunciation of Isaac: Abraham cannot explain his enduring expectation that he will, as God has promised, be the father of a great nation, just as he cannot explain why he intends to sacrifice Isaac. Indeed, these two movements – of resignation and faith – seem to be incompatible with one another, so that keeping both in play together is paradoxical and inexplicable.

Abraham's 'final word'

Having argued forcefully that Abraham cannot speak, Johannes de silentio turns to consider his response to Isaac's question, 'where is the lamb for a burnt-offering?' Abraham's reply that 'God will provide the lamb for the burnt-offering' is, according to the pseudonym, essential to the story: 'Without this word the whole incident would lack something; if it had been different, then everything would perhaps dissolve into confusion' [102]. There is, Johannes claims, a 'necessity of Abraham having to fulfil himself at the final moment, not by silently drawing the knife, but by having a word to say' [104]. So, does Abraham speak, or doesn't he? Can he speak, or can't he?

As we have seen, Luther regards Abraham's reply as an evasive response that aims to prevent Isaac from suffering longer than he needs to. In the light of Johannes de silentio's discussion of aesthetic and ethical concealment, however, we can see that this would be an 'aesthetic' form of concealment that does not stand up to ethical scrutiny. Luther's interpretation does not enable us to regard Abraham's secrecy as distinctively religious.

Johannes de silentio suggests that Abraham's reply to Isaac holds together the contradiction between silence and speech, just as his conduct holds together his resignation and his faith in a 'double movement'. Abraham 'does not say anything, and in this form he says what he has to say' [104]. Indeed, Abraham's words paradoxically express the inexpressible 'double movement'. Johannes' explanation of why this is the case is not especially clear, but I think his interpretation makes sense, at least in the context of his reading of the story as a whole. Abraham says nothing about God's command and his intention to obey it by sacrificing Isaac, which would be the disclosure that Isaac's question calls for, and which ethically is required. But saying to Isaac, 'Actually, you are going to be the sacrifice today' would not be an adequate response, for this would not communicate Abraham's contradictory belief that Isaac will nevertheless be restored. Abraham's reply that 'God will provide the lamb for the burnt-offering' is ambiguous, since on the one hand it signifies the fact that Isaac – a gift which God has indeed provided – is to be the sacrificial 'lamb'; yet on the other hand it expresses Abraham's expectation that God will provide a lamb, and thus restore Isaac to him. 'From this one sees the double movement in Abraham's soul' [105], writes Johannes de silentio. In other words, Abraham truthfully expresses both his resignation and his faith, yet without revealing to Isaac his intention to kill him. Isaac cannot understand his father's words, because he cannot detect in them the movement of resignation which they do, in fact, articulate, albeit indirectly.

As we have seen, Luther thinks that Abraham could have articulated directly the contradiction between God's promise and command – and, indeed, that he did so – and that Isaac would have understood it. Johannes de silentio does not consider this possibility, for he is unwilling to attribute to Abraham words that are not in the biblical text. However, the pseudonym's interpretation of Abraham's 'final word' as it is recorded in Genesis echoes Luther's imaginative reconstruction of the conversation between father and son at the altar, insofar as it involves the truthful expression of a contradiction, a paradox.

Johannes de silentio emphasizes that it is impossible to interpret Abraham's words as indicating his uncertainty or indecisiveness about the outcome of the sacrifice:

> given the way the task is placed upon Abraham, he himself indeed must act; so at the decisive moment he must know what he himself will do, and consequently he must know that Isaac is to be sacrificed. If he has not known this for certain, then he has not made the movement of resignation [let alone the further movement of faith]. Then his words are certainly not untrue, but he is still very far from being Abraham, he is more insignificant than a tragic hero; indeed, he is an irresolute man who cannot make up his mind one way or another and for that reason always speaks in riddles. But a vacillator like that is just a parody of the knight of faith [105].

Abraham's words conceal from his son his intention to kill him at God's command; at the same time, this concealment expresses, openly and clearly, the truth of Abraham's faith. Even though Johannes de silentio insists that 'his silence is not at all to save Isaac' [99], the effect of Abraham's words *is* to preserve Isaac's faith both in him, and in God. At the end of Problem III, Johannes de silentio declares that Abraham's achievement consists in his remaining 'true to his love', and we can see that Abraham's love for both God and his son is reflected in his reply to Isaac, insofar as the 'double movement' of resignation and faith that his enigmatic words express is filled with, fuelled by, both of these loves. Abraham remains true, unfathomably, to these two loves in the face of what is, humanly speaking, an irresolvable contradiction between them.

Johannes de silentio's interpretation of Abraham's 'final word' to Isaac has been analysed by various commentators in ways that diverge considerably from my discussion here. In order to indicate the kinds of issues raised by this section of *Fear and Trembling*, I will briefly outline a couple of alternative responses to it, which differ as much from one another as from my own reading. The first response, presented by Daniel Conway in a recent article entitled 'Abraham's Final Word', is very critical of Johannes de silentio – and, implicitly, of Kierkegaard too. Conway rightly points out that Abraham's final words before the sacrifice is called off are not

'God will provide a lamb for the burnt-offering', but 'Here I am' (Genesis 22: 11), which he says in response to the angel who calls his name. According to Conway, this undermines Johannes de silentio's entire reading of the story of Abraham's sacrifice: he claims that the pseudonym deliberately 'avoids' the final 'Here I am', which 'in fact announces Abraham's decision to disobey his God.'[49] Conway summarizes his own reading as follows:

> Johannes has good reason *not* to extend Problem III to include an examination of the events that transpired at the sacrificial summit of Mount Moriah. Doing so would have obliged him to consider, and perhaps to admit, that the Abraham who released Isaac had either lost his faith or never possessed it in the first place . . . Although Johannes does not admit as much, he is thus obliged to treat the story of the *Akedah* as if it were *two* stories, featuring *two* Abrahams. The first story concerns the knight of faith whose 'final word' is recorded at Genesis 22: 8 . . . The second story concerns Abraham 'the vacillator', who aborts the commanded sacrifice and therefore disobeys his God.[50]

I think this is a misguided reading of both *Fear and Trembling* and Genesis 22, although Conway is not the first commentator to have argued that Abraham's willingness to listen to the angel who tells him to sacrifice a ram instead of Isaac qualifies his obedience to God's previous command.[51] Although it is literally true to say that Abraham's reply to Isaac's question is not in fact his final word, we should remember that in Problem III Johannes de silentio is concerned with the question of Abraham's communication with Isaac – and Sarah, and Eliezer – and more generally with the possibility of human communication within the religious sphere. Johannes de silentio is interested in Abraham's final word *to Isaac*. In this context, then, what Abraham says to God or to the angel is not especially relevant. And Conway's claim that Abraham is a 'vacillator' who 'aborts' the sacrifice and thus 'disobeys' God seems to ignore the fact that Abraham is ordered not to kill Isaac by 'the angel *of the Lord*', God's messenger.

The second interpretation of Abraham's 'final word' that I would like to consider is less discordant with *Fear and Trembling*, although perhaps it still pushes the text too far. Stephen

Mulhall advocates a strongly Christian reading, according to which Abraham's reference to a 'lamb' to be provided by God indicates Jesus, the 'Lamb of God', who will be sacrificed on Golgotha. For Mulhall, Johannes de silentio's 'hints' about the Christian significance of Abraham's faith point to a 'prophetic dimension', to which Abraham himself is oblivious:

> When [Abraham] states that 'God will provide himself a lamb for the burnt offering, my son,' what he predicts turns out to be literally false, since God provides a ram rather than a lamb for the sacrifice on Mount Moriah; but it remains prophetically true, since God later provides the Lamb of God . . . Abraham's ordeal prefigures the Atonement—the Incarnation, Passion, Death, and Resurrection of Christ, God's sacrifice of himself to overcome human sinfulness. God's substitution of a ram for Isaac thus prefigures his substitution of his own Son for human offspring . . . and Isaac's unquestioning submission to his father's will (his carrying of the wood of his own immolation to the place of sacrifice) prefigures Christ's submission to his own Father.[52]

This is an interesting reading of Genesis 22, and the parallels between this narrative and the story of Jesus' death are indeed striking. However, I am not convinced that this reading is implicit in *Fear and Trembling*, and it is certainly not required in order to make sense of the discussion of Abraham's 'final word' presented in Problem III. The Christian significance that Johannes de silentio finds in the story of Abraham is related not, I think, to the content of Christian faith (as Mulhall's interpretation suggests), but to the form of that faith. So, for example, Abraham's expectation that 'God will provide . . . etc.' – that is to say, that Isaac will be restored to him – prefigures the Christian's expectation of forgiveness, of eternal life, of gifts from God, and so on. It is not that Abraham and the Christian expect the same thing, but that in each case expectancy is central to faith. And moreover, in both cases – according to Johannes de silentio – this expectancy is contrary to reason, and relates specifically to the faithful person's singular, individual existence. In these ways, and in others, there is a structural or formal analogy between the faith of Abraham and the faith of the Christian. What is in question in *Fear and Trembling* is the kind of subjectivity that enters into the God-relationship, rather than the historical content of Christian belief. This is borne out, I think, by Kierkegaard's later remark, *apropos* of *Fear and Trembling*, that

> Abraham is called the father of faith because he has the formal qualifications of faith, believing against the understanding, although it has never occurred to the Christian Church that Abraham's faith had the content of Christian faith which relates essentially to a later historical event.[53]

Of course, Mulhall is not claiming that Abraham's 'final word' has a Christian content in the sense that the Hebrew patriarch is actually expressing a belief about the future events that will be recorded in the New Testament. But nevertheless, Mulhall's emphasis on this Christian content does not, in my view, reflect Johannes de silentio's main concerns.

'What did Abraham achieve? He remained true to his love'

The pseudonym's closing remarks in this section of the text mark an end not just to Problem III, but to his analysis of the story of Abraham. His claim that Abraham 'remained true to his love' lies at the heart of *Fear and Trembling*, for this indicates a certain conception of truth according to which Abraham might, perhaps, be saved from condemnation as a murderer. This truth is lived rather than known; it is a kind of truth that belongs to love, as opposed to that which belongs to rational knowledge; it is the truth of faith as opposed to the truth of philosophy. Johannes de silentio asserts not that Abraham *knows* the truth, but that he *is true*. The distinction between the truth of life and the truth of knowledge remains implicit in *Fear and Trembling*, but it is clearly invoked in the opening paragraph of its companion text, *Repetition*. There, the pseudonym Constantin Constantius claims that a new category of truth – 'repetition' – should replace the Greek view that truth is reached through a process of recollection: 'Just as [the Greeks] taught that all *knowing* is recollecting, modern philosophy will teaching that all *life* is a repetition.'[54]

Another feature of the kind of truth that is at stake in Abraham's 'remaining true to his love' is that it involves being true *to* something. Such truth is relational; it signifies faithfulness, fidelity, commitment – to God, to another person, or perhaps to oneself. As the case of Abraham demonstrates, this fidelity is the form of true human love as well as of true religious faith: according to Johannes de silentio's interpretation of the biblical narrative, Abraham is as true to his love for Isaac as he is to his love for God. This suggests that *Fear and Trembling* is concerned as much with the individual's relationships to other people as with her relationship to God. It also suggests, more particularly, that Kierkegaard found in reading the story of Abraham a way to think through the question of his own fidelity to Regine Olsen, as well as the question of what it means to become a Christian. For Kierkegaard himself, it seems, these two questions were inseparable, and as we have seen he regarded his break with Regine as a failure of faith.

Moreover, it is not just that Abraham *is* true, but that he *remains* true. This indicates the constancy of fidelity: throughout his writings Kierkegaard emphasizes the fact that human beings are temporal, always in a process of becoming, and this means that the task of living truthfully is one that stretches through time. This is why Constantin Constantius suggests that lived truth takes the form of repetition: in order to *remain* true to something, or to someone, through time, one must continually repeat one's commitment to this other. In *Fear and Trembling*, Abraham's three-day journey to Mount Moriah expresses this repetition in a concrete way, for every step he takes repeats his 'double movement' of giving Isaac up and expecting to receive him back from God. This idea of repetition is also integral to the logic of the gift, which is an important theme in this text. Isaac is a gift from God in the first place; having received Isaac once, Abraham gives him up – by preparing to sacrifice him – and then receives him back 'a second time' [7]. Abraham 'holds on to' Isaac only because he is given to him repeatedly; the endurance through time of his relationship to his son is grounded in a continual renewal of the gift from God. For his part, Abraham has to repeatedly renounce Isaac in order to receive him back again, for a gift can be given only to someone who does not yet possess it. And the giving of a gift is an expression of love. Abraham can receive the gift only because he believes that God loves him: this, as we have found in earlier sections of *Fear and Trembling*, is the content of his faith.

'There was no one who could understand Abraham. And yet what did he achieve? He remained true to his love.' It is this lived, relational, temporal truth of love that Johannes de silentio wants to place higher than the ethical sphere. According to the pseudonym, the example of Abraham shows that in being true to one's love an individual may transgress ethical requirements, and may not be explicable to others – not even to those to whom one is being true. Such a situation, the pseudonym makes clear, is full of lonely, anxious suffering, and he repeats at the end of Problem III that he lacks the courage to speak or to act as Abraham did. We thus find in Johannes de silentio's idea of 'remaining true to one's love' all the qualities of the heart that were first discussed in his 'Preliminary Outpouring': it is a truth of love, attended by suffering, which demands courage and endures through passionate commitment.

The concealed suffering of faith is caused by love – by the pain of hurting and losing the beloved – but it is also dissolved by love:

> whoever loves God needs no tears, no admiration, he forgets the suffering in the love . . . so completely . . . that there would not be the slightest trace of his pain afterwards if God himself did not remember it; for he sees in secret and knows the distress and counts the tears and forgets nothing. [106]

The ethical sphere is transgressed and unsettled by a 'secret' that is shared only with God. But on the other hand, from a religious point of view it is the inward, private truth belonging to love that underlies the public truthfulness which ethics demands; and where this latter kind of truthfulness is possible, its realization will be precisely the expression of one person's love for another. Johannes de silentio is suggesting that love is higher than the moral law. This does not mean that love cannot provide a motivation to act in accordance with the moral law, but it leaves open the possibility of a conflict, in which the law may be suspended. However, the pseudonym ends his discussion of Abraham with a final formulation of the dilemma that presents this idea in the form of a question to the reader: 'Either there is then a paradox, that the single individual as the particular stands in an absolute relation to the absolute, or Abraham is lost' [106].

EPILOGUE

Abraham is not mentioned in the Epilogue to *Fear and Trembling*. Together with the Preface, this closing section provides a frame that contextualizes Johannes de silentio's re-telling and analysis of the story of Abraham. Two of the key ideas that were introduced in the Preface are repeated here at the end of the book: the concern about the declining value of faith in the modern age, and the attack on the ambition to 'go further' than faith that is associated especially with the Hegelian theologian Martensen. The reader may look back to my commentary on the Preface for a discussion of these themes.

Returning in his Epilogue to the comparison between the declining value of faith in the world of spirit and falling prices in the world of commerce, which he made at the very beginning of *Fear and Trembling*, Johannes de silentio suggests that something needs to be done to raise the value of faith. It makes sense to regard his own interpretation of the story of Abraham as precisely such a strategic intervention: by accentuating the difficulty of understanding Abraham's faith, and of accomplishing it, he puts to his reader the question not just of whether she has already attained faith, but of whether she is even capable of attaining it. The pseudonym claims that 'the present generation [is] perfected in the art of self-deception' [107], and that the problem of the declining value of faith has to be approached with an 'honesty' and 'earnestness' that 'calls attention to the tasks . . . that keeps the tasks young, beautiful, delightful to look upon, and inviting to all, yet also difficult and inspiring for the noble-minded (for the noble nature is inspired only by the difficult)' [107]. The 'task' that Johannes de silentio is concerned with here is the pursuit of what, he claims, is highest in human life: the 'passions' of love and faith. This goes against the view, shared by many philosophers, that reason, not passion, is the most essential aspect of the human being, and that the pursuit of truth through rational thought is the highest human endeavour.

In his Epilogue Johannes de silentio sets up an opposition between two different conceptions of movement. On the one hand, there is a movement of progression, which involves 'going further than faith', and which is associated with Hegel's progressive, developmental interpretation of history. The pseudonym wants to call this kind of movement into question, in part because he believes that it undermines the value of faith. On the other hand, there is the movement that constitutes the task of faith: this is not a move-ment of progression, but an inward, deepening movement that does not go anywhere – and it certainly does not go beyond faith – but is, rather, a movement on the spot, a movement of continual repetition. Johannes de silentio insists that with respect to the task of faith, 'every generation begins primitively, has no other task than each previous generation, and advances no further ... Thus no generation has learned to love from another' [107]. Learning to love – which constitutes the task of faith – is a lifelong project, 'always sufficient for a lifetime' [108]. According to the pseudonym, faith is not a goal that one attains and then rests in:

> the one who has come to faith ... does not come to a stand-still in faith. Indeed, he would be shocked if someone said this to him, just as the lover would feel indignant if one said he had come to a standstill in love, for he would answer, 'I am not standing still at all since I have my life in it.' Yet he gets no further, nor to something else .... [109]

To live is to be in a continual process of becoming, and so to 'have one's life in' something means to return to it and to renew it repeatedly, day after day, and, indeed, moment by moment. For example, loving another person is not something that is accomplished once and for all: one continues to love only insofar as this love is kept alive by being repeatedly felt and expressed.

The final paragraph of the Epilogue invokes, as an example of the supposedly progressive movement of 'going further', the transition in ancient Greek thought from Heraclitus' view that everything is in motion to the Eleatic philosophers' denial of the reality of movement. Plato, in his dialogue *Cratylus*, reports that 'likening the things that are to the flowing of a river, [Heraclitus] says that "you cannot step twice into the same river"'[55]; the Eleatics, led by Parmenides, argued that movement is an illusion, and that everything that exists is unchanging. This is not an example chosen at random, for, as we have seen, the question of movement that apparently polarized these ancient philosophers is echoed in Kierkegaard's critique of Hegelian philosophy. Johannes de silentio's brief discussion of the pre-Socratic debates about motion and change at the end of *Fear and Trembling* is taken up by the pseudonym Constantin Constantius in the opening sentences of *Repetition*: 'When the Eleatics denied motion, Diogenes, as everyone knows, came forward as an opponent. He literally did come forward, because he did not say a word but merely paced back and forth a few times, thereby assuming that he had sufficiently refuted them.'[56] Thus *Repetition* begins where *Fear and Trembling* leaves off – with the question of movement.

The ancient Greek philosophers did not understand how movement could be possible. If, as Heraclitus thought, everything is in flux – not just everything out in the world, but everything within one's own body and mind – then how can there be a self at all? And how can anything be true or false? If, as the Eleatics believed, movement and change are unreal, then how are we to make sense of our experience? How can we gain access to truth if the way things appear to us is an illusion? These are difficult philosophical questions, as you will no doubt find if you try to think them through and answer them.

Kierkegaard was struggling to make sense of such questions, and *Fear and Trembling* articulates this struggle. For him, the most pressing questions were existential and ethical, rather than metaphysical: how can one be true to another, when things are changing – including oneself? How can one make a promise that commits one's future, unknown self to the unknowable future self of another? How can one marry, and have children? Is it possible to do these human things without self-deception? What kind of change does a person undergo when she learns to love – another person, God, perhaps herself? It is not clear that Kierkegaard found answers to such questions. Johannes de silentio's confession that he does not understand Abraham perhaps expresses Kierkegaard's inability to grasp how to make the movements that, he claims, constitute Abraham's faith. Maybe this also expresses, more positively, his recognition that one learns to make the movements only by making them – by leaping into an unknown future. One conclusion that is suggested in the Epilogue to *Fear and Trembling* is that such things cannot be learned by reading books, which would enable each generation to build on the knowledge of previous ones; that each person has to learn how to love for herself, through existing, through suffering, through failing to love and finding the courage to begin the task again.

CHAPTER 3

RECEPTION AND INFLUENCE

Fear and Trembling stands as a relatively recent contribution to a long Judeo-Christian tradition of commentary on the story of the Akedah,[1] but its reconstruction and analysis of Abraham's faith has exerted an enduring influence within philosophy as well as theology. The themes and ideas developed by Johannes de silentio – and also by other Kierkegaardian pseudonyms, in texts such as *Either/Or, Repetition, The Concept of Anxiety, Philosophical Fragments, Concluding Unscientific Postscript* and *The Sickness Unto Death* – have provided some of the conceptual building-blocks for the 'existentialist' tradition that came to dominate European philosophy in the mid-twentieth century. For example, the French writer Albert Camus took up the concept of 'the absurd' that Johannes de silentio uses to characterize Abraham's faith, and applied it to human existence as a whole. Jean-Paul Sartre, as we have already seen, incorporated Kierkegaard's emphasis on decision into his own philosophy – and more recently, the French thinker Alain Badiou has made a Kierkegaardian concept of decision central to his political philosophy of subjectivity. In Germany, Martin Heidegger's influential early work *Being and Time* (1927) drew on the themes of anxiety, repetition and awareness of mortality that we have found in *Fear and Trembling*. All of these philosophers – to whom the term 'existentialist' might be more or less loosely applied – take Kierkegaardian concepts out of their Christian context and develop them within an atheistic framework. But the influence of existentialism is also evident in the work of several twentieth-century theologians, such as Paul Tillich and Rudolph Bultmann.

British philosophy at the beginning of the twentieth century was more receptive to continental thinkers such as Hegel and Bergson than to existentialism, and as it developed over the course of the century it came to be dominated by pragmatism, positivism, and a focus on logical analysis. In fact, Bertrand Russell's classic *History of Western Philosophy*, first published in

1946, makes no mention of Kierkegaard; bizarrely, Russell follows his discussion of Hegel with a chapter devoted to the poet Lord Byron. Perhaps Russell shared Heidegger's view that Kierkegaard was a religious thinker rather than a philosopher. However, Kierkegaard's thought had a profound influence on Ludwig Wittgenstein, who himself remains one of the most influential modern thinkers within British philosophy. Wittgenstein was not a Christian, but he had a religious or spiritual temperament, and his reflections on Christianity are distinctly Kierkegaardian. In his *Lectures on Religious Belief* he echoes Johannes de silentio in his emphasis on his own inability to comprehend a subject that nevertheless fascinates him. Unlike many philosophers in the Anglo-Saxon tradition, Wittgenstein's difficulties in understanding religious belief do not lead him to dismiss it. In the notes published under the title *Culture and Value*, he writes that faith is 'what Kierkegaard calls a *passion*'; that trust is the basis of religious belief; and that 'Christianity is not a doctrine, not, I mean, a theory about . . . but a description of something that actually takes place in human life'.[2]

Kierkegaard's most famous intellectual heirs are not, as a rule, the most attentive and insightful readers of his work. In this chapter we will take a step back from *Fear and Trembling*, in order to reflect on the ideas it presents and the questions it poses, and to ask ourselves whether we agree or disagree with Johannes de silentio – and with Kierkegaard. For this purpose, I will draw on a small selection of the very large – and continually growing – body of secondary literature on the text that is available in English, which will convey a sense of the variety of interpretative directions that have been taken by scholars.

Before we turn to these commentators, however, we should note that there are several features of *Fear and Trembling* that make our critical task especially difficult. First, although the text is explicitly polemical, it is not easy to establish what, and who, its targets are. This means that we cannot simply assess Kierkegaard's criticisms of his opponents – asking, for example, whether his representation of Hegel's philosophy is accurate, and whether his attack on it is justi-fied – without engaging in some interpretative work to identify these opponents. Commentators continue to debate whether the charac-terization of 'the ethical' presented by Johannes de silentio is Kantian or Hegelian. (For what it's worth, my view is that it is primarily

Hegelian, since it regards ethical duties in terms of the fulfilment of specific social roles, but that – as the proliferation of Kantian readings of the text demonstrate – the issues raised by Johannes de silentio are certainly relevant to Kant's moral philosophy too.) Similarly, it is only quite recently that commentators outside Denmark have recognized that Danish Hegelians, particularly Martensen, are the focus of at least some aspects of the pseudonym's critique of modern philosophy's pretensions to 'go further than faith'.[3]

A second reason why it is difficult to gain some critical purchase on *Fear and Trembling* is that it is essentially open-ended and inconclusive. As we have seen, and as I will explain further in this chapter, this is part of a deliberate strategy on Johannes de silentio's part: he repeatedly presents the reader with a dilemma, with a choice between remaining within the ethical, and recognizing a 'higher claim' that would make it possible to admire Abraham and, more generally, to accord a special and distinctive role to religious faith. This gives the text an openness that makes it rather elusive. And as well as opening up this space for the reader's decision, *Fear and Trembling* also contains a space, an indeterminate gap, between Johannes de silentio and Kierkegaard. Many readings of the text end up falling into one, or both, of these holes. Or perhaps it is, on the contrary, a question of allowing ourselves to be drawn into these openings, so that a refusal to do so inhibits our understanding of the text. In any case, it seems to be difficult to find a firm footing, a solid base from which to develop either an interpretation of *Fear and Trembling*, or a critical assessment of it.

I will now sketch an overview of the structure of the text in a way that will help to clarify our task of evaluating it.

FAITH, ETHICS, AND JOHANNES DE SILENTIO'S DILEMMA

We can identify two distinct but closely related questions at the heart of *Fear and Trembling*. First, what is the nature of faith? And second, what is the relationship between faith and ethics; between religious life and ethical life? Both of these questions are embedded in a particular historical context: we need to remember that they are being asked in 1843, in response to a certain cultural milieu that is, on the one hand, clearly Christian, and that is, on the other hand, characterized – in Kierkegaard's view – by a shift in attitudes and by a decline in values that has perhaps not yet become fully explicit.

As we have seen, Johannes de silentio's response to the question about the nature of faith involves the claims that it consists of a 'double movement' of resignation and expectation; that this double movement is contradictory and, at least from the point of view of an outsider, absurd; that this absurdity is not just theoretical but practical, or existential, since it holds together loss and gain, suffering and joy; that faith involves the expectation of a gift; and that it requires a 'paradoxical and humble courage'. Now, it is not obvious that this characterization of faith leads directly to a particular response to the second question, about the relationship between ethics and religion. However, the story of Abraham shows that a person who has such a faith is prepared to do something that is unacceptable from an ethical point of view. This suggests that this faith cannot simply be reduced to the ethical sphere, understood in terms of the individual's duties to obey universal laws and to act for the good of the community as a whole.

Having made this distinction between the two basic questions at stake in *Fear and Trembling*, we may glance back over the text in order to see how they are brought together. The structure of the text is dialectical, as its subtitle indicates. First we have the Preface, which articulates concerns about the declining value of faith, without yet stating what faith is or raising the question of its relationship to ethics. 'Tuning Up' then gets us in the mood by introducing the story of Abraham and suggesting that he cannot be understood. Here, the repetitions of Abraham's story and the focus on his existential situation – the fact that he must make a choice about how to respond to God's command to sacrifice Isaac – draw our attention away from the outcome of the story, and so begin to suggest that his decision to kill his son is ethically questionable. Next, Johannes de silentio's 'Tribute to Abraham' specifies certain inward qualities that constitute the ingredients of faith: love, expectancy and struggle. The pseudonym also emphasizes here the significance and value of faith, suggesting that if there were no 'eternal consciousness' in a human being – no consciousness of God, no relationship to God, no possibility of faith – then life would be empty and human beings would be in despair. This is followed by 'A Preliminary Outpouring from the Heart', where Johannes continues to develop his account of faith by describing the movements of resignation and faith. Abraham's faith, we are told, consists not in giving up Isaac, but in expecting to receive him back.

We can see how all this leads up to the dilemma articulated in the three Problems: *either* there can be a teleological suspension of the ethical, *or* Abraham – and the example of faith he provides – is lost; *either* there is an absolute duty to God, *or* Abraham and his faith are lost; *either* faith cannot be subject to the ethical requirement for disclosure, *or* Abraham and his faith are lost. The stakes are high: so far in *Fear and Trembling* we have been urged to value Abraham's faith above all else, to regard it as the highest human possibility, and we have been told that without faith there is only despair. It is important to pay close attention to the lines that make the transition to Problem I, where faith is described as 'a paradox that is capable of making a murder into a holy act well pleasing to God, a paradox that gives Isaac back to Abraham' [46]. This indicates that if Abraham had acted only in resignation, he would have been simply a murderer. His faith *transforms the significance of his action*. It elevates him above the ethical sphere. This is not because his faith means that he does not *want* Isaac to die – the knight of resignation does not *want* to lose the beloved, either – but because faith *expects* that Isaac will live.

With this transition, we pass from the question about the nature of faith to the question about the relationship between ethics and faith. The comparison in Problem I between Abraham and the tragic heroes shows that the former is outside the ethical sphere, while the latter remain within it and are justified and praiseworthy in ethical terms. Abraham's faith is shown to be structurally similar to the faith of the first Christians, insofar as it involves 'the distress, the anxiety, the paradox' [58, 66] of an opposition to the ethical that is haunted by the possibility of being mistaken. The main point of both Problem I and Problem II is to demonstrate that such faith cannot be reduced to the ethical sphere – as it is in Kantian and Hegelian philosophy – and that it is either immoral, or else relates immediately and absolutely to a *telos* that is higher than ethical duties. Of course, in developing this claim, Johannes de silentio continues to flesh out the nature of faith, but it is the question of its relationship to ethics that is now in the foreground.

Problem III brings these two questions fully together. Faith is shown to be an inexpressible paradox, and the concealment that belongs to faith is shown to be entirely different from the concealment proper to the aesthetic sphere. Faith, we are told, is *not* the aesthetic. But it does not meet the ethical requirement for disclosure. If genuine faith is neither aesthetic nor ethical, then it either does not exist at all – and thus what passes for faith in the story of Abraham is in fact just wicked or deluded violence – or else the individual's relationship to God is lived out in a sphere that is distinct from, and higher than, the ethical domain.

Johannes de silentio's dilemma articulates this distinction between the ethical and religious spheres. This should be understood in the context of a particular historical situation, which the pseudonym returns to in his Epilogue. The readers he is addressing lived in a Christian society, where ethical and religious life were, in practice, one and the same. That is to say, the shared communal values, customs and practice – what Hegel terms *Sittlichkeit* – were Christian values, customs and practices. The social roles and relationships which gave to individuals their moral duties and responsibilities were embedded in such a Christian culture. On the face of it, there was no concrete need to decide between ethics and religion. However, this historical situation was a contingent state of affairs. As Johannes de silentio indicates, there was a time when Christian teachings were not identical with *Sittlichkeit*, namely when Jesus was living, when he was put to death as a subversive criminal, and when the disciples who followed him sacrificed their family ties and faced persecution. Paul, for example, the author of the earliest Christian scriptures, was imprisoned and eventually executed. And, more to the point, there may be a time in the future when this Christian *Sittlichkeit* gives way to a different form of ethical life – perhaps a thoroughly secular morality. Of course, it might be perfectly possible that, *in practice*, an individual could maintain her relationship to God while at the same time fulfilling her ethical role within her community: it cannot be right to argue that a person has faith if and only if she is actually required to 'suspend' the ethical, and presumably Abraham has faith before he is commanded to sacrifice Isaac. But if the sphere of faith and the sphere of ethics are *in principle* distinct, then it is also possible that an individual will face a conflict between her duties to God and her ethical duties. The story of Abraham exemplifies this possibility.

Kierkegaard thought that the fact that Christianity (at least in its external movements) and communal life happened to coincide in nineteenth-century Denmark concealed the decision that, in his view, was essential to the task of becoming a Christian. People could regard themselves as Christians just by going along with given customs and practices, by participating in institutions such as the Danish Church, by using a certain shared vocabulary. The dilemma presented so vividly in *Fear and Trembling* holds apart the ethical and religious spheres, and so discloses the Christian decision as something inward, something to which each individual has to respond without the security provided by a comfortable Christian culture. This does not mean that the religious life must be individualistic or other-worldly: on the contrary, as we have seen, the relationship to God should be lived out in the world, through relationships with other people. How this is to be done is, I think, the central problem of *Fear and Trembling*. And moreover, the analysis of 'the present age' that Kierkegaard presents in later texts expresses a concern for social fragmentation, for a breakdown of meaningful relationships between people.[4]

IN DEFENSE OF THE ETHICAL

We may now be better placed to respond critically to *Fear and Trembling*. In my commentary on the text I have challenged various aspects of the text, such as the apparently inconsistent account of the significance of history (see my discussion of Johannes de silentio's Preface), and the neglect of embodied and communal aspects of the religious life (see, for example, the section on 'A Tribute to Abraham'). Here, however, I will focus on the questions that emerge from the fact that the position which Johannes de silentio occupies is not a straightforward defence of Abraham, but a movement from one side to the other of a dilemma between remaining within the ethical, and acknowledging a claim higher than ethical duties. We need to ask whether the reader is compelled to accept this dilemma. Notice what a harsh, difficult dilemma it seems to be: *either* we admit that a murder of an innocent child can be an admirable, holy act, *or* there is no such thing as faith (because it is swallowed up by ethical duty). When Johannes de silentio expresses it in such terms he is deliberately accentuating the most shocking, extreme implication of his basic dilemma concerning the nature of the individual's relationships to God and to other people – and we should not lose sight of his more comforting claim that 'it is only by faith that one acquires a resemblance to Abraham, not by murder' [25]. However, it might still seem that the dilemma only allows us to admire Abraham by following Luther in praising his 'blind faith', his refusal to reflect rationally on the divine command. Is the reader of *Fear and Trembling* really forced to choose between this Lutheran view, on the one hand, and the Kantian view, on the other hand, that Abraham was simply wrong to do what he did?

The pseudonym's dilemma rests on a certain account of faith, and a certain account of the ethical. Is faith really as absurd as he suggests? And is the ethical sphere he characterizes the only one available to us? Might there be an expanded conception of the ethical that is able to accommodate religious faith? Several commentators have responded to *Fear and Trembling* by arguing that its account of the ethical is flawed. One such response is articulated by the French philosopher Emmanuel Levinas, who criticizes both the account of the ethical and the interpretation of the story of Abraham presented in *Fear and Trembling*. Levinas states that he is 'shocked' by Kierkegaard's 'violence', and argues that Kierkegaardian thought has shaped the 'hard masculine tone' of modern existentialist philosophy 'through its intransigent vehemence and its taste for scandal':

> Kierkegaardian violence begins when existence, having moved beyond the aesthetic stage, is forced to abandon the ethical stage (or rather, what it takes to be the ethical stage) in order to embark on the religious stage, the domain of belief . . . That is the origin of the relegation of ethical phenomena to secondary status and the contempt for the ethical foundation of being which has led, through Nietzsche, to the amoralism of recent philosophies.[5]

Levinas's reading of *Fear and Trembling* is not especially detailed or careful, and in this quotation he seems to overlook the way in which the ethical exerts a compelling claim throughout the text. But nevertheless, Levinas makes some important points. He argues that Kierkegaard shares with Hegel a conception of the ethical as 'essentially general', as requiring 'our incorporation and dispersal into generality'[6], and his critique of *Fear and Trembling* focuses on his rejection of this account of the ethical:

> As a consciousness of our responsibility towards others, the ethical does not disperse us into generality. On the contrary, it

individualizes us, treating everyone as a unique individual, a self. Kierkegaard seems to have been unable to recognize this, because he wanted to transcend the ethical stage, which he identified with generality.[7]

We might want to question this emphasis on generality in Levinas's reading, however: isn't Johannes de silentio's Abraham 'tempted' by very concrete, specific ethical requirements – his duty to his only son, and to the future generations of his people that have been promised to him by God?

Levinas offers an alternative reading of the Genesis narrative that accords with his own account of the ethical as an individualizing call to responsibility to others. Instead of focusing on Abraham's willingness to obey God, and the inward movements that, according to Johannes de silentio, this involves, he argues that the climax of the drama on Mount Moriah is

> the moment when Abraham paused and listened to the voice that would lead him back to the ethical order by commanding him not to commit a human sacrifice. That he should have been prepared to obey the first voice is of course astonishing enough; but the crucial point is that he could distance himself from his obedience sufficiently to be able to hear the second voice as well.

This suggestion that Abraham's ability to hear the second command implies a 'distance' from his obedience to the first is, I think, problematic: Abraham simply obeys each command as he receives it. But this does not undermine Levinas's main point, which is that the story of Abraham may be read as showing how

> Death has no dominion over a finite life whose meaning is derived from an infinite responsibility for others . . . It is only here in the ethical that an appeal can be made to the singularity of the subject, and that life can be endowed with meaning, in spite of death.[8]

Like Kierkegaard, Levinas regards the highest task of human life as involving an 'infinite' dimension, but for the latter this is to be located within the ethical sphere, in the individual's responsibility for other people.

In fact, Kierkegaard also regards ethical requirements as 'infinite', but for him the fact that such requirements exceed our finite capacity to fulfil them points beyond the ethical sphere. In the 1845 text *Stages on Life's Way* we find a succinct expression of the issue: 'The aesthetic sphere is the sphere of immediacy, the ethical the sphere of requirement (and this requirement is so infinite that the individual always goes bankrupt), the religious the sphere of fulfilment.'[9] The French philosopher Jacques Derrida, in his book *The Gift of Death*, both develops Levinas's idea of an infinite ethical demand, and attempts to bring Levinas and Kierkegaard closer together. (Derrida, like Levinas, attributes *Fear and Trembling* to Kierkegaard rather than to Johannes de silentio, and overlooks the dilemmatic form of the text.) According to Derrida,

> Kierkegaard would have to admit, as Levinas reminds him, that ethics is also the order of and respect for absolute singularity, and not only that of . . . generality . . . He cannot therefore distinguish so conveniently between the ethical and the religious.[10]

But similarly, Levinas's attribution of infinite otherness to human beings undermines the distinction between the divine and human 'other', and thus 'his ethics is already a religious one'. For both thinkers, argues Derrida, 'the border between the ethical and the religious becomes more than problematic'.[11]

Notice that, in spite of Derrida's analysis, Levinas's account of the ethical and his reading of the story of Abraham do not necessarily bring together the ethical and religious spheres that are so sharply distinguished in Johannes de silentio's dilemma. For Levinas, Abraham fulfils his 'infinite responsibility' to Isaac only to the extent that he 'distances himself' from his obedience to God. This means that Levinas's criticism actually endorses the idea, central to *Fear and Trembling*, that the relationship to God and the demands of the ethical sphere are distinct in principle, and thus might possibly conflict in practice. But on the other hand, Levinas also seems to be following Kant in suggesting that the relationship to God is fulfilled only in the ethical life, although his account of that ethical life is at least superficially different from Kant's. His reading of Genesis 22 ends up looking like a milder version of Kant's much more strident analysis, according to which Abraham ought to disobey God's command for the sake of his ethical duty.

Some more recent discussions of *Fear and Trembling* have echoed aspects of Levinas's analysis of the text. Howard J. Curzer follows the French thinker in offering an ethical reading of Genesis 22. His rather unorthodox interpretation of the story of the sacrifice insists that Abraham is not a man of faith who transgresses his ethical duty, but, on the contrary, a 'faithless moral superhero'. Curzer argues that in Genesis 22 God is 'testing Abraham's ethics', and that Abraham passes this test by disobeying God's command to sacrifice Isaac. On this reading, 'the Abraham of the *akedah* turns out to be a sophisticated moral revolutionary who boldly rejects a horrible practice', who when he tells Isaac that 'God will provide a lamb for the burnt-offering' is 'implicitly saying, "Get a sheep ready, God, because child sacrifice is wrong, and I am not going through with it."'[12] Curzer's argument is certainly refreshing, but his interpretation turns out to rest on the claim that the angel's announcement that Abraham will be blessed 'because you have done this and have not withheld your son . . . because you have obeyed my command' (22: 16–18) was wrongly transcribed. 'The location of the word "not" in this passage must be an ancient typo', asserts Curzer.[13] Of course, it is always possible that a biblical text, like any other text, contains errors, but speculation about where such errors occur on the basis of a certain reading of the text in question is likely to undermine that reading, rather than strengthen it. Be that as it may, the claim that Abraham is not wholly obedient to God throughout Genesis 22 is, as I suggested in response to Levinas, difficult to accept.

On a more philosophical note, Stephen Mulhall echoes Levinas insofar as he also challenges the account of the ethical at work in *Fear and Trembling*, arguing that '[Johannes] de silentio's idea that Abraham cannot speak . . . merely inverts and hence implicitly presupposes the Hegelian notion that the domain of the ethical and the domain of the universal are one and the same.' In Mulhall's view, while the pseudonym 'takes himself to be defending the specificity of faith in relation to the ethical', he is actually 'distorting his account of faith in a way which precisely corresponds to Hegel's distorted characterization of the ethical as exhaustive, as the only intelligible form, of spiritually meaningful existence.'[14] However, while Levinas's reading of *Fear and Trembling* rests with this account of the ethical, and makes it the target of his criticism of the text, Mulhall identifies a 'covert message' to the effect that in Christianity the individual's relationship to the ethical changes, because of the recognition of sin:

> Acknowledging our sinfulness means acknowledging our inability to live up to the demands of the ethical realm; acknowledging Christ means acknowledging that those demands must nevertheless be met, with help from a power greater than our own. In other words, faith returns the ethical to us, but our existence within that realm has shifted its centre of gravity: we are no longer self-supporting, but rather suspended from an external, absolute, divine point of reference or telos.[15]

Even this brief glimpse at Mulhall's sophisticated analysis of *Fear and Trembling* suggests that Levinas's critique is rather simplistic and superficial. If, with Levinas, we substitute an infinite ethical demand for an infinite religious demand, then, at least from Kierkegaard's Christian perspective, this leads only to despair, since human beings are not able to fulfil even finite ethical requirements, let alone infinite ones. It is this inevitable falling short of moral duties that is at stake in the question of the relationship between ethics and religion: if the religious life is no more than the ethical life, then what happens to our relationship to God when our relationships to others break down, when we fail in our duties to them? (Of course, this question could be dismissed by those who do not accept the possibility that human beings do have a relationship to God: perhaps all that can be said in this case is that we simply muddle through, try not to repeat our mistakes, and do our best to forgive each other.) According to C. Stephen Evans, the 'main point' of *Fear and Trembling* is that religious faith cannot be reduced to a life of moral striving – and this, he argues, is crucial because

> for some people, the possibility that "ethics" is not the final word is very important, for if ethics is the final word, then their lives are hopeless . . . for some people at least, the ethical view of life seems to founder on the discovery that they are incapable of fulfilling their social roles in the prescribed manner.[16]

For Evans, this is a specifically Christian idea, but as we will see there are ways of developing it which do not rely on a certain theology.

Mulhall is right to emphasize that *Fear and Trembling* challenges the idea that human beings are morally self-sufficient, and he may also be right in attributing to Johannes de silentio the view that 'faith could never require the violation of ethical duty, although it might require its transfiguration'. However, this reading seems to overlook the parallels drawn in the three Problems between Abraham's faith and Christian faith. Isn't Johannes de silentio suggesting, in Problem II, that the disciples who left their families were violating an ethical duty? If we want to follow Mulhall's interpretation, then we may need to make a stronger distinction than he does between the pseudonym's perspective, which is outside faith, and the perspective from within faith. From within the ethical sphere, Abraham's actions indicate a teleological suspension of the ethical; but from this position, there can be no teleological suspension of the ethical, since the ethical 'has nothing outside itself that is its *telos*' [46] – and therefore Abraham is lost. From a religious perspective, Mulhall argues, faith does not violate ethical duties and thus does not require the ethical to be 'suspended'. This suggests that Mulhall's position reflects just one side – the religious side – of Johannes de silentio's dilemma, and thus represents his own decision in response to it. But until we have each made our own response, by positioning ourselves within either the ethical or the religious sphere, the dilemma seems to remain.

THE VALUE OF TRUST

Some commentators have attempted to defend Abraham by emphasizing his trust in God, rather than his obedience. This is certainly true to *Fear and Trembling*, which as we have seen finds Abraham's greatness not in his obedience to the divine command to kill Isaac, but in his trusting expectancy that God will nevertheless fulfil his earlier promise. Focusing on Abraham's trust may give us one way of admiring him without resort to a Lutheran advocacy of 'blind faith', and trust might also provide a criterion of ethical value that is common to both religious and non-religious perspectives. An ethical theory based on virtues – positive character traits such as justice, generosity, courage and honesty – may be more hospitable to Abraham than an ethics of duty, and perhaps trust might be included in a list of such virtues.

One commentator who argues in this way is Robert M. Adams, who raises the question of why the movement of faith is admirable – 'not everything difficult is admirable, after all' – and suggests that it is Abraham's trust in God that makes his faith praiseworthy.[17] However, this only raises the further question, why is trust admirable? Of course, if the God-relationship is already recognized as the highest *telos*, then trust gains its value as part of that *telos*: if God is offering a gift, it is good to be able to receive it, for this receptivity *is* the actualization of the God-relationship. But if we are appealing to the value of trust in order to justify the view that the God-relationship is the highest *telos*, then we need to say more than this. Surely it is only good to trust a person who is trustworthy? According to Johannes de silentio, however, Abraham's greatness consists in the fact that he expected 'the impossible', and his suggestion that expecting the impossible is 'greater' than expecting what is possible and probable implies that trust which has little or no rational basis is superior to trust in something more secure. Praising Abraham's trust in God is, it seems, open to the Kantian objection that Abraham should have trusted his reason to guide him, and thus refused to believe that the command to kill Isaac really was divine.

Another commentator, Jung H. Lee, argues that when we read the story of the sacrifice in the wider context of Abraham's life and ongoing relationship to God, we can see that Abraham does have grounds for his trust. Lee emphasizes the mutual fidelity and responsiveness demonstrated by Abraham and God throughout the Book of Genesis, and suggests that

> trust and care, *rather* than blind obedience to arbitrary and unintelligible divine commands, defines Abraham's moral framework and enables him to endure his 'trial'. In the trust which Abraham exhibits towards God, he reveals his confidence in the goodwill and competence of God to take care of Isaac . . . This is why Abraham is not a murderer; this is why Abraham is not lost.[18]

One problem with identifying grounds for Abraham's trust in this way is that it leads straight to the objection – which Kant would surely raise – that God's command to sacrifice Isaac should itself be taken as a reason for Abraham to withdraw his trust. When there is so much at stake, is it sensible to trust someone on the basis of his or her reliability hitherto? But having said this, Abraham's trusting expectancy does not simply follow from the fact that in his experience God has proved himself to be reliable. The fulfilment of the promise that Abraham and Sarah will have a son does not just persuade Abraham that God can be trusted, but changes his horizons of possibility, expands his conception of what is possible, and allows him to believe that 'for God everything is possible' [39]. Abraham's faith provides a paradigm of Christian belief in this respect: a person who believes that God incarnated himself in Jesus, and that the latter was resurrected after his crucifixion, ought to have an infinitely expanded sense of possibility in relation to her own future. From a Christian perspective, the Incarnation is an indication not only of God's infinite power, but also of his love, and thus a belief in this event could provide a basis for the kind of personal trust that Abraham demonstrates.

This still, however, leaves the risk of being mistaken: Abraham has to trust himself in order to be confident that the command really is from God, that he has heard it correctly, that he loves Isaac with his whole heart. Likewise, the disciples had to trust their own judgement that Jesus was the right person to follow, and that their decision to leave their families was not motivated in the slightest degree by indifference towards them. And in fact, Kant's criticism of Abraham's obedience focuses less on the question of God's reliability than on this question of whether he can trust himself – and for Johannes de silentio too the latter question is at least as important as the former. If Kierkegaard is right to regard self-deception as integral to human nature, then this accentuates the difficulty of trusting oneself, of discerning one's true motivations. For example, one's own inner duplicity might make it hard to distinguish between trusting someone, and wishfully hoping that what they say is true. This is not so much an argument against Johannes de silentio's interpretation of Abraham, as the very problem he is grappling with in *Fear and Trembling*.

It is important, I think, to be wary of adopting a purely intellectualist approach to this issue. Perhaps the best way to respond to Kant's uncompromising scepticism is to point out that just as one's trust in another person grows gradually through time as one gets to know her, so one can develop trust in oneself by becoming increasingly familiar with one's thoughts, feelings, motivations and so on. This does not eliminate the possibility of being mistaken, but indicates a practical response to precisely this possibility. Within the religious traditions there are practices – prayer, confession, meditation, for example – that support this task of self-understanding, as, indeed, there are analogous secular practices and techniques, such as those employed in psychoanalysis and cognitive behavioural therapy. Johannes de silentio himself highlights the significance of this cultivation of self-knowledge when in Problem III he praises the monastic life as a commitment 'to explore every single secret thought . . . and call forth . . . the dark emotions that still lie concealed in every human life' [88]. And in Kierkegaard's journal of 1843 we find a reference to this kind of practice:

> I sit and listen to the sounds in my inner being . . . To synthes-
> ize them is a task not for a composer but for a man who in the
> absence of larger demands upon life restricts himself to the
> simple task of wanting to understand himself.[19]

Religious teachings and beliefs are embedded in ways of life that incorporate such practices.

Like Adams and Lee, Sharon Krishek regards Abraham's trust in God, rather than his obedience, as central to his faith, and she goes further in developing an account of why this trust is admirable. She argues that 'the *test* that Abraham withstands does not consist in his willingness to kill his son, but rather in his *trust* in God's promise.'[20] Her interpretation of the relationship between faith and ethics in *Fear and Trembling* is very close to Stephen Mulhall's in its denial that faith is opposed to ethics, and in its emphasis on human beings' inability to fulfil ethical requirements:

> not only does Abraham's faith *not* violate any ethical ideal, it
> presents the highest way of fulfilling it. The ideals remain the
> same, but our appropriation of them in the context of faith is
> changed completely . . . Thus, the essential element that

distinguishes between a merely rational approach to ethics and a religious approach (the approach of faith) is trust. An ethics that remains within the limits of human understanding and capacities alone finds itself bankrupt when facing an unfathomable obstacle on the way to fulfilling its ideals. We need the trust that is involved in faith to be capable of holding fast to the possibility of this fulfilment.[21]

What is particularly compelling about Krishek's reading is the way in which she understands the ethical sphere in terms of love, rather than just in terms of the fulfilment of roles and duties. This is faithful to *Fear and Trembling*, in spite of the fact that Johannes de silentio's conception of the ethical does, as Levinas, Derrida and Mulhall argue, incline towards 'generality'. The text, as we have seen, is populated by people involved in personal relationships: think of Sarah and Tobias, Agnes and the Merman, Agamemnon and Iphigenia, the mother who weans her child. More to the point, Krishek's inclusion of love within the ethical is truer to the way human beings live. It is quite easy to see that being a good mother, a good husband, or a good friend is a matter not just of responsibility towards another person, but of loving them. But in other social roles, too, there is the possibility for responsibility to be animated by love: love for one's work, for one's home, for justice, for nature, for one's country, for one's football team, and so on. It is this love that makes human being-in-the-world a source of both suffering and joy, and of course these are important themes in *Fear and Trembling*.

One of the strengths of Krishek's reading is that it brings together the two questions that I mentioned above: the question of the nature of religious faith, and the question of the relationship between ethics and faith. As we have seen, several commentators find in *Fear and Trembling* the Christian idea that human beings are in a state of sin that prevents them from fulfilling their ethical requirements. What Krishek's discussion of the text accentuates is that we are prevented from loving not just by self-interest, which might be regarded as a moral defect, but also by fear of loss. Drawing on a recent essay by John Davenport,[22] she argues that only faith, in the sense of trust, can enable a person to continue to love in the face of loss:

We may now be in a position to understand why the desirable renewed relationship with the finite deserves the title 'faith'. To use Davenport's terminology, the ethical ideal that concerns us here is that of maintaining a relationship of *love*. The obstacle in the way of fulfilling this ideal is *loss*. And finally, the way to fulfil the ideal notwithstanding the obstacle of loss is *faith*. Namely, the way of . . . holding fast to the finite while completely releasing any claim on it, the way of trusting the fulfilment of even the most unattainable of our ethical wishes.

. . . We live in a complex reality of bestowal and deprival . . . a reality that offers us splendid goods but sometimes also takes them away, leaving us in pain and sorrow. We therefore need the unique language of faith – profoundly attentive to our twofold bond with God and finitude – with which we can talk and listen to the world. This dialogue contains the infinite pain involved in releasing everything, but also the intense joy of getting a firm hold on everything back again. Thus, it is only faith that manages to give a real place for the existential, and ultimately religious, intuition regarding the world's receptivity to us. This intuition is the basis for the desirable relationship – the faith-full (faith-pervaded) relationship – we should aim to sustain with everything given to us, and with the beloved one in particular.[23]

Of course, Krishek's reading of the text cannot solve the problem of *how* one might get into the position of 'trusting the fulfilment of even the most unattainable of our ethical wishes'. Again, this question of *how* – 'how one entered into [faith], or how it entered into one' [5] – is precisely the question that is raised by Johannes de silentio, and to which he does not find an answer: 'How [Abraham] entered into [the paradox] is just as inexplicable as how he remains in it' [58]. It may be true that the trust described by Krishek is the only way to live happily in the world, rather than be consumed with anxiety about the loss of the beloved. But there is clearly a difference between seeing that it would be good to believe something, and actually being able to believe it. If human beings are unable to fulfil ethical demands – whether these are understood in the narrower sense of moral duties, or in the expanded sense that includes loving others in the face of the prospect of losing them – then this limitation does not provide grounds for trust, even though it does show why trust is desirable. After all, in Kant's philosophy we find an acknowledgement that human beings inevitably fall short of the moral law alongside an insistence on the autonomy of the ethical sphere – an insistence which, according to Johannes de silentio, renders God 'an invisible vanishing-point, an impotent thought' [59]. Kant does in fact advocate religious belief – in an immortal soul, and in a just God who will reward virtue with happiness – since this makes possible the moral perfection and justice that are impossible in this lifetime. But this is quite different from the belief in 'fulfilment' *in this world* that Abraham exemplifies and that constitutes, for Johannes de silentio, the task of Christian faith. So it seems that Krishek's reading only goes so far as to show what is at stake in the pseudonym's dilemma: it shows us that if we are unable to admire Abraham, then we stand to lose the faith or trust that enables us to enjoy our transient relationships to the full.

It also seems that, when we focus on trust, we remain within a religious framework. After all, Abraham trusts a God who provides for him and who promises him great things. It is, of course, important to be able to trust other human beings, but what is in question here is trust in something that exceeds the finite human domain. Or perhaps not: after all, every other person's freedom to love lies beyond one's own power, and thus trust is always in a sense transcendent. But in *Fear and Trembling* what is expected and trusted in, both in Abraham's particular situation, and in the case of the Christian believer, is the continuation of life itself, in the face of death; the restoration of the gift, in the face of loss. Perhaps some people might make sense of the idea of a trusting relationship to life itself, which would be a faith that as each moment slips away a new one will take its place, so that Abraham's expectation that 'God will provide' comes to stand for the trust that life will continue to give itself. This naturalistic interpretation has its limitations insofar as what is at stake in Abraham's faith is not just the renewal of life, but its restoration – the gaining back of something that was genuinely lost. However, even this may be understood naturalistically, as the restoration of lost time through forgiveness. Ordinarily understood, the past is lost to us: we cannot take it back, cannot repeat it, and this is an especially painful loss when we recall our mistakes and missed opportunities. Of course, forgiveness cannot literally restore a lost past, but it might transform one's relationship to the past, so that earlier actions cease to be a source of guilt and resentment, and even become instead an opportunity to develop wisdom and compassion. This applies both to those who are forgiven, and those who forgive.

HUMBLE COURAGE

While Abraham's trust in God has received a lot of attention from commentators keen to defend *Fear and Trembling* from charges of irrationalism and immorality, his courage – and more generally the courage of faith – is little discussed, in spite of Johannes de silentio's numerous references to it. Courage is a secular virtue not immediately associated with the religious life: we often hear expressions of praise for the courage of a soldier, or of a fire-fighter, or of someone 'battling' a serious illness. But what these examples indicate is that courage is a virtue especially, although not solely, related to a confrontation with death. Courage is a response to some kind of vulnerability and threat: as Johannes de silentio puts it,

> every moment to see the sword hanging over the beloved's head and yet to find, not rest in the pain of resignation, but joy by virtue of the absurd – that is miraculous. The one who does that is great, the only great person. [43]

Courage is also an important virtue in relation to trust. The difficulty of sustaining trust – in God, in religious teachings, in another person, in oneself – points to the need for courage. Courage responds to risk and uncertainty as well as to vulnerability. Given the 'fear and trembling', or anxiety, that Johannes de silentio emphasizes in his interpretation of Abraham, it should not be surprising that courage plays a central role in his account of Abraham's heroism. The use of the word 'knight', with its military connotations, to describe a person who makes the movement of resignation or the double movement of faith, expresses the significance of courage or bravery.

Of course, if Abraham's courage is to be taken as a sign of his greatness, then we need to ask ourselves what is good about courage, just as we raised the question of the value of trust. First, though, we should clarify what courage is. It involves the capacity to face danger or difficulties without retreating. Like all virtues, courage is a middle term between two extremes; according to Aristotle, who remains the most influential philosopher of virtue, courage is the middle term, or the mean, between cowardice and recklessness in the face of danger. 'Abraham arrived neither too early nor too late' [29]. Courage is, so to speak, the right amount of spiritedness: too little of this quality will prevent a person facing up to danger, while too much of it will lead to a foolhardy kind of risk-taking. The virtue of courage also involves the wisdom that recognizes what it is appropriate to fear, and what is worth fighting for – and even risking one's life for.

Courage is a traditional virtue, but it certainly has a place within the expanded conception of the ethical in *Fear and Trembling*, which, as Krishek argues, includes love for particular others as well as duties towards them. Corresponding to this expanded conception of the ethical is an expansion of the concept of sin to include fear of loss as well as selfishness and perversity (that is, the inclination to do what one knows is wrong). The theologian John Milbank argues that, 'where Augustine located the transcendental sin as "pride," which already thinks to subject the infinite to its own grasp, Kierkegaard substitutes fear, which swims in the medium of acknowledged uncertainty.'[24] Insofar as such fear leads to an anxious flight from the fact of mortality, the traditional Christian understanding of sin as a failure to be true to God, and thus to oneself insofar as one is constituted by one's relationship to God, might be glossed as a failure to be true to what one really is – to one's contingency, finitude, vulnerability.

While Krishek claims that 'the obstacle in the way of fulfilling the [ethical] ideal [of love] is loss', it would be more accurate to identify this 'obstacle' as *fear of* loss – and this shifts the focus from trust in transcendent restoration or fulfilment to courage in the face of one's own fear. Fear of losing the beloved – symbolized in *Fear and Trembling*, as we have seen, by 'the sword hanging over the head of the beloved' – can prevent people from loving, and also, importantly, from allowing themselves to be loved by others. This is brought out particularly in Johannes de silentio's discussion of the story of Sarah and Tobias, for while the pseudonym acknowledges Tobias's courage in loving Sarah, he praises far more highly Sarah's courage in letting herself be loved by Tobias, by virtue of 'the great mystery that it is far more difficult to receive [love] than to give [it]' [91]. Fear of loss undermines not only the individual's own ethical life, but ethical life as such, since it can prevent others from loving, and thus from fulfilling their own ethical requirements. For Johannes de silentio, the virtue of courage that belongs to faith is the capacity first to confront one's fear of loss and to accept the inevitability of the loss of the beloved; and then to accept the beloved back in the form of a gift – a gift from God, a gift from life, a gift from death, or a gift from love as it is incarnated in each living being. The first phase is the movement of resignation, the second is the movement of faith.

In his recent book *Radical Hope: Ethics in the Face of Cultural Devastation*, the American philosopher Jonathan Lear offers a discussion of courage that resonates with Johannes de silentio's account of faith's courage. Rather as *Fear and Trembling* uses the story of Abraham to reflect on questions about faith, ethics, and the human condition, so *Radical Hope* uses the true story of a tribe of American Indians, the Crow, in order to reflect on some similar questions. Although Lear does not discuss Kierkegaard at any length, he takes up the idea of a 'teleological suspension of the ethical' in order to characterize the Crow's response when their traditional way of life came to an end, and more generally his understanding of the human condition resonates with *Fear and Trembling* in its emphasis on finitude and vulnerability. Lear's answer to the question of the value of courage focuses on these features of human life:

> Courage is a virtue, I think, because it is an excellent way of coping with, responding to, and manifesting a basic fact about us: that we are finite erotic creatures. By *finite* I mean to point to a family of limitations that characterize the human condition: we are not all-powerful or all-knowing; our ability to create is limited; so is our ability to get what we want; our beliefs may be false; and even the concepts with which we understand the world are vulnerable . . . By *erotic* I follow a basically Platonic conception that, in our finite condition of lack, we reach out to the world in yearning, longing, admiration and desire for that which (however mistakenly) we take to

be valuable, beautiful and good . . . [We may consider courage] as the ability to live well with the risks that inevitably attend human existence. To be human is necessarily to be a vulnerable risk-taker; to be a courageous human is to be good at it.[25]

If courage has value as a good way to respond to vulnerability, in *Fear and Trembling*, this means confronting and accept transience. Courage is a middle way between clinging to the beloved, and withdrawing from her, both of which are attempts to avoid the pain of loss. One point we can add to Lear's analysis is that there is a stillness in courage: considered as a middle way between fearful flight and reckless, thoughtless combat, courage involves a willingness to stand and look whatever is frightening in the eye. Such courage is a condition for the development of wisdom, for only in this stillness can one see things clearly, size up the nature of one's situation, and find the most appropriate response to it. Kierkegaard seems to express such a view when his pseudonym Vigilius Haufniensis writes, in *The Concept of Anxiety*, that 'every human being must . . . learn to be anxious.'[26] The point here is not that anxiety is a good thing, but that, given that anxiety is part of the human condition, one should learn to *be* anxious: to remain in anxiety rather than to flee from it. According to Vigilius Haufniensis,

> whoever has learned to be anxious in the right way has learned the ultimate . . . Then the assaults of anxiety, even though they be terrifying, will not be such that he flees from them. For him, anxiety will be a serving spirit that against its will leads him where he wishes to go.[27]

What is particularly interesting about Lear's discussion of courage is the way in which he extends the idea of human vulnerability and finitude to the ethical sphere as such. When in the 1880s the Crow tribe moved onto a reservation, their traditional nomadic life of hunting and fighting against other tribes was destroyed. Of course, their situation raises political questions, but Lear is most interested in its philosophical significance. As the experience of the Crow tribe demonstrates, it is always possible that a way of life, which includes the shared concepts that structure one's understanding of a good life, may come to an end. As Lear argues, 'Even when we try to think about the world we inhabit, think about ourselves and our lives, we take a risk that the very concepts with which we think may become unintelligible.'[28] This vulnerability of the ethical sphere not only demands a response of courage, but calls for the possibility of a claim from beyond any given *Sittelichkeit*. Lear draws on Johannes de silentio's notion of a teleological suspension of the ethical in order to explain that the Crow could only survive, and maintain at least the possibility of flourishing, if they were 'willing to give up almost everything they understand about the good life.' He argues that 'This was not a choice that could be reasoned about in the pre-existing terms of the good life. One needed some conception of—or commitment to—a goodness that transcended one's current understanding of the good.'[29]

This is, I think, pertinent to *Fear and Trembling*, especially when we consider the text as responsive to a particular historical situation. Of course, the concrete situation of Christians in nineteenth-century Europe appears to be very different from, and even the opposite of, that of the Crow tribe during the same period. While the Crow way of life was collapsing, Christians were, according to Kierkegaard, complacently settled in Christendom, a society in which the Christian faith coincided with institutions, customs, communal values, and so on. But it was precisely this apparent security that covered over the essential vulnerability that Lear describes so well. In articulating his stark dilemma between the loss of faith and the immanence of the ethical sphere, Johannes de silentio urges his readers to confront the possibility that the ethical might not coincide with the task of becoming a Christian.[30] This possibility, as he indicates, is instantiated in the situation of the earliest Christians, and in the twenty-first century we can see very clearly how it may be instantiated again. Today we live in a world in which people pursue their tasks of becoming Christians, or Muslims, or Buddhists, or socialists, or philosophers, or whatever, within societies where 'the ethical' does not coincide, and may well conflict, with these tasks. Might it even be the case that the task of becoming *a human being* involves the possibility of a higher claim than that of ethical life?

It should be noted that the courage to which Johannes de silentio refers is a certain kind of courage. According to the pseudonym,

A purely human courage is required to renounce the whole of temporality in order to gain the eternal . . . but it takes a paradoxical and humble courage next to grasp the whole of temporality by virtue of the absurd, and this is the courage of faith. [41]

What does this 'paradoxical and humble courage' involve? While we may ordinarily think of courage as strength of will (or of the heart) in facing up to danger and fighting against what threatens us, the courage of faith takes the form of receptivity rather than resistance. It is passive as much as it is active; not merely strong-hearted, but open-hearted. Abraham is able to hear the angel calling him, not because of a lack of obedience to God's command or an overriding moral conscience, but because, even as he raises his knife over Isaac's body, his heart is sufficiently quiet and attentive. His courage enables him to listen.

George Pattison, a philosopher and Kierkegaard scholar, discusses this distinctive form of courage in his book *Thinking About God in an Age of Technology*, where, as the title suggests, he explores – as Kierkegaard does – the task of religious thinking, and existing, in a specifically modern context. Pattison emphasizes the need for courage in undertaking this task, and points to the element of passivity within this courage:

The question of God remains a question whose outcome cannot solely depend on our willing. Instead, thinking about God must wait upon its object . . . and its courage is the courage of waiting. In the *Upbuilding Discourses* that also modelled a kind of thinking about God, Kierkegaard put constant emphasis on just this element of patience and, in doing so, exploited the etymology of the Danish word for patience, *Taal-mod*, a word that contains within itself a doubling of courage and patience, meaning, literally, 'courage to bear'.[31]

According to Pattison, 'If courage needs the restraint of patience, patience too needs the force of courage if it is to be true to itself and to be able to bear the strain of its long wait.'[32] In this way, incidentally, he indicates how the wilful strenuousness associated with existentialist thought – its 'hard masculine tone' which, as we have seen, Levinas complains about and attributes to *Fear and Trembling* – is tempered in Kierkegaard's own thought by an emphasis on what might be regarded as a quieter, more feminine form of courage.

In his discourses 'To Preserve One's Soul in Patience' and 'Patience in Expectancy', which were published together in March 1844, Kierkegaard explores the connection between trust, patience and courage in a way which suggests that these all belong together within faith. 'Patience teaches trust in life,' he writes.[33] Although the titles of these discourses suggest an emphasis on patience over courage, Kierkegaard insists that 'patience is just as active as it is passive,'[34] and the first discourse in particular abounds with references to power, danger, fear, and struggle with death – with images of warriors and battles. For example, it is clear that it is courage which is in question when we read that:

> If a person discovered the danger while all speak of peace and security, if he discovered the horror and after having used the healthiest power of his soul to make himself fully aware of it, again with horror before his eyes, now developed and preserved the same strength of soul as one who fought in peril of his life, the same inwardness as the one who fought with death—yes, then we shall praise him . . . My listener, surely you have also struggled in this conflict . . . .[35]

In these discourses, as in *Fear and Trembling*, the knight of faith's 'paradoxical and humble courage' is presented, to Christian readers, as a specifically Christian virtue. But it is not confined to this context: after all, it is already there in the faith of Abraham, and it may also be a part of ethical life for a non-religious person. However, this courage would be a feature of ethical life which answered to ethical demands while also acknowledging and responding to the ethical sphere's own limitations and fragility. It seems that *Fear and Trembling* has something to teach us about such a radical and responsive kind of courage, although we may need to re-examine Johannes de silentio's distinction between a 'paradoxical and humble courage' and a 'purely human courage'. Can we regard the courage of faith, with its distinctive quality of receptivity, as a purely-human possibility?

CHAPTER 4

FURTHER READING

The texts recommended here represent a relatively small selection from a large body of literature relating to Kierkegaard's philosophy in general, and to *Fear and Trembling* in particular.

WORKS BY KIERKEGAARD

If *Fear and Trembling* is the first of Kierkegaard's texts you've read, you might like to look next at *The Concept of Anxiety*, *Philosophical Fragments*, *The Sickness Unto Death*, or *Eighteen Upbuilding Discourses*.

INTRODUCTIONS TO KIERKEGAARD'S THOUGHT

Carlisle, Clare. *Kierkegaard: A Guide for the Perplexed* (London: Continuum, 2006).

Evans, C. Stephen. *Kierkegaard: An Introduction* (Cambridge University Press, 2009).

Hannay, Alastair. *Kierkegaard: The Arguments of the Philosophers* (London: Routledge, 1982).

Hannay, Alastair and Gordon Marino (eds). *The Cambridge Companion to Kierkegaard* (Cambridge University Press, 1998).

Pattison, George. *The Philosophy of Kierkegaard* (Chesham: Acumen Publishing, 2005).

BIOGRAPHIES OF KIERKEGAARD

Garff, Joakim. *Søren Kierkegaard: A Biography*, translated by Bruce Kirmmse (Princeton University Press, 2005).

Hannay, Alastair. *Kierkegaard: A Biography* (Cambridge University Press, 2001).

Kirmmse, Bruce (ed.). *Encounters with Kierkegaard: A Life as Seen by His Contemporaries* (Princeton University Press, 1996).

Lowrie, Walter. *A Short Life of Kierkegaard* (Princeton University Press, 1942).

TEXTS ON AND RELATED TO KIERKEGAARD'S
FEAR AND TREMBLING

Adams, Robert M. 'The Knight of Faith' in *Faith and Philosophy* 7 (1990), 383–95.

Buber, Martin. 'The Question to the Single One' and 'The Suspension of Ethics' in Will Herberg (ed.), *Four Existentialist Theologians* (New York: Doubleday Anchor, 1958).

Conant, James. 'Putting Two and Two Together: Kierkegaard, Wittgenstein and the point of view for their work as authors' in T. Tessin and M. von der Ruhr (eds), *Philosophy and the Grammar of Religious Belief* (London: Macmillan, 1995).

Crocker, Sylvia Fleming. 'Sacrifice in Kierkegaard's *Fear and Trembling*' in *The Harvard Theological Review* 68 (1975), 125–39.

Davenport, John and Anthony Rudd (eds). *Kierkegaard After MacIntyre: Essays on Freedom, Narrative and Virtue* (Chicago: Open Court, 2001).

Derrida, Jacques. *The Gift of Death*, translated by David Wills (The University of Chicago Press, 1995).

Green, Ronald M. 'Enough is Enough! *Fear and Trembling* is *Not* about Ethics' in *Journal of Religious Ethics* 21 (1993), 191–209.

Hall, Ronald L. *The Human Embrace: The Love of Philosophy and the Philosophy of Love. Kierkegaard, Cavell, Nussbaum* (The Pennsylvania State University Press, 2000).

Krishek, Sharon. *Kierkegaard on Faith and Love* (Cambridge University Press, 2009).

Levinas, Emmanuel. 'Existence and Ethics' in Jonathan Rée and Jane Chamberlain (eds), *Kierkegaard: A Critical Reader* (Oxford: Blackwell, 1998).

Lippitt, John. *Kierkegaard and Fear and Trembling* (London, Routledge, 2003).

Milbank, John. 'The Sublime in Kierkegaard' in *The Heythrop Journal* 37 (1996), 298–321.

Mooney, Edward F. *Knights of Faith and Resignation: Reading Kierkegaard's Fear and Trembling* (Albany, NY: State University of New York Press, 1991).

Mulhall, Stephen. *Inheritance and Originality: Wittgenstein, Heidegger, Kierkegaard* (Oxford University Press, 2001).

Perkins, Robert L. (ed.). *Kierkegaard's Fear and Trembling: Critical Appraisals* (The University of Alabama Press, 1981).

—. *International Kierkegaard Commentary: Fear and Trembling and Repetition* (Macon, GA: Mercer University Press, 1993).

Phillips, D. Z. and T. Tessin (eds). *Kant and Kierkegaard on Religion* (London: Macmillan, 2000).

Rée, Jonathan and Jane Chamberlain (eds). *Kierkegaard: A Critical Reader* (Oxford: Blackwell, 1998).

Rudd, Anthony. *Kierkegaard and the Limits of the Ethical* (Oxford: Clarendon Press, 1993).

NOTES

1 OVERVIEW OF THEMES AND CONTEXT

1. See Søren Kierkegaard, *Eighteen Upbuilding Discourses*, edited and translated by Howard V. Hong and Edna H. Hong (Princeton University Press, 1990), pp. 49–101.
2. For a reading of *Fear and Trembling* in the light of *Three Upbuilding Discourses*, see George Pattison, *Kierkegaard's Upbuilding Discourses: Philosophy, Literature, Theology* (London: Routledge, 2002), pp. 193–202.
3. Note, however, these lines from Psalm 2: 'Serve the Lord with fear, with trembling kiss his feet' (New Revised Standard Version); 'Serve the Lord with fear, and rejoice with trembling' (King James Version).
4. *Papirer* X B 2 (1851).
5. Kierkegaard, *Concluding Unscientific Postscript* translated by Alastair Hannay (Cambridge University Press, 2009), p. 268.
6. See Søren Kierkegaard, *Eighteen Upbuilding Discourses*, edited and translated by Howard V. Hong and Edna H. Hong (Princeton University Press, 1990), pp. 103–58.
7. Ibid., p. 265.
8. For Regine's side of the story, see Bruce Kirmmse (ed.), *Encounters with Kierkegaard* (Princeton University Press, 2006), pp. 33–54.
9. *Kierkegaard, Journals and Papers*, translated by Howard V. and Edna H. Hong (Indiana University Press, 1976), 5663 (1843). Hereafter referred to as JP..
10. Kierkegaard, *Concluding Unscientific Postscript*, p. 266.
11. JP VI 6491.
12. Kierkegaard, *Concluding Unscientific Postscript*, p. 252.
13. See Kierkegaard, *Repetition*, translated by Howard V. Hong and Edna H. Hong (Princeton University Press, 1983), p. 131.
14. JP V 5664.
15. See the 'Supplement' to *Fear and Trembling* in the Hong and Hong edition of the text (Princeton University Press, 1983), p. 243.
16. Plato, *Symposium*, 207d.
17. Immanuel Kant, *Religion within the Boundaries of Mere Reason*, edited and translated by Allen Wood and George Di Giovanni (Cambridge University Press, 1998), p. 166 (emphasis in original).
18. *Luther's Works*, volume 4; edited by Jaroslav Pelikan (Saint Louis: Concordia 1964), p. 95.
19. Ibid., pp. 92; 114.
20. Ibid., p. 113.
21. Martin Luther, *The Book of Concord*, edited by T. Tappert (Philadelphia: Fortress Press, 1959), p. 578.

22. Kierkegaard's *Journals and Papers*, 6598 (1850).
23. Søren Kierkegaard, *Two Ages*, translated by Howard V. Hong and Edna H. Hong (Princeton University Press, 1978), pp. 75–8.
24. See Friedrich Nietzsche, *The Gay Science*, translated by Walter Kaufmann (New York: Vintage Books, 1974), §§125, 343.
25. See Johan Ludvig Heiberg, *Om Philosophiens Betydning for den nuvaerende Tid*, Copenhagen 1833. *ASKB* 568. For an extended discussion of Heiberg's work, see Jon Stewart, *Kierkegaard's Relations to Hegel Reconsidered* (Cambridge University Press, 2003), pp. 50–8.
26. See Bruce Kirmmse (ed.), *Encounters with Kierkegaard*, pp. 196–7. The original source is H. L. Martensen, *Af mit Levnet* [From My Life] (Copenhagen: Gyldendal, 1882–1883), vol. 2, pp. 140–2.
27. JP 1559 (1849).
28. For a discussion of this line of interpretation, see John Lippitt, 'What neither Abraham nor Johannes de silentio could say' in *Proceedings of the Aristotelian Society Supplementary* Vol. 82, 2008, pp. 79–99. Section V of Lippitt's paper (pp. 92–7) is entitled '*Fear and Trembling's* Hidden Christianity', and discusses the views of various commentators such as Louis Mackey, Ronald M. Green and Stephen Mulhall, who have identified a specifically Christian message in the text.
29. Ibid.
30. See Luther's lectures on Genesis in *Luther's Works*, volume 4, pp. 113–16. Here, Luther relates the contradiction between God's promise concerning Isaac and the command to sacrifice him to the contradiction between life and death, and suggests that Abraham manages to 'reconcile' the former contradiction just as the latter contradiction is reconciled in the story of Jesus' death and resurrection, and in the promise of salvation given to Christians: 'Those contradictory statement cannot be reconciled by any human reason or philosophy. But the Word reconciles these two, namely, that he who is dead lives . . . it is something wonderful and impossible for reason to believe that God can, and wants to, do away with death and change it into life'.

2 READING THE TEXT

1. See Jon Stewart, *Kierkegaard's Relations to Hegel Reconsidered* (Cambridge University Press, 2003), pp. 110–11; 242–6; 307–8.
2. Søren Kierkegaard, *Concluding Unscientific Postscript*, translated by Alastair Hannay (Cambridge University Press, 2009), p. 257.
3. Ibid., pp. 311–12.
4. In Alastair Hannay's translation of *Fear and Trembling* the title of this chapter is 'Attunement'; in the Hongs' translation it is 'Exordium'.
5. Holy Bible, New Revised Standard Version, Gen. 22.1–19.
6. See Kierkegaard's critique of 'the present age' in *Two Ages*, for example, pp. 68, 77, 91.

7. For an attempt to link each parable of the mother and the child to the version of Abraham's story they follow, see L. Williams, 'Kierkegaard's Weanings' in *Philosophy Today*, 42, 3 (1998), 310–18.
8. JP V 5664.
9. See Kierkegaard, *Fear and Trembling*, translated by Howard V. Hong and Edna H. Hong, pp. xxvii–xxviii.
10. JP VI 6388.
11. JP I 908
12. JP V 5640.
13. In Alastair Hannay's translation of *Fear and Trembling,* the title of this chapter is 'Speech in Praise of Abraham'; in the Hongs' translation it is 'Eulogy on Abraham'.
14. See Kierkegaard, *Repetition*, p. 214.
15. Ibid., p. 304. This passage is not from the text of *Repetition*, but from a draft letter written, in the name of Constantin Constantius, in response to J. L. Heiberg's comments on the book.
16. See Mt. 19.26, Mk 10.27, Lk. 18.26.
17. See *The Sickness Unto Death*, translated by Howard V. and Edna H. Hong (Princeton University Press, 1980) p. 40 (emphasis in original).
18. In Alastair Hannay's translation of *Fear and Trembling*, the title of this chapter is 'Preamble from the Heart'; in the Hongs' translation, it is 'Preliminary Expectoration'.
19. See Kierkegaard, *Concluding Unscientific Postscript*, trans. Hannay, pp. 261–2.
20. Kierkegaard, *Concluding Unscientific Postscript*, translated by Alastair Hannay, p. 33.
21. Robert Merrihew Adams, 'The Knight of Faith' in *Faith and Philosophy* 7 (4) (1990), 383–95; 386.
22. See Andrew Cross, '*Fear and Trembling*'s unorthodox ideal' in *Philosophical Topics* 27 (2) (1999) 227–53; 238.
23. John Lippitt, *Routledge Philosophy Guidebook to Kierkegaard and Fear and Trembling* (London: Routledge, 2003), p. 68. See pp. 66–76 for his discussion of this issue, in response to Andrew Cross.
24. Sharon Krishek, *Kierkegaard on Faith and Love* (Cambridge University Press, 2009), p. 79.
25. Ibid., p. 78.
26. Ibid., p. 80.
27. Ibid., p. 81.
28. JP 6958 (1850).
29. Kierkegaard, *Concluding Unscientific Postscript*, translated by Alastair Hannay,. p. 307.
30. JP VI 6718
31. *Hegel's Philosophy of Right*, translated by T. M. Knox (Oxford: Oxford University Press, 1952), §360; pp. 222–3.
32. Ibid., §4; p. 20.
33. Immanuel Kant, *Groundwork for the Metaphysics of Morals*, edited by Thomas E. Hill, Jr. and Arnulf Zweig (Oxford: Oxford University Press 2002), chapter one: 13; p. 203.

34. Immanuel Kant, *The Conflict of the Faculties* . . ., translated by Mary Gregor (University of Nebraska Press, 1992), p. 115
35. Kant, *Religion Within the Boundaries of Mere Reason*, edited and translated by Allen Wood and George Di Giovanni (Cambridge University Press, 1998), p. 166.
36. These are alternative English translations of the German word *Geist*.
37. Hans Lassen Martensen, *Den christelige Daab* [*The Christian Faith*] (Copenhagen: 1843), p. 23. See Kierkegaard, *Philosophical Fragments*, p. 316 for the Hongs' English translation of this passage.
38. See Kierkegaard, *Philosophical Fragments*, pp. 94–8.
39. *Luther's Works*, vol. 4, edited by Jaroslav Pelikan, p. 112.
40. Ibid., p. 113.
41. See Jean-Paul Sartre, *Being and Nothingness*, translated by Hazel E. Barnes (London: Routledge, 2003), pp. 70–94.
42. Jacques Derrida, *The Gift of Death*, translated by David Wills (University of Chicago Press, 1995), pp. 61–2.
43. Ibid., p. 72.
44. Kierkegaard, *The Sickness Unto Death*, p. 30.
45. Kierkegaard, *The Sickness Unto Death*, p. 22.
46. Kierkegaard, *Concluding Unscientific Postscript* (trans. Hong and Hong), p. 269.
47. William Shakespeare, *King Richard the Third*, Act I, scene I.
48. Ibid., Act I, scene I.
49. Daniel W. Conway, 'Abraham's Final Word' in Edward F. Mooney (ed.), *Ethics, Love and Faith in Kierkegaard*, pp. 175–95; p. 189.
50. Ibid., pp. 190–1.
51. For example, Emmanuel Levinas, whose reading of *Fear and Trembling* I will discuss in my closing chapter, argues that Abraham can hear the angel's call to him only because he 'distance[s] himself from his obedience' to God's earlier command. See Levinas, 'Existence and Ethics' in Jonathan Rée and Jane Chamberlain (eds), *Kierkegaard: A Critical Reader*, (Wiley-Blackwell, 1998), pp. 26–38; pp. 34–5. More recently, Howard J. Curzer has offered a stronger version of this reading in 'Abraham, The Faithless Moral Superhero' in *Philosophy and Literature* 31 (2007), pp. 344–61.
52. Stephen Mulhall, *Inheritance and Originality: Wittgenstein, Heidegger, Kierkegaard* (Oxford University Press, 2001), pp. 379–80.
53. Ibid.
54. Kierkegaard, *Repetition*, p. 131.
55. Plato, *Cratylus*, 402a.
56. Kierkegaard, *Repetition*, p. 131.

3 RECEPTION AND INFLUENCE

1. For discussions of these traditions of commentary on Genesis 22, see Louis Jacobs, 'The Problem of the *Akedah* in Jewish Thought'

and David A. Pailin, 'Abraham and Isaac: A Hermeneutical Problem Before Kierkegaard', both in Robert L. Perkins (ed.), *Kierkegaard's Fear and Trembling: Critical Appraisals* (University of Alabama Press, 1981), pp. 1–9 and pp. 10–42.

2. Ludwig Wittgenstein, *Culture and Value* (University of Chicago Press, 1980), pp. 53; 72; 28 (ellipsis in original).

3. This appreciation of the significance of the Danish Hegelians is due largely to the work of Jon Stewart, especially his 2003 book *Kierkegaard's Relations to Hegel Reconsidered.*

4. See Anthony Rudd's *Kierkegaard and the Limits of the Ethical* (Oxford: Clarendon Press, 1993), pp. 113–73 and especially pp. 117–31, for an excellent summary of Kierkegaard's critique of modern society which relates it to the theoretical question of the relationship between religion and ethics that is at stake in *Fear and Trembling.*

5. Emmanuel Levinas, 'Existence and Ethics' in *Kierkegaard: A Critical Reader*, edited by Jonathan Rée and Jane Chamberlain, pp. 26–38; p. 31.

6. Ibid., pp. 31–2.

7. Ibid., p. 34.

8. Ibid., pp. 34–5.

9. Søren Kierkegaard, *Stages on Life's Way*, translated by Howard V. Hong and Edna H. Hong (Princeton University Press, 1988), p. 476.

10. Jacques Derrida, *The Gift of Death*, translated by David Wills (University of Chicago Press, 1995), p. 84.

11. Ibid., p. 84.

12. Howard J. Curzer, 'Abraham, The Faithless Moral Superhero' in *Philosophy and Literature* 31 (2007), pp. 344–61; pp. 350–1.

13. Ibid., p. 351.

14. Stephen Mulhall, *Inheritance and Originality: Wittgenstein, Heidegger, Kierkegaard* (Oxford University Press, 2001) p. 382.

15. Ibid., pp. 386–7.

16. C. Stephen Evans, 'Faith as the Telos of Morality: A Reading of *Fear and Trembling*' in Robert L. Perkins (ed.), *The International Kierkegaard Commentary on Fear and Trembling and Repetition* (Macon, Georgia: Mercer University Press, 1993), pp. 9–27; p. 20.

17. See Robert M. Adams, 'The Knight of Faith', in *Faith and Philosophy* 7 (4) (1990), p. 392.

18. Jung H. Lee, 'Abraham in a different voice: Rereading *Fear and Trembling* with care' in *Religious Studies* vol. 36, no. 4 (2000), 377–400; p. 393.

19. JP 5651 (1843).

20. Sharon Krishek, *Kierkegaard on Faith and Love* (Cambridge University Press, 2009)p. 106 n.

21. Ibid., pp. 106–7.

22. See John J. Davenport, 'Faith as Eschatological Trust in *Fear and Trembling*' in Edward F. Mooney (ed.), *Ethics, Love and Faith in Kierkegaard* (Indiana University Press, 2008), pp. 196–233.

23. Krishek, *Kierkegaard on Faith and Love*, p. 107.
24. John Milbank, 'The Sublime in Kierkegaard' in *The Heythrop Journal* 37 (1996), 298–321; p. 310.
25. Jonathan Lear, *Radical Hope* (Harvard University Press, 2006), pp. 119–23.
26. Søren Kierkegaard, *The Concept of Anxiety*, translated by Reidar Thomte (Princeton University Press, 1980), p. 154.
27. Ibid., p. 159.
28. Lear, *Radical Hope*, p. 120.
29. Ibid., p. 92.
30. C. Stephen Evans's reading of *Fear and Trembling* also emphasizes this aspect of the text: 'Insofar as God transcends the social order, and insofar as the social order attempts to deify itself and usurp divine authority, there is a necessary opposition between faith and "reason", just as there is a tension between faith and what in *Fear and Trembling* is called "the ethical" . . . From the perspective of faith, the relativity and historical character of "reason" and "the ethical" become clear, and new ways of thinking and acting open up, which may be judged by society as "irrational" and "unethical" but may be seen by the "single individual" as fulfilling in a more authentic way the ideals that society itself claims to support'. See Evans, 'Faith as the Telos of Morality', p. 24.
31. George Pattison, *Thinking About God in an Age of Technology* (Oxford University Press, 2005), pp. 121–2.
32. Ibid., p. 122.
33. Søren Kierkegaard, *Eighteen Upbuilding Discourses*, edited and translated by Howard V. Hong and Edna H. Hong (Princeton University Press, 1990), p. 192.
34. Ibid., p. 187.
35. Ibid., p. 201.

INDEX